Curriculum Philosophy and Theory for
Music Education Praxis

Curriculum Philosophy and Theory for Music Education Praxis

Thomas A. Regelski

Oxford University Press is a department of the University of Oxford. It furthers
the University's objective of excellence in research, scholarship, and education
by publishing worldwide. Oxford is a registered trade mark of Oxford University
Press in the UK and certain other countries.

Published in the United States of America by Oxford University Press
198 Madison Avenue, New York, NY 10016, United States of America.

© Oxford University Press 2021

All rights reserved. No part of this publication may be reproduced, stored in
a retrieval system, or transmitted, in any form or by any means, without the
prior permission in writing of Oxford University Press, or as expressly permitted
by law, by license, or under terms agreed with the appropriate reproduction
rights organization. Inquiries concerning reproduction outside the scope of the
above should be sent to the Rights Department, Oxford University Press, at the
address above.

You must not circulate this work in any other form
and you must impose this same condition on any acquirer.

Library of Congress Cataloging-in-Publication Data
Names: Regelski, Thomas A., 1941– author.
Title: Curriculum philosophy and theory for music education praxis /
Thomas A. Regelski.
Description: New York : Oxford University Press, 2021. |
Includes bibliographical references and index.
Identifiers: LCCN 2021012494 (print) | LCCN 2021012495 (ebook) |
ISBN 9780197558706 (paperback) | ISBN 9780197558690 (hardcover) |
ISBN 9780197558720 (epub)
Subjects: LCSH: Music—Instruction and study—Philosophy. |
Curriculum planning.
Classification: LCC MT1 .R418 2021 (print) |
LCC MT1 (ebook) | DDC 780.71—dc23
LC record available at https://lccn.loc.gov/2021012494
LC ebook record available at https://lccn.loc.gov/2021012495

DOI: 10.1093/oso/9780197558690.001.0001

The manufacturer's authorised representative in the EU for product safety is
Oxford University Press España S.A. of El Parque Empresarial San Fernando
de Henares, Avenida de Castilla, 2 – 28830 Madrid (www.oup.es/en or
product.safety@oup.com). OUP España S.A. also acts as importer into Spain
of products made by the manufacturer.

I dedicate this book to the memory of my parents, Barbara and Adam Regelski, who started, then nurtured my interest in art, music, and words. I hope they would have been proud of my achievements.

Loving thanks to my wife, Kaisa Kononen, for her support and help in many ways during the long gestation of this book.

Finally, thanks to my former student Kent Knappenberger, Westfield (NY) Central School and Academy, winner of the first (2014) GRAMMY Foundation Music Educator Award. He thinks I had something to do with his success, but I've learned more from his praxis, much of which is reflected in this book. I was a mindful cupid in assigning his future wife to him for student teaching; that's my lasting thanks to him.

Music is of and for life:

"As a kid, I was lucky enough to know a gaptoothed [sic] band director named Byron Gillette. . . . I thought he was teaching me to play a trumpet when actually he was teaching me to live a life. My sister and I recently recalled life under his baton, and we felt the same debt piled up over nearly half a century. . . . She's now a life-shaping educator herself." David Von Drehle (2019)

When nurturing music for life:

"You cannot aim at something,
cannot work to get it,
unless you can recognize it
once you have got it."
John Searle (2018).

"It" must be clear in mind, whether for a student's practicing or a teacher's praxis.

"The Germans are the only people who presently have come to use the word *aesthetic* to designate what others call the critique of taste. They are doing so on the basis of a false hope conceived by that superb analyst Baumgarten. He hoped to bring our critical judging of the beautiful under rational principles, and to raise the rules for such judging to the level of a lawful science. Yet that endeavor is futile." Immanuel Kant, *Critique of Pure Reason* (1781)

Any attempt to teach aesthetic "good taste" in music is equally futile!

Contents

Preface	ix
1. Basics of Curriculum	1
Introduction	1
Preliminary Considerations	7
Curriculum	9
Three Types of Curriculum	9
"Hidden Curriculum"	12
Curriculum as Philosophy	13
2. Traditional Philosophical Foundations of Curriculum	17
Preliminary Considerations	17
Idealism	18
Idealism and the music curriculum	19
Realism	28
Realism and the music curriculum	28
Neo-Scholasticism	33
Neo-Scholasticism and the music curriculum	35
Closing Perspectives	38
3. 19th and 20th Century Philosophical Foundations of Curriculum	41
Preliminary Considerations	41
Existentialism, Phenomenology	41
Christian existentialism	43
Humanistic existentialism	46
Humanistic Psychology and Existential Theory	51
Existentialism, phenomenology, and the music curriculum	55
Pragmatism	59
Pragmatism and "artful living" through music	65
Pragmatism and the music curriculum	69
4. Contemporary Perspectives for Curriculum Theory	77
Preliminary Basics of Praxis and Practice Theory	77
Theoria	78
Technē	79
Praxis	81
Praxical knowledge	83
Ethics of school music as praxis	85
Duty Ethics	86
Consequentialism	87

viii Contents

Virtue Ethics	89
The virtue of praxis	91
Music as a social praxis	92
Action Learning	96
Postmodernity	98
Modern*ity*	98
Modern*ism*	100
Postmodernity and modernist art and music	100
Postmodern tendencies	103
Postmodernity and the music curriculum	108
Metanarratives "deconstructed" and the transformation of schools	109
Music Appreciation Reconsidered	115

5. Curriculum Models from Educational Theory — 117

Preliminary Considerations	117
Basic-Studies/Essentialism	118
Perennialism	121
Progressivism	123
Reconstructionism and Critical Theory	128
Reconstructionism	128
Critical Theory	129
Summary	135

6. Curriculum as and for Praxis — 137

Preliminary Considerations	137
Dimensions of a Praxical Curriculum	139
Three dimensions and their criteria for a curriculum	140
An Example Modeling a Praxis-Based Curriculum	143
Rubrics	144
Discussion	145
Concluding Perspectives	149

Notes	153
References and Further Reading	177
Index	183

Preface

The dedicated study of music is only one step needed to enter the profession of music education. Music audition standards and SAT scores alone do not predict in-service success! Inevitably other important knowledge and skills are left out of professional training, which is mainly focused on musicianship and performance skills, with relatively little time given to school music studies. Curriculum theory, for example, is typically ignored in favor of this or that, single-minded 'delivery' method.[1] There are many texts about curriculum theory, but none provides a survey specifically oriented to music education's special nature. Thus, the need for this volume is demonstrated by the typical absence of curriculum studies in preparing music educators.

Curriculum *theory* is in effect curriculum *philosophy* since much of it deals with philosophical and related theories. And any account of these philosophies is also bound to be decidedly philosophical. This book is thus not a textbook that pretends to offer 'neutral' knowledge. Knowledge (even in textbooks) inevitably has a point of view. There is no view from nowhere. Everyone is somewhere in the history of ideas, language, culture, and their implications on thinking and writing.

This book, thus, is a monograph for pre- and in-service teachers in the expectation that they are interested in and can use such principled knowledge. The pre-service teachers are projected to be U.S. students in their junior and senior years of music education studies, typically ages 20 and older. I believe they are capable and in need of understanding this philosophical analysis of curriculum. It offers a point of view generally oriented to Pragmatism and especially to what will be explained as *praxis*. Its survey of traditional philosophies (Chapter Two) relies on the method of "critical philosophy" of the noted German philosopher Immanuel Kant (1724–1804). Critical philosophy critiques philosophical claims to expose their weaknesses. For contemporary themes and issues it relies on Critical Theory (explained later) and engages in "ideology critique" to reveal the "false consciousness" that accepts curricular theory and models without critical interrogation.

A few in-text *scholarly citations* (inside parentheses) are used to cite sources for quotations, but otherwise are for further reading and perhaps are of interest only to scholars. *Notes* rarely cite references. Most are extensions of the text at those points (labeled COMMENTARY in the note itself) and true examples (TRUE STORIES) from my over 50 years of experience with the practical aspects of teaching: not the Ivory Tower, but the implications of curriculum theory for the everyday praxis of everyday teachers. Some notes offer possibilities (IDEAS) for application. Possibly unfamiliar technical terms are briefly explained (DEFINITIONS). These notes thus offer important information that will be missed by ignoring them. The "test" of understanding them will take place in front of school students.

Many years of publishing and teaching have guided the content of the book. Small parts have been extracted and edited from previously published peer-reviewed articles. I've observed schools in several countries and believe that many of the issues addressed are relevant beyond North America, however different in particulars. Though intentionally short, this book summarizes much of what otherwise is spread out over my 130+ published journal articles and six books. It is the culmination, then, of a research program I've followed since the 1960s, when I taught general and choral music in middle and high school (rural and city) and wrote my first published article in the *Music Educators Journal*. My PhD in Comparative Arts/Aesthetics has always afforded me somewhat of an outsider's view of scholarship in music education and supports my present philosophical and praxical argument. My musical background as a pianist and choral conductor informs my musical insights.

My heartfelt thanks go to 30 years of former students at the SUNY Fredonia School of Music—too many to name—from whose student teaching and lives I have learned so much. And thanks to the MayDay Group, whose leading members have been a touchstone of new thinking about the field and often a confirmation of my outside-the-box wanderings. Herein, I also update some of my earlier positions: publications should be printed on paper that self-destructs after 20 years! Note: Herein I adopt "praxical" for my brand of what is otherwise called "praxial," to recognize its emphasis on music as a social praxis, teaching as praxis, and the importance of social phenomenology.

Note to Professor: If time is limited, a lecture/discussion/outline of Chapters One and Two can precede a reading assignment of Chapters Three through Six. A handout of the four types of curriculum (from Chapter One) should be discussed with an emphasis on the hidden curriculum. Also important to Chapters Three through Six is to establish the critique of "delivery" methods, the term is used in later chapters. Chapters One, Three, and Five can be assigned in sections to students who prepare a handout on their topic, make a short presentation to the class, and lead a discussion.

In-service students can analyze favored teaching practices according to one or more of the philosophies presented.

Pre-service teachers can analyze and critique music education practices which they experienced during their school years as per the particular philosophical positions described herein. Special attention should be devoted to methods and curricular content that were wed to the three traditional philosophies covered in Chapter Two.

Typical needs (e.g., rehearsal plans and choices of literature) should be proposed according to the praxical themes discussed in the later chapters. For example, what will the differences be between a lesson predicated on praxical themes rather than the three traditional philosophies?

The model in Chapter Six should premise proposed curricular statements for other likely teaching needs, and for assessment records of progress in those needs.

Helsinki, Finland
May 2021

1
Basics of Curriculum

Introduction

Curriculum decisions are the foundation of education. They determine the knowledge, understandings, skills, attitudes, and values judged important to learn. They importantly provide the criteria for evaluating students' learning—that is, whether an individual lesson has been effective (according to curricular criteria), especially over the long term (past graduation). Instructors who don't recognize students' *failure* to learn have no basis for judging the *success* of their instruction. Beyond their musical competencies, a curriculum is, therefore, the most important responsibility facing music educators. It is a responsibility that goes well beyond the skills of simply 'delivering' an individual lesson, one that accounts for (or should) beneficial outcomes for individual students, graduates, and ultimately the world of musicing.

Oddly, however, curriculum theory per se and design for music education have been largely overlooked in undergraduate music education.[1] And it is usually no more on the radar of in-service teachers. In general, then, at neither the undergraduate nor the in-service level is *curriculum theory* directly emphasized. The U.S. politics governing school curriculum are constantly in public view (e.g., U.S. "No Child Left Behind," "Common Core"). Nonetheless, music educators have traditionally been on the sidelines of curriculum theory and practice.

Compared to raucous public debates about curriculums for history, biology, and literature, this lack of concern for a music education curriculum is symptomatic of a troublesome detachment of music education itself from the commitments of *general education*: what is worth learning and to what pragmatically functional ends for all students. Considerable scholarly commentary does exist in our field on specific issues such as social justice, gender, race, and inequality. But whether this specialized and, to teachers, often difficult discourse reaches the typical music classroom too often goes unobserved from the Ivory Tower. Formal theorizing about such important issues cannot be easily applied to everyday instructional efforts and consequently can fail to make a lasting difference in the instruction offered. Too often, such narrowly focused scholarship may advance a researcher's academic career, but not a teacher's everyday planning decisions. And, in any case, teachers often don't read this scholarship. Thus, the need to base instruction on *warranted theory* gives way, unfortunately, to this or that single-minded method advocated by a professor. Had the student attended a different school of music, the music education methods offered would likely vary considerably, often being totally at odds with the methods taught elsewhere! This amounts to an anarchy of methodolatry.

Consequently, the answers to important curricular questions are taken uncritically from the status quo and from "do it this way," "it works," and other taken-for-granted traditions.[2] "It works" too often only means that the lesson plans could be 'delivered' in some school, but any curricular ends to be served are typically not specified. (This is especially the case with displays of "show and tell" methods at music teacher conferences.) "Best practices"—that are akin to fanciful claims of *the* best way to raise a child—are promoted as recipes for lessons to be 'delivered' as though on an assembly line.

No matter the differences between students, student bodies, instructors, important variables of class size, communities (rural, exurban, suburban, city, inner city), schedules (instructional time), and resources, and any considerations for authentic, pragmatic musicianship—these and other variables are ignored due to the axiom "teachers teach the way they were taught." This model, as shall be seen in what follows, is not a good criterion for preparing modern school students for their futures—in our case, as musically educated and thus more inclined and able to make music as part of their everyday adult lives.

"Praxis," in the curricular sense, will be detailed in Chapter Four. For now, it is not to be confused with just any "practice" or habitual behavior (i.e., the "practice" of wearing a hat). Praxis, instead, refers to and is usually translated as "action" (pl. praxes, actions). The actions in question for music curriculum are those productive of enhanced musicing and musicianship that lead to students' musical "agency." "Agency" is *musicing*, a verb form that emphasizes active doing (performing, composing, listening, collecting, organizing playlists, etc.).[3]

As will be detailed in Chapter Four, praxis includes an *ethical criterion*, a decidedly thoughtful and *care-full* [sic] act that is ethically responsible for effectively serving those for whom the action (praxis) is undertaken—and importantly, in *doing no harm* in the process. In schooling, "no harm" means that students, for example, should not be 'turned off' by instruction, criticism, competition, and drill; instead, they should be 'turned on' to music. "Mathophobia" is typically a result of harmful instruction, and the same is the result for students who quickly quit instrument lessons or tune out in general music classes. In medical practice (i.e., praxis), of course, there should be no harm to the patients. Thus, "mal*practice*" is literally a matter of "mal*praxis*," of not following ethically warranted "standards of care."

Praxis-focused teaching stresses the development of functional knowledge, competencies, and attitudes that facilitate life-long musicing. Its focus is "Action Learning" (Regelski 2004; Chapter Four in this book)—promoting 'real-life' musicing, that is, musical praxes that are typically engaged in by students later as adults. Its premise is to get students *into action* musically in ways that serve them outside of school and into later life.

Instead, as many readers remember, the next rehearsal and concert are most often the focus of ensemble directors and their students. And the next lesson, from a commercial music "textbook series" or typical *delivery method* lesson plans (e.g., purchased from the Internet), dictates daily practice by many music educators who are committed to offering activities they claim are "teaching concepts." These methods are committed to 'delivering' lessons according to recipe or formulaic means and without planned curricular assessment for any actual learning that might result—especially learning lasting beyond the short-term duration of a given lesson.

Such *delivery lessons* often do not take the form of 'real music' (e.g., Orff Schulwerk, classroom "rhythm bands") and supposedly promote concepts, but lasting musical relevance is dubious. "Good teaching" in this well-worn paradigm amounts to the 'delivery' of supposedly 'good' lesson *plans*, not in the "authentic assessment"[4] of *musical learning* of a lasting kind. The 'goodness' of plans, especially those said to be "best practices," are mistakenly judged to be best in *advance* of instruction, not in terms of typical results in this or that school.

"Methodolatry" is my neologism describing the taken-for-granted uncritical acceptance of systems or collections of '*delivery methods*'. If the lesson is delivered successfully according to a 'good' plan, the uncritical assumption is that valuable musical learning will result—just as some parents uncritically assume spanking the child will result in good behavior when all it does is result in crying and a fearful relation to what should be a bond between parent and child. This mistake, unfortunately, is also the typical criterion for student teaching observations: how well a student-teacher 'delivers' a lesson *plan—irrespective of curricular criteria* (which often do not exist).

Student teaching thus institutionally often creates the conditions of and continued reliance on delivery methodolatry—habits adopted from cooperating teachers that are carried forward into the first teaching position. In neither ensembles nor general music classes is curricular attention typically paid to *lifelong learning*. Instead, the effects of such instruction typically reach a dead end with the completion of required general music classes[5] and with the graduation of ensemble members.

Among the issues leading to this problematic situation is the lack of scholarly literature *specifically* about curriculum. As a result, methods classes[6] (and sometimes their professors) are lacking in the foundations of curriculum theory enough to assist pre-service and in-service teachers. Instead, the routinized delivery methods of methodolatry are stressed and the notion instilled that 'good teaching' amounts to the successful 'delivery' of 'good' lesson *plans*, often based on a featured method or as prescribed by university professors. What such lessons lead to in terms of accumulated, lasting results over the years (if anything!) is lost in the random and disjointed 'delivery' of individual lessons, fruitlessly accumulating over time—like filling a wastebasket with good intentions. Thus, for example, despite a heavy emphasis on singing and music reading in classroom music classes (i.e., general music), students in North America often fail to learn to sing 'in tune' (on pitch) or read music effectively.[7] How many beginning instrumental students quit before very long?

In pre-service classes focusing on directing and conducting ensembles, the assumption is widespread that "curriculum" is simply the overall *literature* studied for concerts. Asking an ensemble teacher to see their curriculum is met with a bemused look: what a dumb question! Consequently, six to eight years of such concerts (two to four years in elementary and middle school ensembles and four years of high school for students who don't drop out along the way) is the dominant focus and sole result. Except for a rare few who become university music majors (often enabled with out-of-school individual lessons), student ensembles, then, rarely have a musical impact on individual members that lasts beyond graduation. Adult graduates of these ensembles rarely seek or create opportunities to continue performing, and their listening preferences are no different than the taste choices of those who were not in an ensemble.

Inherited practices dominate (i.e., again and again, "Teachers teach as they were taught"). Students entering their teaching practicum have been exposed in their methods or pedagogy classes to "best practices," but rarely is the curricular goal of such idealized lessons stressed. What lasting outcomes are such lessons the "best" on the way to achieving? As a result, in their student teaching practicum, they often submit to imitating the methods of their cooperating teachers: their lessons are 'delivered' successfully when school students find them most like those of the cooperating teacher.

In other words, *imitating the cooperating teacher* is seen as the best way to survive the student teaching practicum with good recommendations.

Instruction recommended in university methods classes that departs from the norm of a cooperating teacher is professionally risky for the novice. For example, the student-teacher who rehearses a choir using methods that teach and improve music reading will be thoroughly defeated when conducting choruses of a cooperating teacher that are used to being taught their literature by rote drill.

Typically, then, 'delivery' of lessons based on the examples of their cooperating teachers is learned regardless of the methods or pedagogy classes professors have recommended! As first-year teachers, such graduates are then inevitably faced with teaching situations, conditions, and challenges that are usually very different from those they experienced in their school years, pre-service method classes, and the teaching practicum. Thus, a first-year teacher's struggle begins where the 'good plans' of methods class and student teaching are no longer reconciled with new teaching conditions.

This incongruous variation between teaching situations goes well beyond the usual differences between communities, student bodies, schedules, and resources. In fact, unlike most other *"helping professions"*—those that exist to benefit the public (social work, medicine, therapy)—much of music education is characterized by what can be called without exaggeration instructional and curricular *anarchy* with teachers "doing their own thing." We hope such anarchy doesn't exist, say, in dentistry.

This multiplicity is often seen even within a school system: the bigger it is, the more diversity there will be, especially lacking a mutually agreed-upon curriculum guide. Sociologists of education long ago noted that a school "system" often amounts to a collection of different one-room schools under one roof. This is especially the case for music education.[8] Even experienced educators who move to a new job contend with the inherited status quo of the previous teacher that is usually different than their habits. And often, their preferred 'delivery methods' are at first unsuited to the new circumstances and variables.

What follows surveys the field of curriculum studies. It begins with an analysis of curriculum basics and their implications for music education. Then, it follows a consideration of traditional philosophical roots of curriculum—foundations that still impact contemporary curriculums, most often in negative ways! This survey (Chapter Two) will follow the model of "critical philosophy" mentioned in the Preface. Chapter Three addresses 19th- and 20th-century philosophies and their potentials for music curriculum. Chapter Four explains contemporary perspectives of curricular theories that, while not philosophy as such, have ancient philosophical roots and important implications for curriculum design. Chapter Five outlines the differences between a range of typical educational curricular models and their prospects for curriculum theories (including Praxis and Critical Theory). Chapter Six presents a praxis-based curriculum model that incorporates many of the most favorable contributions of the earlier surveys.

Many themes appear repeatedly given different contexts by each philosophy and theory. Take special notice of these overlapping themes as cumulative evidence of their substance and relevance (e.g., praxis, chamber musicing, transmission vs. transformation, authoritarian vs. authoritative, action ideals, concept teaching, intentionality, methodolatry, and *an* experience). Each gains new importance in a new philosophical context. They address music educators in a variety of specialties, as well as readers concerned with community musicing.

Typical readers are expected to be diverse in their experiences and expectations. Music education students often enter the profession with a range of prior assumptions. Some enter because their parents, with an eye on potential careers, wouldn't let them study music otherwise; competitive music careers are risky. Others have enjoyed summer camp experiences working with children and doing so with music seems like a good idea. Still others who are good at performing realize that performance or composition careers are unlikely and music education becomes their second choice. Some will see themselves as following in the footsteps of favored teachers who are their models. Only a very few enter teaching to be better than the models they had in school!

Among the diversity of such readers will be those who may feel defensive or uneasy with critiques of their embracing of many hand-me-down approaches to teaching music, and they need forewarning that these uncomfortable moments, and what follows them, are key opportunities for professional growth and new insights. They should be all the more attended to, rather than dismissed or resisted as Ivory Tower theorizing. "Critical philosophy" encourages *further thought* by identifying unwarranted theories and hand-me-down methods and curriculums that create a range of instructional problems and impede the assessment of effective learning and effective teaching. It is more than likely that some *moments of such discomfort or challenge will arise*, and these readers are encouraged to set aside previous convictions and to attempt to understand the philosophical criteria at stake. Many of these moments are fuel for discussion in music education classes.

Readers' questions or doubts that arise along the way are likely to be addressed in later chapters. The book covers much more than has informed the prior thinking of most readers, especially their own experiences of school music—whether as students or in-service teaching. Models of favored teachers are always in mind. But what about the many students who were not as positively affected in their own adult musical choices and lives by those favored models: what were the problems that caused them to drop out? While focusing on philosophy, the book also reinforces many conclusions reached by psychological and sociological premises for music curriculum. These, however, are not the focus of attention.

I anticipate that readers will be pre- and in-service teachers (ages 20 and upward) seeking a useful understanding of curriculum theory and design—although doctoral students and professors may also be interested (perhaps more in the scholarly references and themes). Given the anticipated audience, the minimal in-text scholarly citations usually identify sources quoted, and some have notes to further references. Notes, on the other hand, provide important comments extending discussions in the text and even suggestions for thought relevant to the fullest understanding. And given the possibility that some readers will be using this book in classes having other assigned readings, the text is reasonably concise despite its coverage of much of the history of Western philosophy.

Preliminary Considerations

Instructors in all fields of music education often continue to employ passed-on methods, materials, and "tricks of the trade." They assume that delivering 'good methods plans'—declared as 'good' *in advance of use*—somehow automatically produces 'good results'. Ignored is the long-term, cumulative sense of a curriculum. Instead, "successful teaching" is mistakenly judged only by the 'delivery' of the lesson plan. Performance ensembles that come closest to the kinds of musical results teachers were accustomed to in their musical training are therefore taken as models of musical success.

References to "programs" among many ensemble directors usually do not entail anything even remotely involving "curriculum." "Program" at best refers to the "feeder system" where only *some* elementary students continue in middle school, then even *fewer* in high school. Very typical of any such program, then, is a notable and predictable decrease in the numbers of participating students at each subsequent level. The demands of "presentational" criteria for concerts require more dedicated practice and rehearsal that lead less committed student musicians to drop out.[9] Thus, the dropout rate between starting students and those in the high school ensemble is typically great.

Unlike ensembles that engage only a small percentage of the student body, many general music classes teach "concepts" said to improve "music appreciation" (addressed in Chapter Four) or music reading for purposes of eventual ensemble membership. These classes supposedly address the musical needs of *all* students but are typically unnoticed by the public or administrators. But the degree to which they stimulate student interest enough to promote future musical interests is doubtful. Hence, the inclusion of music in the overall curriculum as part of the "general education" of *all* students is almost everywhere marginalized! Instead, attention goes to the few in performing ensembles—because they appear in public and showcase the director's efforts. Parents may remark about the quality of the football half-time marching band, but not about the K–6 general music curriculum.

But even ensembles are instructed according to taken-for-granted assumptions that deserve considerations from curriculum theorizing. Again, in over eight years of, say, band, the de facto 'curriculum' amounts only to the literature performed. Instruction is thus focused on "bringing off" the next concert successfully *as a group*, and not specifically the lifelong functionality of the musical knowledge, skills, and attitudes that *individuals* (e.g., the tuba players) have gained as a result. Typically, the *averaging effect of large numbers* aurally conceals the weaker abilities of many individuals in any large ensemble. Accordingly, the larger the group, generally the better it sounds. In comparison, chamber music groups with one to three students per part require more of each player and promote independent musicianship for lifelong learning.

There is therefore little doubt, then, that many members of even the best-sounding ensembles fall far short of *individual* musical competence that would allow (or motivate) them to continue to be musically active upon graduation. And the narrowness of the literature leaves most graduates similarly lacking the skills of *listenership*. "Music" extends beyond an ensemble's concert literature. All ensembles rehearsing at the same time in the school day (often for scheduling ease) prevents interested and able students from being in more than one, and directors will sometimes compete for select students (or students have to alternate on some schedule). Directors choose concert literature according to the present amateur abilities of students, and as a result, they do not usually encounter the more advanced repertory heard in professional concerts and from CDs.[10] But *listening is a praxis of its own*, and audience listening experiences are typically not part of students' ensemble curriculum.[11]

Justifying school music education requires such results to be a legitimate part of general education. While *advocacy* usually advertises high-minded aesthetic benefits, the reality is that too often, school curriculums do not promote notable, continuing benefits—aesthetic or otherwise. Music education is thus in a progressively serious deficit compared to other classes where studies are expected to have lasting pragmatic results. It leads to the resistance of taxpayer and administrative support for the inclusion of music studies in general schooling. Much of such school music, notably band and orchestra, is typically very expensive, especially for students whose parents can't afford the instruments. Taxpayers, then, can wonder why they should financially support such students' musical education.

Curriculum

The common English term "curriculum" stems from the ancient Latin *currere*, meaning "to run." The contemporary idea of curriculum includes two complementary dimensions: the action of conveyance (running, progressing to an important destination), and what message of importance or useful outcomes are that destination.[12] This twofold dimension leads to much confusion in education, curriculum, and assessment of instruction and learning. For example, it has resulted in confusion resulting from assuming that the process of merely 'delivering' instruction is synonymous with "teaching." Leading proponents of 'delivery methods' mistakenly refer to the collection of their favored strategies, activities, and "best practices" as a 'curriculum'—which is akin to confusing the tools and materials of carpentry with what is built! It leaves out the provision of learning outcomes for students in favor of teachers' plans for 'delivering' instruction.

Furthermore, commercial materials for general music classes and instrumental "methods series," make similarly mistaken claims for the simple 'delivery' of activities and lessons to the status of a curriculum. Most have favored philosophical subthemes of which teachers are unaware, often premises based in aesthetic philosophy. However beneficial and otherwise useful such individual lesson plans may seem to be, at best they provide only a series of options for the *process* of conveyance. But they most certainly do not automatically address the praxical *product* criterion for "curriculum" described in the following pages.

Three Types of Curriculum

There are three types of curriculum references, with a fourth kind looming worryingly in the background.

1. First, a FORMAL CURRICULUM GUIDE is a document that describes a course of study in a level of detail that conveys the "content" (knowledge,

understanding, skills, attitudes, and values) to be addressed by instruction. This level of detail expresses the *action potential* that the curriculum is proposed to advance: the *agency* of what the student should be able to *do* (or do better or with more appreciation) as a result of instruction. This action potential of a *curriculum* distinguishes it from a *syllabus* that only outlines content to be 'covered'. The same is true of "spiral curriculums" that claim to visit the same 'concepts' at ever-higher levels.[13]

Those who, as is sometimes said, those who "write curriculum" are engaged in the process of producing a formal document intended to guide instruction to well-considered curricular ends. When writing curriculum is done cooperatively by multiple teachers, the curriculum document produced is intended to guide and coordinate their instruction, so that each is addressing the same skills and knowledge in their classes. Methods may differ, but the curriculum guide—its action potentials—is the unifying factor.

In many subjects (e.g., language arts, mathematics), the curriculum often comes in "prefabricated" ("prefab") form as commercial publications adopted by the school. In large schools, teachers may not even be consulted about such adoptions.[14] Instrumental "methods series" can often be examples of such published materials parading as curriculum, ever-moving to the next tune. In some countries, education ministries produce a curriculum of generalities, the details of which are left up to educators in a particular school to fill in co-operatively. Such flexibility does not avoid the need for clarity and specificity to guide curricular results.

The *horizontal* alignment of curriculum coordinates teachers at the same level (e.g., in different classrooms or buildings). With a *vertically* aligned curriculum, the curriculum of lower levels is designed to merge with the curriculum at the next highest level. A *linear curriculum* that attempts a perfect fit of early with later levels is, however, difficult to achieve.

Furthermore, having produced a formal curriculum is not the same as successfully *using* it. Thus, many music teachers who have produced a "curriculum"[15]—often at the insistence of an administrator or as a paid summer assignment—do not necessarily use it at all.[16] One reason for this lack of follow-up is that they produce documents that are far too detailed, far too ideal to be used, or too vaguely stated to be meaningful. Instruction predicated on behavioral objectives (e.g., "the student will be able to . . ."), or, in the U.S., state and "Common Core" standards, risks becoming one-shot lessons that fail to provide "readiness," or meaningful follow-up lessons that eventually result in functional competence.[17]

2. The second distinction, the INSTRUCTED CURRICULUM is the actual instruction given. It often refers to what the instructor 'delivers' in the absence of a musically holistic, structured sequence of lessons. Importantly, then, a useful distinction can be recognized between "instruction" and "teaching." *Because not all instruction results in learning, not all instruction results in teaching.* In comparison, a "goalie" in sports who rarely stops opponents' scoring attempts only has the title of "goalie" but fails to fulfill the described function. "Teachers" too risk only holding their title despite not reliably facilitating learning. Therefore, it seems useful to use the term "teaching" mainly for "instruction" that results in learning.[18] Without this distinction, instructors are all too apt to conclude, "I taught it to them, but they didn't learn it because of . . . [any number of scapegoats]"—meaning that they only "delivered" a lesson.[19]

In the case of a formal curriculum guide, it is too easy to identify as 'teaching' the mere "covering" of the 'content' intended—falsely meaning that lessons about the learnings in question only were 'delivered'. Of course, despite the best of intentions, the lack of effective learning can be due to various constraints, such as class size, limitations of resources, scheduling, etc. However, such predictable constraints need identification and allowances in the preparation of a curriculum guide. A curriculum for playing guitar where two students must share one instrument, or where students don't have an instrument to practice between classes, cannot expect the same results as for one student per guitar or having a guitar (lent by the school or owned) for practicing.

3. Finally, there is the learned or ACTION CURRICULUM—meaning what the students actually and notably *learn* from instruction. Here, "learn" means "can DO something new or better—or more often or with more enthusiasm—as a result of instruction." Therefore, improved musical agency leads to the ability needed for one or more forms and levels of musicing to bring personal levels of satisfaction. This is not to diminish (as behaviorism[20] did) all manner of mediating variables such as attitudes, values, abstract thinking, affects, feelings, intuition, metacognition, supervisory knowledge, and the like. Such variables are important to the degree that they inform and serve to facilitate concrete and discernible changes in students' musical functioning *as a result of instruction.*

"Hidden Curriculum"

While the formal curriculum guide is the *explicit* curriculum, the "HIDDEN CURRICULUM" is the unspoken (tacit) or implicit curriculum that, in effect, is "soaked up" informally (inductively) by students every minute of every day in every class. It takes the form of attitudes, values, and certain other kinds of learning, habits, and behaviors that result from the *institutional structure* of formal schooling itself: the norms, beliefs, rules, routines, and social structures of daily school life. "The hidden curriculum consists of implicit messages given to students about socially legitimated or 'proper' behavior, differential power, social evaluation, what kinds of knowledge exist, which kinds are valued by whom, and how students are valued in their own right."[21] It also sends implicit messages "through the 'silences' of what is left out" (deMarris & LeCompte 1990, 242).

While not publicly stated as objectives of schooling, the hidden or tacit "purpose of the hidden curriculum is to produce specific outcomes for later life, particularly to prepare students to accept as legitimate specific patterns of social behavior, positions in the social class structure, attitudes toward gender roles, and occupational placement" (deMarris & LeCompte 1990, 243; full details, 242–247). Inability (or unwillingness) to follow the hidden curriculum—aka "discipline problems"—can more likely result in student failure than poor academic work. Success with the hidden curriculum thus often determines how well students do in their studies.

So much about the hidden curriculum is so taken for granted that *it is often invisible to teachers* as well! They absorbed much of it uncritically in their school days (hand raising: "Wait to be called upon to speak"!).[22] Some of its influences may be idiosyncratic for a particular teacher—for example, certain assumptions concerning 'good music' may lead to the conclusion that only Eurocentric music is suitable for study. "Silence" about popular, ethnic, and everyday musics in effect *teaches* students that these other musics (often musics they identify as "theirs") are not worthwhile enough to include in the curriculum.

Other influences are typically more widespread—for example, the overwhelming acceptance by music educators of traditional large ensembles as the preferred format for performance instruction, thereby ignoring chamber groupings for various kinds of music (folk, ethnic, jazz, etc.). Thus are strings altogether ignored in small schools lacking numbers for an orchestra, instead of including chamber groupings of various sizes. The grammar of the hidden curriculum, in other words, is dominated by its implicit enacting of all manner of *institutional power*, which conditions in a variety of ways whether learning takes place at all, and if so what learning was gained and what 'good' it has for students.

It is useful to consider the sources and wielding of power in the university school of music in preparing musicians and music teachers, and what the different needs are for each curricular group. What is the hidden curriculum at that level? To what ends?

Unfortunately, a massive number of hidden curriculum goals are widespread in schools. One addressed by social critics is that the *regimentation* (bells, timed periods, dress codes, attendance taking, uniform conduct, etc.) is central to the hidden curriculum of providing *good workers* for society. The hidden curriculum also tends to focus on middle-class values, often to the detriment of students from lower socioeconomic classes (e.g., lack of home computers, not owning one's instrument, unaffordable prom dresses, music typically heard at home, children of working-class [or out-of-work] parents) in classes of middle-class teachers (deMarris & LeCompte 1990, 244–246).

Some critics of U.S. public schooling see the hidden curriculum as destroying students' natural joy of learning, their curiosity, and their personal interests and initiatives (Gatto 2017). In this account, the routines, the rigor, stultifying boredom, *an*esthetizing tedium, and irrelevance to students' interests supersede any rewarding, pragmatic outcomes. They "turn off" too many students to the benefits of learning and lead to a range of problems in the school day. Such memories from school days should serve as a warning to new teachers who "buy into" the hidden curriculum. Advice from experienced teachers ("Don't smile until Christmas," "Never turn your back on a class," etc.) often signifies the hidden curriculum.

The differences between (1) the formal curriculum guide, (2) the instructed curriculum, and (3) the action curriculum, all conditioned by the background of factors of the (4) hidden curriculum, point out the kinds of consequential considerations that are typically overlooked or minimized by otherwise well-meaning music educators in typically providing daily instruction. Without considerations informed by philosophical and other theoretical possibilities from social theory and psychology, teachers will continue to run afoul of various kinds of unexpected consequences, many of which are negative.

Curriculum as Philosophy

Choosing what to include in a curriculum is a matter of deciding among possible *values*—what musical learning is most valuable to students and society. The most basic curricular decisions, therefore, involve answering this critical question: *What of all that could be learned is most worth including in instruction—and to what useful ends?* There is always more to learn than there is time or resources! In consequence, not all musical knowledge and skill are equally valuable to all students everywhere.[23] Ultimately, then, curricular planning amounts largely to a process of judging some potential learning to be more valuable to individual students and society than other locally available possibilities.

The domain of values, of course, is a notably difficult terrain to negotiate: status quo values are usually taken for granted and often defended against new alternatives. In education, this resistance leads formal schooling to be a very conservative institution, often protecting and *transmitting* the status quo more than meeting the *transformative* needs of the present and future. Being philosophically informed about the bases and criteria for unavoidably value-laden curricular decisions clarifies thinking and assists instructors in the direction of greater discernment, effectiveness, and consistency.

The study of values is called *axiology,* a subdiscipline of philosophy. Curricular thinking inescapably involves the criteria involved in making value judgments concerning what is most worth learning from instruction. Therefore, *curriculum planning and choices are unavoidably philosophy in action (philosophical praxis)*. The theories to follow in later chapters, then, reflect the impact on education of different philosophies. Social perspectives (theories and values), as we shall see, also have their role to play in newer curricular trends.

Most teachers probably don't think of themselves as involved with philosophizing, but the fact is that their philosophical choices of musical and social values are often taken for granted. "Following the pack" does not, in the least, mean they have avoided important philosophical conundrums. In truth, *every music educator is "doing philosophy" every day* in the classroom or rehearsal! Whatever instruction they offer is unavoidably couched in terms of some usually taken-for-granted philosophical position *of which they are unaware.*

Not being prepared by inclination or training to examine the philosophical soundness of what they offer, music teachers are unaware of the philosophical, practical, and social implications of the often-uninformed philosophical choices they make for their curriculum. For example, facts and information *about* music are usually confused with music as *praxis*—with musicing. Teaching concepts is teaching verbal abstractions that only refer, after the fact of experience, to musical praxis. And performing is automatically regarded as good in itself and as the best, most direct route to "music appreciation." It is neither.

Instruction in the "rudiments" or "theory" of music regularly falls prey to such misleading results, such as when "common practice" music theory is falsely advanced as practical—for example, the senior music education major in a piano class who thought G^6 in the "lead sheet" was a "first inversion" G chord! Traditional rudiments of "theory" are regularly taught as facts to the exclusion of functional symbology relevant to many musics of today. Consequently, the theories behind, for example, "perfect" intervals are not typically disclosed to students.[24] And it is entirely unappreciated by many who offer instruction in music theory that "music has from its beginnings [in Ancient Greece] been connected with philosophical theory" (Alperson 1994, 195). Thus, even the very question of "What is music?" (e.g., Alperson 1994; Erskine 1944) is inescapably philosophical.

This being the case, the teacher who presumes to teach "music," but who is philosophically uninformed about what it *is*, is open to creating and suffering all sorts of confusing results. Is "the music" the score? The resulting sounds? Or sounds as experienced as "music" according to sociocultural context? Is musical "meaning" autonomous to "works" and uncomplicated by extrinsic variables (words, sociality, and historical variables), or is it socially constituted in every instance from the very beginning, always fulfilling valued social needs that determine its creation and use? Is music an architecture of sound and thus purely formal, or is it "expressive of" human experience? Is musical "expression" (e.g., sadness) *in* the notated score, or *in* the listener? These, and many more important questions, too often go unexamined in the thinking of many music teachers.

For example, a general music curriculum that focuses on "Great Works" is often dull for students in comparison with a curriculum that addresses music as an important and always contemporary *social praxis*—as something they can *do* now and later in life. Many teachers, however, take for granted that "music" *is* simply the "score" (i.e., the notation) and proceed to emphasize music reading—only to wonder why the right notes still don't sound "musical." And they ignore musics that do not use notation—probably most of the music in the world.

Others who claim to "teach music" often focus so much on technical skills (scales, exercises, drills, and études) that asking them about the difference between a "*music* lesson" and, say, a "*piano* lesson" seems absurd—only to complain when performances demonstrate a technical command that exceeds evidence of musical insight or artistry.[25] How many students give up lessons because they wanted to study *music* and not *technique* as though for its own sake? Doesn't a wise choice of music itself offer ample opportunities for progressive technique development? Piano virtuoso and conductor Daniel

Barenboim recounted that his father, who was his teacher, taught that there were plenty of scales and arpeggios in Mozart's piano literature, and therefore, he successfully focused on selected literature for his son's technique development.

Most consequential of all is the question of musical meaning and value. Is meaning and value (a) aesthetic, autonomous, intrinsic, and immanent to (in) the sounds of musical "works" (i.e., "absolute music") or (b) a social and cultural *praxis* in which individual 'works' are not autonomous of life, but rather are particular instances of cultured, socially situated processes and meanings that are, at least in a significant way, extrinsic to the sounds of the moment? The former philosophy of music contends that music is *aesthetic* in meaning, while the latter philosophy roots music in and as *praxis* and always social in origin, meaning, and value.

The first alternative premises *music education as aesthetic education* (MEAE), while *praxis theory* premises music (and teaching) as a vital and always contemporary (i.e., dynamically relevant) *social action*. The first is satisfied in believing that mere contact with music—performing, classroom listening lessons—is automatically aesthetic and therefore somehow advances "aesthetic responses." Those who follow the contrary path approach music not as a *museum culture* of "Great Works" but as a *living culture* of social relevance that continually constitutes and transforms today's culture. The practical consequences of such philosophical distinctions for curriculum decisions are considerable, and the challenges of curriculum design for music education profit from being placed in a philosophical context and judged according to warranted philosophical criteria.

2
Traditional Philosophical Foundations of Curriculum

Preliminary Considerations

Traditional philosophies of curriculum and schooling fall into three broad families: Idealism (perhaps more easily understood as idea-ism), Realism, and Neo-Scholasticism. A hodge-podge of these three has characterized formal schooling since its very beginning. While they tend to be more influential today in higher education, they are often still prominent in public school instruction beginning with the elementary years. And their implications gain in accumulated effect as students progress through the more advanced years of musical schooling.

Such old-fashioned philosophy can lead some students to quit at the earliest legal age. Others drop out mentally, misbehave, and don't do their school "work." Why? Learning is a natural joy to children. The brain is constructed to scan for novelty in its range of activities: new experience for the brain is the seeds of new learning! **The brain cannot *not* learn!** When blocked from the novelty-seeking natural to it, as too often is the case in schools, the brain turns its attention to other sources of stimulation: staring out the window, restlessness, acting out, doodling, talking with classmates, etc. Consequently, educators need to explain why students *don't* learn and why schools make learning into "work" instead of a *natural exploration of the world by their brains and minds*. Part of the answer is the problematic continued legacy of the traditional philosophies examined in the following chapters.

The foundations for Idealism and Realism originated in Ancient Greece, with Plato and Aristotle, respectively. For its part, Scholasticism coincided with the rise of schools and universities that flowered, usually in conjunction with a Catholic cathedral (thus called "cathedral schools"). They participated readily in the recovery from Muslim translations of Greek texts of Aristotle's philosophy, to which St. Thomas Aquinas (and other religious scholars) called attention. All three traditional philosophical foundations of curriculum theory, individually or in combination, lead today's institutionalized schooling to be extremely conservative.

Idealism

Idealism is a philosophical family, all variations of which hold that 'reality' is a mental and immaterial "form"; it might have better been called idea-ism. Idealism's (ideal) "forms" of immaterial ideas or concepts should not be confused with idealist*ic* kinds of utopian (impractical) thinking. An Ideal form of a tree is one's mental composite over time of traits shared by all trees, including huge sequoia and little bonsai. Such Ideal forms are regarded as the essence of 'reality': when referring to a "tree," we rely on our Ideal form (schema, concept) as its essence.

As universal and abstract, such pure ideas are believed to apply everywhere, and in every realm of human activity. In this broad and diverse philosophy, then, *ideas are regarded as more substantially 'real' (and thus more important) than tangible things of the material world.* An idea (Ideal form) is eternal and unchanging (e.g., idea/concept of "table"), while the things of the material world (this or that table) are physically affected by age or vary according to short-term fashion. Instead, for Idealism, the ideas and thoughts of the mind (usually conveyed through words) are emphasized. 'Truth' for Idealists takes the form of ideas that have logical and internal consistency. Knowledge, for Idealism, is not gained through experience but depends on rational thinking (rationalism is shared with Realism and Neo-Scholasticism), intuition, and transmission (after successful disputation) by learned authorities.

Idealism has centrally influenced Christian theology. The Platonic idea(l) of the immaterial "soul" is central to Christian faiths. Accordingly, Idealist-influenced truth and values have been revealed and taught over history by religious authority. In Christianity, through the late medieval age, this authority was the Catholic Church. The Bible also reflects religiously oriented Idealism and, despite its emphasis on spiritual and metaphysical realities (even miracles), relies on *words* for transmitting such truths and values to the masses.

For Protestant denominations, the Bible, *sola scriptura* (only scripture), not popes and priests, is the authority that directly reveals "the Word" of God to all believers. "In the beginning was the Word, and the Word was with God, and the Word was God" (John 1). However, starting with the first Christians, the Bible has often been intensely disputed. Early Christianity experienced what early Catholicas authorities and church councils ruled to be heresies: their beliefs were stricken from Catholic theology (e.g., Gnosticism). After the Protestant Reformation, the fragmentation of Protestant denominations and the proliferation of sects gained momentum (each reading the Bible according to its preferred doctrine), and the teachings of the Bible spread with the invention of the printing press. Similarly, scriptures in other religions are accepted as a source of the revealed 'truths' of their religious traditions (e.g., Talmud, Koran, Book of Mormon), the Ideals that guide them.

Accordingly, Idealists' values involve eternal ideas of "the true, the good, and the beautiful" (as often quoted in history)—common claims associated with Idealism—that are not just universal but characterize the Universe itself! Ethical living, then, is congruent with the natural principles of the universe as revealed to those studied in such matters—among them, "professors" whose theses *profess* their conclusions about truth, goodness, and beauty and living the good, namely moral, life.

However, despite claims to universality, professors' "theses" required a successful "thesis defense" against opponents to earn a "doctor" of learning. This sanctioning by a thesis defense is followed by even more "disputations" that today involve scholarly "disciplines" whose members, through *peer review* (by other professors who have passed the same hurdles), dispute or accept and condone their ideas for published research.

Luther promoted his "95 theses" against the Catholic Church of the time by the "social media" of the time, the newly invented printing press. And he was very adept at using it to promote his ideas. The printing press also spreads printed music and graphic art. Since then, publishing (professing) one's scholarly ideas "theses" in scholarly journals and books (this book, among them) has defined what it means to be a "professor." However, the sheer multiplicity of ideas in the liberal arts and humanities represents an insuperable challenge to claims for the universal status of Idealism.

Idealism and the music curriculum

In the Idealist framework of knowledge and valuing, favored are a priori ideas that exist apart from sensory perception (experience) of the tangible world and the human body. *A priori* ideas or knowledge, then, exist independently of (prior to) experience: for example, basic axioms of arithmetic (2 + 2 = 4 is a priori). *A posteriori* knowledge, in contrast, arises from (post-) experience: for example, learning from *experi*ments across the history of science (e.g., the speed of light).

For Idealists, *art* features ideals, universal ideas, or abstract forms. In Ancient Greece, sensory perceptions (of *aisthesis*) were judgments of knowledge made by the senses (e.g., sweet vs. sour, and thus concepts of "taste"). This understanding of aisthesis was mistakenly pilfered in the 18th century by the spread of *aesthetic theories*. These stress, then, *rationally derived concepts of art and music*. However, these concepts often rely only on the oft-used metaphor that compares experiences of art and music according to different "tastes."

What is 'beautiful' is said to arise as somehow capturing the world of Ideals: Ideal 'reality' as perfectly reflected by the artist; a still-life painting reveals not just these fruits and flowers, but the Ideal essence of them. These reflections are focused on capturing the realm of ideas in pure form by 'idealizing' sensory perception of perfect, unchanging Ideal forms ('pure beauty') that derive from eternally fixed (Ideal) principles. Addressing music's "forms," it follows for Idealists, is key to "music appreciation," and attending to form is held to be the proper way to listen—a problem for listeners of contemporary musics that have no form to guide a listener. Nonetheless, form analysis study is often the basis of the training of musicians, and common forms (e.g., sonata allegro) are the bases of music appreciation texts and courses.

In schooling, *'intellectual' learning* is most important, since the rational mind governs the acquisition of knowledge. Focus is on, then, the student's 'intellectual' development of "received" facts and information passed on by books and scholars. In the beginnings of schooling in many countries (e.g., the U.S.), such teaching was offered only to the select few whose minds could understand the abstractions offered in schools. For these children of the upper class whose parents could afford private "preparatory schools" (preparation for a guaranteed, elevated class in life), Greek and Latin, higher mathematics, rhetoric, art history, and literary classics were the norm. With the beginning of compulsory schooling, practical and vocational skills and Bible studies were instead taught to the masses.[1]

The Idealist's curriculum characteristically studies the liberal arts and humanities: the supposedly best ideas of human history. This also puts an emphasis on 'pure' mathematics. But, since most ideas are encoded in words, an Idealist-leaning curriculum relies mainly on discourse. Literature (philosophy, essays), then, is seen as a leading source of the history of "great ideas." The lecture (old French for "reading") thus prevails as the chosen method of transmitting ideas from the humanities and liberal arts into the minds (or at least the notebooks) of students. Curriculum, then, is focused on sustaining the academic status quo based on the dominance of the past. New ideas are therefore often at first resisted, and Idealism-based schooling tends everywhere to be a very conservative social institution. Its separation of the mind from the body favored rational processes and denied the important role of the body as a source of knowledge (e.g., empirical science, aisthesis in music).

Since teachers' minds are more highly developed, they can best transmit the propositional 'knowledge' of an Idealist curriculum to students. The curriculum is predicated largely on ideas—largely verbal, formal, or mathematical—and instruction, in turn, is given to techniques of various kinds for *transmitting* ideas (information) to students from instructors, books, or computers. The use of the computer should not be allowed to disguise its all-too-traditional use in simply making easily available and then transmitting knowledge (ideas, information, etc.). Other uses of computers allow interactivity and drills (e.g., aural skills training). But the knowledge is still 'delivered' using technology rather than by an instructor.

It is not important for Idealists that learning, knowledge, and skills be *useful* in any practical sense (but "common practice" music theory is, in fact, not at all common today). As a result, it often begins and ends being what students call "merely academic"—the "Academy" was the name of the school where Plato taught, named after *Academus*, a Greek war hero. Such academic ideas, theories, and learning—as defined by experts, authorities, and teachers, according to transmission from the past—are therefore taught as "good for their own sake," as part of being "well educated" (also the focus of Basic-studies and Essentialism covered in Chapter Five). Schools, in this framework, exist to protect, preserve, and pass on authorized knowledge from the past, rather than to effect change or meet the demands of contemporary life.

An Idealist curriculum, then, is a matter of transmission of the accepted status quo of knowledge to learners. Idealism has been a dominant philosophy of music. It has resulted in many divergent *aesthetic theories* that stress the intellectual, cerebral, cognitive, and symbolic values of music—values that, despite certain key distinctions, tend to overlap with Realist and Neo-Scholastic aesthetic theorizing (both described later in this chapter). An *aesthetic ideology* and *an orthodoxy* dominated by Idealist strains have thereby arisen and dominated music education from the top levels down to elementary schools.

According to the aesthetic orthodoxy, 'good music' is the 'art music' approved by highbrow Culture. Musical "meaning" involves ideas that are intrinsic to ('built in') music's sounds as governed by the score, and that exist for their own sake—for contemplation alone. An "aesthetic distance" must, therefore, be maintained—that is, an *aesthetic attitude* that seeks musical contemplation for its own sake, not for personal reverie, sociality, use, or pastimes. Such *detachment* separates ("pure") musical contemplation from any other 'extrinsic' functions and interests (e.g., dancing) or personal uses (e.g., mood regulation). This is extremely difficult to achieve with young people: for adolescents, not only is music *not* detached from life, but also it is a central means of defining Self, managing moods, and maintaining peer relations.

Despite the fixation on words in academic subjects, in Idealist aesthetic theories, words set to music are *extrinsic* because they refer to 'extra-musical' (verbal, abstract, formal, and often humanly relevant) concepts and ideas—usually love, nature, and God. Consequently, solo/choral music is rendered further down *Idealist aestheticians' hierarchy* that has instrumental chamber music and solo literature at the top, most valued as pure "music alone" (Kivy 1980). Such "absolute" music, as it is called, is said to transcend a particular time, place, or person in favor of universal meanings of a metaphysical or cognitive kind—depending on the aesthetic theory, of which there seem to be as many as there are aestheticians!

"Absolute" music is held by aesthetes to be socially unconditioned and complete in itself, with no connection to extra-musical concepts or meanings: simply a sonorous structure existing only to be contemplated by concert audiences. Musical "Nationalism" is demoted aesthetically by absolute music theorists for its reliance on national history, themes, and folk music (e.g., Copland's *Appalachian Spring*). "Program music" is similarly diminished in its 'aesthetic value' for its connection to stories and visual sources (e.g., Mussorgsky's *Pictures at an Exhibition*, Saint-Saëns's *Carnival of the Animals*). Arguments about the value of program music (Liszt's "symphonic poems") versus absolute music (Brahms's symphonies) were the source of great philosophical ferment among composers and aesthetes toward the end of the 19th to early 20th century. Nonetheless, teachers' plans for listening lessons tend to favor program music rather than absolute music, precisely because of its extrinsic bases in stories and pictures—life-based themes students may have more interest in than absolute music's abstract formal relations.

Popular, folk, improvisatory, and similar kinds of vernacular, indigenous, and functional musics are certainly "music." However, the *aesthetic hierarchy* of musical value (see Figure 2.1), as speculated on by aesthetes, puts the standard Eurocentric 'art music' repertory of absolute instrumental chamber music and solos at the very top. Symphonies share the wordless purity of chamber music (until, at least, some late Romantic-era symphonies with choral sections) but gain in audience appeal by the impressive impact of large ensembles. Vocal (art song, opera) and choral music are of lesser value due to their musically extrinsic words, and thus are lower on the hierarchy shared with Program and Nationalist music. And jazz, folk, and popular genres are grouped on the bottom—though not by students who rank such musics as their major musical value). It is worth observing that audiences of classical

---

SPECULATIVE AESTHETIC HIERARCHY

High — **Chamber music and solos**—'pure music', small scale, intimate audiences

Symphonies and Concertos—absolute music, but size is appealing; large audience

Art song and choral music—meaning tied to words; musical value thus reduced

Opera—extrinsic interest in scenery, action, dramatic or humorous storylines

Program and Nationalistic music—based on stories, images, and folk music

Marches, ceremonial, and occasional music*—serves social uses

Religious music—serves liturgy or otherwise has a religious text and meaning

Jazz (?)—not notated, entertainment not 'art', performed in bars and social clubs

Ethnic music—tied to ethnic tunes, dances, or words, easily appreciated by listeners

Low — **Popular music**—for entertainment, popularity soon fades, sung easily understood,

*Music serving specific social occasions; e.g., patriotic music; Tchaikovsky's *Festival Coronation March* (D major, TH 50, ČW 47), commissioned by the city of Moscow for the coronation of Tsar Alexander III, 1883.

Figure 2.1

music seem to most value music that has words or programmatic and nationalist references, along with familiar standards from the standard symphonic repertory of absolute music. This, at least, is the hypothesis of teachers' selections of music for listening lessons.

In the Idealist view, "music" is a composite idea (like "tree"); all "music" supposedly has a shared "essence" or intrinsic nature. Though we find "trees" acceptable, the very idea of a plurality of "musics," each of a distinctive type, violates such Idealistic *essentialism*. We easily refer to "laws," but "musics" is, by Idealism's long-term influence, rejected in favor of a supposedly shared "essence" of all music(s). Thus, we have the misnomer of "music education," not *musics* education.

Furthermore, while some people confer legitimacy as "music" on jazz, popular, ethnic, and similar aesthetically "lowbrow," "downtown" musics, it is only through this claim that such musics compare in some trivial way with aesthetic criteria. In other words, even though its creators have other than aesthetic criteria and intentions in mind, some so-called "aesthetic properties" of an immediately accessible nature (e.g., "tunes" not "themes") supposedly emerge naturally and spontaneously, thereby ensuring some trivial aesthetic experience requiring little or no study or experience. Popular musics are for aesthetes disqualified or at the bottom of the aesthetic hierarchy simply due to their easy accessibility. Such musics supposedly can't be worthy if anyone can access them without training and connoisseurship. That bias seems to be waning and popular musics are studied more in music education today, especially in Europe, and today's educated listeners are musical omnivores compared to the snobs of yesteryear.

In contrast, aesthetic experience is said to be cerebral, intellectual, and abstract and to deal in 'musical ideas'. In aesthetics, no one seems to agree what exactly a "musical idea" (or "aesthetic idea") is: a motif, a theme, a phrase, a section, a 12-tone set, a movement, or an extended passage. Nonetheless, depending on the aesthetic theory, listeners are expected to either (a) follow along with the unfolding formal "development" of ideas or (b) synthesize their listening in a final realization and appreciation of the overall form.

These two theories, of course, are contradictory. Moreover, aesthetics consists of such contradictions and philosophical dead ends (aporia): aestheticians disputing each other in journal articles and books read by other aestheticians interested in philosophical word games. They agree only in lamenting that theories of musical value rooted in praxis gain value through confirmation by ethno-musicology, sociology of music, cultural studies, and anthropology of music! These disciplines are typically offered in only a very few U.S. university schools of music; in general, you need to go to Europe to study the sociology of music, for example.

However, powerful bodily based feelings, frissons ('chills'), somatic residuals, and other embodied experiences are, if anything, treated by Idealist and other formalist aesthetic traditions with deep suspicion—as though merely satisfying bodily appetites, or as superficial "entertainment" (i.e., "ear candy")—and seen as distractions from the 'real' meaning of music, which is said to be one or another kind of cerebral ideation. Consequently, as critics too numerous to mention have pointed out, Idealist aesthetic philosophies of music separate the mind ('musical ideas' as contemplated by intellect) from the body (sentience, aisthesis) and give precedence to the former while denying or disparaging the value of the latter.

The body is also denied in notably important ways by a downplaying of the act of performance. Certainly, performers are respected; without them, aesthetes could hear no music. But listening and composing are accorded the highest value: the composer's creativity is said to encode purely musical (aesthetic) ideas into notation on the page that the performer then only creates instances of—though interpretively distinctive. With the contemplation of music for its own sake as the ultimate value, performance is accorded a secondary status as mainly (or merely) replication of a *composer's* notated creation (*viz.*, the score equals "the music"). Performance, then, is regarded as a matter of facile fingers—as a kind of athletic discipline, for example, scale drills and other technique-building "exercises" (études), being, in effect, musical calisthenics. The "musical ideas" are "there" *in* the score to be realized in performance, however creatively idiosyncratic or compelling the performer's interpretation may be.[2]

More to this point, in university schools of music (in the U.S. at least), studio lessons and ensemble participation are not accepted as fulfilling "general education" or "liberal arts" requirements—those courses that teach the "great ideas" and scientific discoveries composing the various disciplines. Hence, studio lessons and ensembles are often regarded by many in the humanities as "professional training" ("digital dexterity"), not as conveying liberalizing or humanizing *ideas*. Music history courses—especially the boiled-down kind called "music appreciation"—are sometimes accepted for humanities/general studies requirements for nonmusic majors, but oddly are considered as professional "training" for music majors.

Various aesthetic theories have been taken for granted as supporting music education, at least in North America. In some countries (e.g., Germany), "aesthetic education" refers instead to praxis, to performing and to 'making music'. This they contrast to teaching disciplined traditions of "music appreciation" (boiled-down history and theory) as supposedly needed for properly backgrounded contemplation of "Great Works." Nonetheless, music teachers in many other countries have focused almost exclusively at the secondary levels on performance ensembles to the exclusion of listening—or for that matter composition studies.

It is abundantly clear that the small percentage of all students who choose to take part in ensembles find making music together to be an agreeable *social activity*, but their 'tastes' appear to remain unchanged. Do they listen, for example, to choral, string, and band/wind literature outside of school, or as adults? They might if provided as part of the ensemble curriculum with playlists and even assignments for listening, and if the school library had CDs of such exemplary listening. *Listening is a distinctive praxis of its own*! It deserves intensive development.

Unfortunately, the conditions for making music in large ensembles are difficult to organize in adult life after graduation. To begin with, too often community ensembles don't always exist, which prompts the question, why is there not a compelling demand in every community? And where amateur ensembles do exist, scheduling large ensemble rehearsals and concerts into busy adult life can exclude those having interest but who can't find time for amateur musicing due to job and family. Chamber musics (e.g., duets, trios) are much easier to schedule.

However, since most graduates have not had significant opportunities in school to discover the joys of solo and chamber groups performing literature that interests them, the evidence in any community is that very few continue to perform after graduation from school despite their prior attraction to large ensembles as school-based *adolescent social activities*. Virtually all advocacy of music education in schools most often relies on assumptions of music education's aesthetic benefits (MEAE). However, without any overt evidence for judging 'aesthetic growth', such claims are simply false. Instead, the lack of carry-over of music studied in school to graduates' adult musicing is evidence of the abject failure of aesthetics-based advocacy of school music.

General (classroom) music teachers, on the other hand, tend to "teach concepts" as the assumed cognitive bases for the kind of musical contemplation described by aesthetic ideals (e.g., Schwadron 1967; Reimer 2003[3]). Therefore, students are subjected to "activities" that supposedly teach the "concepts" of melody, harmony, form, timbre, and a host of other *words* (terms), such as "program music," "unity in variety," "rounded binary," "sonata form," "development," "cadence," "counterpoint," and the long list of musical jargon that has filled four intense years of the teacher's preparation.

However, much of what music educators have studied in becoming "professional musicians" is assumed *by them* to be the only or best route to "music appreciation." Many of those studies, though, consisted of professional verbiage and technical terminology that even they don't regularly contemplate as audience members: "Oh, nice double fugue"; "V^7 to flat-major VI—what an interesting chord substitution." Yet they persist in assuming that such "background knowledge" is the key to everyone's appreciation, and that appreciation is solely a matter of high-minded contemplation and connoisseurship.

Concepts, however, are not a priori abstractions or words that need to be 'filled out' by musicing furnished by class activities. Studying words used to describe conceptual activity (e.g., high/low), then, is of no value. There's nothing "high" about 'high' pitches; only the number of acoustical cycles per second is colloquially a 'high' number (A440 cps is a larger/'higher' number than the smaller/'lower' pitch of A220 cps). To some people (even some musicians) high pitches sound "thin" while 'low' pitches sound thick (e.g., piccolo vs. tuba). And when students' notated music is flat on the desk, "high" is "out" (in front of them), not "up." Worse, "high/low" references to pitch can get confused with dynamics (i.e., "Turn *down* the TV, it's too *high*").

Concepts are observed in action—in their effective doing (praxis). "Pitch" awareness is a matter of a student's ability to "match pitch" consistently and play in tune. And "melody" is observed in a student's recognition of a familiar tune and singing it or playing it by ear, in tune. "Beat" is seen by those who "keep a steady beat" performing familiar literature or marching. Difficulty with vocal "pitch matching" for some young singers requires individual coaching (see Regelski 2004, 196–199), while other students improve naturally with ensemble performance.

However, in contradiction to contemplative models of appreciation, social psychologists of music conclude that it is precisely the *social value* of music (i.e., praxis) that most attracts young people (Zillmann & Gan 1997). But keep in mind that such 'extrinsic' social values are viewed by Idealist and related aesthetic traditions as detrimental to the 'ideal' fullness of aesthetic responding. However, peer group musical affinities and personal identification with certain musics (most often popular styles) are in total contrast with Idealist aesthetic theories.

The social psychology of music also confirms the social existence of "taste publics" and "taste cultures" (Russell 1997) that reflect adult *social tastes* denied by aesthetic theories and confirmed by praxis theory (described in Chapter Four). In other words, ordinary "music lovers" of varying educational backgrounds find a host of interests in and from musics and musical values that are denied or downplayed by the Idealist-dominated *aesthetic orthodoxy* and its partiality for abstract ideas and *formalism*, and for refined "aesthetic emotion," which is (as described later in connection with "Realism") not actually "emotion."

"Formalism" in musical aesthetics contends that musical meaning depends on perceiving, comprehending, and hence appreciating formal musical relationships (themes, harmonies, rhythms, development, etc.) and consequently that musical meaning is the result of intellect and training. Formalism is usually the basis for "form and analysis" university studies and for attempts of music appreciation texts to describe "ideal" musical forms. They take, for example, an early Mozart movement as the "ideal" model for all music said to be 'in' (idealized) sonata form—often *Eine Kleine Nachtmusic*, a divertimento that in any case was a praxical, background 'diversion' for aristocrats' soirees. Yet "sonata form" is not a cast or mold, and each sonata is unique—fortunately. At best, knowledge of this or that "form" is useful mainly in following the music as it unfolds, where similarities of later moments with earlier ones give a sense of "shape" to what otherwise would be an incessant flow of ever-new musical gestures.

Idealist-leaning aestheticians, along with those inclined to Realism, hold that music is expressive of emotional states of mind (e.g., sadness). More to the point, such an "expressionist" theory claims that music is expressive of *aestheticized* emotions and feelings. These, however, are qualified to emphasize that music is expressive of idealized emotions: *cognitions* of emotional states (i.e., the essence of sadness in the abstract or in general), not real emotions (actual sadness). This is better discussed later in connection with Realism.

We might assume that turning to the philosophy of Realism, more familiar bases for music and curriculum might be encountered, but this is not the case.

Realism

For Realists, *aisthesis* (sensory experience) reveals the world as they believe it 'really' is.[4] They believe that the accuracy or details of our sensory observations may change over time (e.g., with technology, experience, or science) but not the material world itself, which is stable. Aristotle, disagreeing with his teacher Plato, taught that "form" could not exist without "matter" to be formed—the cognitive giving of form to sensory experience is the *in-form*ations (inward forms) of aisthesis.

Unlike Plato, Realism accepts, then, that the material world of things is independent of mind. Accordingly, the physical world and natural laws are the source of truth and knowledge—instead of mind and ideas. Realism, therefore, is a source of modern empirical science. Values and truth, for Realists, are also derived from the discovery and observation of natural laws and, given the stability of the material world, are absolute and unchanging.

However, there is one important variety of Realism. *Pragmatic* or *Internal Realism*[5] is notably different from the *direct Realism* described throughout this section. Pragmatic Realism agrees with direct Realism that the material world of things exists independently of our concepts—that trees exist apart from our ideas of them (and make a sound when they fall even if no one hears it). However, Pragmatic Realism qualifies that our knowledge of them (e.g., walking into a tree in the dark and knowing their variety) is nonetheless always embodied (via pain, touch, vision) and thereby acclimatized by the language, society, and previous pragmatic experiences. We never know 'treeness' as an Ideal form or thing-in-itself (as per Idealist essentialism).[6]

Realism and the music curriculum

The natural world "out there" is also the source of criteria for judgments of beauty. Beautiful art and music, then, represent (*re*-present) the patterns and arrangements of the natural world. Realist aesthetics posit that "aesthetic properties" exist independently of the mind. 'Good art', then, reveals the orderliness and rationality (laws) of the natural world. In consequence, Realist aesthetics are sometimes called "naturalistic aesthetics."[7] Ethical values also arise from the study of the natural order in the universe, and given an unchanging universe, moral laws are regarded as eternal, not relative to time, place, society, or person.

Schooling exists, similarly, to transmit an authoritative understanding of the logic and order of the universe—as validated and transmitted by instructors, curriculum committees, scholarly authorities, and textbooks. Mathematics and the social and natural sciences are especially stressed, and transmitting 'facts' and information is given primary importance in all subjects. Knowledge and truth, then, as with Idealism, arise outside of and prior to the learner's experience and are transmitted and passively received in school. While some instruction may use activities, experiments, demonstrations, and the like, the knowledge thus gained is inert (pre-fab), and it is expected to be accepted, not questioned. Learning, then, is a matter of accepting a priori or "given" truths and 'facts', not personally constructed, relevant meanings.

In dealing with music, Realism faces many obstacles. These difficulties may well explain the fact that few philosophers have felt comfortable proposing philosophies of music that reflect the Realist aesthetic leanings described previously. The first problem faced by a Realist aesthetic of music is the fact that while musical sounds do have *physical* properties, music is *not* simply acoustics. In consequence, hearing sounds *as* "music" is not simply a function of the auditory mechanisms of the brain. It is not the biological mechanisms of hearing that convert sound into "music," but the cultural tunings of the *social mind* that result from being born into a world of tonality or microtonality and socially influenced brain mechanisms. A host of other social variables distinguish "music" from "noise." The social *use* of music enhances all forms of sociality.

The social mind is a cognitive mind-set conditioned (pragmatically) by one's social and environmental milieu. Some thoughts cannot arise outside of one's location in the world and its language and culture: for example, the many different qualities of snow that inform the lives of residents of northern climates whose lives depend on the distinctions. In Iceland, techniques for rotting fish result in a culinary favorite. In Finland, most doors open outward, and in England, people are well used to driving in the left lane and likewise walk to the left on sidewalks. Music, in like fashion, is a socially constructed and embodied experience. Not surprisingly, then, what is "music" in one culture is often very strange to those in another where the social mind and the social reasons for creating music at all are often quite different.

The social mind is especially conditioned by language, social institutions, social interactions with significant others (particularly family and the community), and experiences in the shared geographical and climatic environment and its impact on the mind and body. Philosophically, the "social mind" also includes bodily responsiveness: what, why, when, and how the body is a source of both musical inventiveness and musical responsiveness. In consequence, the "social mind" acknowledged by sociological and philosophical Pragmatism (Searle 1998; Mead 2015) is not just brain anatomy (M. Johnson 1987). Moreover, with the exception of imitative effects (e.g., bird-like calls), music does not refer directly to (represent) the things of the world. Even "program music"—music inspired by stories and visual images—relies heavily on titles and other hints to the listener who otherwise would have no experience with what the music is supposedly "expressing" (e.g., Debussy's *La Mer*, for desert peoples).

Similarly, Realism diverges from the purities of "formalist" (Idealist) aesthetic theories (i.e., music as pure form, as balance, proportion, and symmetry, an "architecture of sound"). Instead, it offers "expressionist" aesthetic theories. However, the feelings, ideas, and emotions that music is said to 'express' are quite evidently not in fact "real"—not the same as in everyday experience, As Peter Kivy (1980) notes, the drooping visage of the St. Bernard dog's face does not express its sadness (Figure 2.2). It is anthropomorphized

Figure 2.2 The face of the St. Bernard is sad

and "looks sad" to human observers. The dog may be happy or content. This sanctifying of emotions separated from their bodily origins is claimed to be the purpose of art: somehow emotions are neutralized or intellectualized and thereby 'purified'.

Music, if this reasoning is correct, does not *express emotion* (notation is not capable of 'having' human emotion) but is said to be somehow "expressive of" this or that emotion (Kivy 1980). Philosopher Susanne K. Langer argues that music sounds as feelings feel, that music cognitively offers *presentational symbols* of feelings (Langer 1977), and, therefore, music's sounds seem to (somehow) resemble how human emotions are felt. It is difficult, however, to map the ongoing experiences of emotional feelings in life with music, especially since personal feelings can be so variable. Worse, labeled (discursive) feelings (e.g., anger) present themselves differently to different people at the same time, and differently to the same people at various times. Langer's argument just cannot be sustained to explain the diversity of feelings and forms of musical "expression." Her "presentational symbols" are altogether too cerebral and removed from the actual dynamics of felt life. Her theory has thus garnered much criticism rather than approval from philosophers. In fairness, however, many analytic philosophers do not regard aesthetics as even being systematic philosophy.

Consequently, upon apprehending, say, what we describe as anger or sadness in music, we do not find ourselves actually angry or sad. We only observe or contemplate some seeming similarity that is said to be from and of the composer whose creativity and intellect put it *in* "the music" (i.e., in the score). It is not, therefore, from and of the listener who, instead, supposedly only experiences a cerebral conveyance of the composer's expression of 'felt life'. "That is why the emotion felt in listening to music has been called aesthetic emotion, *intellectual emotion*. . . . It is not the real thing somehow" (Broudy 1991, 81; italics added). As a result, Realist aesthetics hold that music suggests or implies images and ideas by symbolically presenting expressivity and sound rationally and logically.

For example, musical movement can seem analogous to the movement in the physical world: for example, *andante* as walking, "L'Éléphant" in Saint-Saëns's *Carnival of the Animals*, a lumbering waltz for double basses and piano, marked "allegro pomposo (Debusy,. 'Jimbo's Lullaby'), in *Childrens Corner Suite*." Such "musical movement" is experienced as expressive of the emotions that accompany physical movement (Broudy 1991, 81) without, somehow, actually engendering the authentic, lived emotion. Thus, while music is experienced as such "in" or "by" the social mind, in the Realist's view musical experience does not call attention to or take the sentient form of holistic bodily experience. Consequently, as with Idealist aesthetic theory, Realist aesthetics results in disembodied products of perception that are appreciated based upon some symbolic, cognitive, or intellectualized association with lived experience.

As a philosophy guiding music curriculum, Realism strongly—as with Idealism—emphasizes *connoisseurship*. Music deemed to be 'good' by the "experts of successive ages" is 'exposed' to students in the hypothesis that it will "enhance the pupil's enjoyment of music and life" (Broudy 1991, 91–92). According to Realism, whatever *pragmatic* values music other than the Eurocentric repertory might have for religious or social occasions are not to be confused with *aesthetic* values, which should be the sole focus of formal music education (Broudy 1991, 77). The emphasis, again, like Idealism, is largely on contemplative listening. This disembodied account of musical meaning again relegates music to a secondary realm. Realist philosopher Harry S. Broudy (1991) hardly mentions performance in his "realist" criteria for music education. Instead, meaning for his Realism resides objectively "in" the score, the work, apprehended only in a detached and mainly cognitive or cerebral form.

This claim for musical meaning brings about a final problem especially associated with Realism as a basis for a school-based music curriculum. If the 'higher' and 'richer' forms of human experience 'expressed' musically in a score by a composer are the true bases for musical valuation, it is difficult to account for how *students of school age* are supposed to recognize, associate, or identify with such complex adult states of mind. How, then, are they to value them since they have not yet had such rich and mature personal experiences? You do not educate students for future life by exposing them to, say, 'anger' in music.

The music they *can* and *do* relate to is regarded aesthetically as immature and inferior. Nonetheless, the comprehension and discrimination needed to develop good taste and appreciation are supposedly developed better through listening because young performers lack the technical skills to properly fully realize the aesthetic value of 'good music' through their underdeveloped performances. For similar reasons, however, amateur, recreational, lay, vernacular kinds of music and music-making are ignored for lacking aesthetic depth. In contrast, when exposed to the "Great Works" of the traditional repertory, "musical training affords the learner a basis for objective and informed judgments about certain aspects of musical quality" (Broudy 1991, 86).

This idea of music education as a "training" for *backgrounded connoisseurship,* while sharing some features of Idealism (i.e., idealized emotions), also bears similarity with the Neo-Scholastic philosophy.

Neo-Scholasticism

Scholasticism is a philosophy that developed in the late medieval age with the very beginnings of what we know today as schooling. "Scholasticism" usually refers to the presuppositions of a single philosophy taught in the universities of late medieval Europe, presuppositions found useful by philosophers working outside those universities in the late 16th and early 17th centuries. As such, there is, strictly speaking, no such doctrine as Scholasticism, only a matter of dealing with questions or truth, faith, and reliable knowledge. However, the tag "Scholasticism" was later adopted by self-styled neo-Scholastics of the late 19th and early 20th centuries who remained committed to doctrines whose origins can be traced back to Aristotle. It may now be necessary to speak of Neo-Scholasticism,

Today's references to "scholar," "school," and "scholastic," share this medieval legacy. It is thus the source of some of the most basic habits and traditions of today's schools and schooling. For example, the "lecture" (old French for "reading," Latin *lectio*) stems from medieval times when hand-copied books were in short supply. So those *professing a thesis*, called, appropriately, "professors," directly read their treatises (theses) to student followers, called "bachelors, in part" because they were free to accompany or attend the professor's journeys between cathedral schools. Experienced followers who had learned a scholar's theses and arguments were called "masters" and supplemented the professor's lectures, kind of graduate assistants. They helped new learners before striking out on their own as authoritative "professors" of the master's (or their own) professed theses—usually religious or related to religious precepts. In later centuries, the reading aloud of a distinguished text was the primary step in instruction followed by a period of reflection, and then questions could be asked of the professor. The resolution of questions depended on logical disputation.

These "professors" and their followers congregated at major crossroads of Europe in connection with Catholic cathedrals and monasteries. Although today's rank of a PhD (doctor of philosophy) didn't exist, the honorific title "doctor" was used to address the most respected of such professors.[8] Today's trappings of bachelor's, master's, and doctoral degrees—such as caps and gowns, maces, deans and chancellors (all the attire, protocol, and nomenclature of medieval church schools), and the lecture method—are not, however, the only remnants of scholasticism that survive. Scholasticism is firmly rooted in formal schooling around the world, especially in universities.

Scholasticism, in its prime (13th to 14th centuries), benefited greatly from the rediscovery of Greek philosophy. Scholars (court musicians too) served in the courts as evidence of the elevated learning of the King or Pope. Muslim intellectuals had preserved Greek philosophy and conveyed it to European scholars in what is today southern Spain and Greece. They also brought to medieval Europe from northern Africa the ancestors of the viols and guitars, and they decisively influenced European scholarship. Some were influential scholars in their own right.

The intellectual life of the late medieval age soon came to be concerned with disputes between various monastic orders over translations and points of disputation with Greek philosophers. This intellectual contentiousness was particularly the case between Franciscans and Dominicans: they carried on the Greek contrast between Platonic Idealism (by then, Neoplatonism—today's source of "Platonic Love") and Aristotelian Rationalism. Franciscans (first St. Bonaventure, later St. Augustine) argued for the Neoplatonic emphasis on an immaterial (Ideal) "soul" and the immateriality of God. Worldly reason, then, had to be tempered by faith. Dominicans, in contrast, using the newly available translations of Aristotle's texts, emphasized reason. St. Thomas Aquinas synthesized Aristotelian rationalism with Christian doctrine. His theology (also known as Thomism) became definitive for Catholic theology until the present day.

Neo-Scholasticism today is a contemporary term rooted in following the medieval scholastics' emphasis on rational knowledge, disciplined training of the intellect, training in the ancient "classics," and subjects that have a rational organization (e.g., mathematics, Greek, Latin). It has so much in common with Realism that in its traditional Catholic form it is sometimes called "scholastic" or "religious Realism." And in its continuation in later secular forms seen in liberal arts and humanities in universities, it is sometimes known as "classical Realism" or "rational humanism."

Scholasticism had important roots in Aristotle. His *aisthesis* or sentient knowledge supported Realism (and, later, science). Key also was his three-part *deductive* logic of the syllogism, the first two terms of which are taken to be true:

[If] All humans are imperfect.
[And] This author is human.
Therefore, this author is imperfect.

Inductive logic, in contrast, derives conclusions by generalizing from observed evidence. Unlike the certainty of deductive logic, inductive logic deals with degrees of probability: "All swans are white" states a probability that requires surveying all swans. In consequence, different individuals faced with the same observations of evidence might well arrive at different conclusions. For example, people have different opinions of schools depending on their experiences of schooling. On the other hand, deductive reasoning nonetheless depends on inductive or experiential knowledge that defines the first two terms of deductive logic:

> Women have babies.
> That person had a baby.
> Therefore, she is a woman.

As with medieval scholasticism, a conception of humans as *rational* underlies Neo-Scholasticism—which often comes as news to teachers of middle schoolers! In this view, the ability to think rationally is the noblest and most valued capacity that humans possess. Thus, the mind can seize upon truth logically in the form of self-evident ("*analytic*") truths (e.g., "If A is larger than B and B is larger than C, then A is larger than C") or via scientific or empirical thinking ("*synthetic*") truths that depend on experience for testing and confirmation (e.g., "Snow is cold"). The *tension between rationalism* and *empiricism*—between analytic and synthetic knowledge—usually antithetical, results for Neo-Scholasticism in considerable overlap with Idealist and Realist theories and therefore with their aesthetic assumptions for music education.

However, purely rational knowledge, analytic truth, is seen by Neo-Scholastics as having a higher logical status than empirical knowledge because it is a priori and independent of the subjective impurities of people's sensory knowledge (aisthesis). As with Idealism and Realism, bodily knowledge is distrusted for being subjective; reason rises above such subjective differences. For Neo-Scholasticism, values ultimately depend on rationality: accordingly, the "good life" is in harmony with reason. Therefore, base desires and emotions should be under the control of rational intelligence and of making rational choices for living. Thus, political conservatives often believe that falling into poverty is a failure to live rationally. (Tellingly, the very rich think the same about the middle classes.)

Neo-Scholasticism and the music curriculum

The creations of artists, artisanal skills, and intellect can reach beyond pure reason to intuitive insights that are then developed by reason. *Technē*, a term from Aristotle's time (explained in detail in Chapter Four), is the skill and applied theory of "excellent making," the practiced *craftsmanship* of the arts. Such artisanship is undertaken on behalf of the applied arts, but not for its own sake. Technē is concerned with (excellent) *making* (e.g., things and performances), in contrast to *praxis* (also detailed in Chapter Four), which is concerned with (excellent) action that involves promoting the well-being of *people* (e.g., students) served by the praxis. Pastoral praxis, for example, is concerned with the effects of a pastor's actions on the lives of parishioners. Technē also includes the skills of rational communication and rhetoric, both of which require logic.[9]

Much music, in Ancient Greece, was a technē of the common classes and regarded (by notables) as inferior to the liberal arts practiced and enjoyed by aristocrats. Its choral music was an intoned text somewhat like Gregorian chant. Appreciation of artistic creation took the form of intellectual interest, stimulation, and its gratification or fulfillment. "Good taste" in art and music, for Neo-Scholasticism, is a rational accomplishment gained through appropriate study, training, and cumulative experience, and accordingly is the purview of only qualified connoisseurs.

In schooling, the development of students' rational faculties requires studies of the leading "disciplines" and sources of learning (e.g., the "Great Books"). These disciplines structure the knowledge of their domain in coherent, rationally organized and presented (disciplined) terms—though ongoing developments contribute new knowledge to the accumulative status quo of disciplines over time.[10] Such expansion engages scholars who, in the best traditions of scholasticism, "profess" and "dispute" according to ever-more progressive theses and interactions, thus incorporating new knowledge and theories into existing disciplines—sometimes even expanding the discipline into a new one (e.g., biochemistry, ethnomusicology).

The "disputation" of a thesis is among the hallmarks of scholasticism, even today. What started as face-to-face disputations between "professors" are now the defences of doctoral degrees, where the aspirant's thesis is defended before critical faculty (and, in some places, interested audiences).[11] More frequently, it appears in peer-reviewed publications that challenge or expand upon status quo findings and understandings. The more research articles and books of a professor accepted for publication by peer review—and the standards of those publications as judged by their refusal rates—the greater the authority of the professor.

Accumulated authority takes the form of a hierarchy of ranks: lecturer, assistant professor, associate professor, full professor, distinguished or university professor, holders of endowed professorships or "chairs"—the "endowed" meaning it comes with money to support the holders and their research. For Neo-Scholasticism, "professing" without such "authority" from a record of distinguished publication is scholarly purgatory. Students, unfortunately, often don't know about the publishing records of their professors and book authors and just assume their authority (see, e.g., https://scholar.google.com/intl/en/scholar/citations.html: Thomas A. Regelski).

Through studying these disciplines and their highly developed logic, it is believed that the student develops disciplined habits of thinking that inform and guide the good life—the educated life guided by reason. Systematic subjects such as mathematics and foreign languages (at one time, Greek and Latin) and, in particular, the "great ideas," the "Great Books," and Western musical, literary, and artistic "masterworks" are particularly favored in the belief that they promote the best achievements of humankind (Adler 1994). The watchword for Neo-Scholasticism is the *discipline* that results from rigorous *training*. As a result, school students are regularly "exposed" to and expected to study and master subject matter in which they may have no interest because they anticipate no important, immediate, or eventual practical or personal relevance beyond faculty claims for improved reasoning.[12]

Scholasticism had its origins in the waning years of the Middle Ages when art and music were praxis and served a wide variety of social, celebratory, and—especially—religious and courtly functions. Neo-Scholasticism, therefore, has no clear philosophy of art or aesthetics and tends to share an often untidy (contradictory) mix of Idealism and Realism—sometimes focusing on rational ideas (formalism), and sometimes on intuitions of feeling (expressionism). Schools around the world still tend to be committed to the original scholastic ideal and model of promoting rational thinking and mental discipline through transmitting the truths and knowledge codified in the traditional intellectual (academic) disciplines.

In this Neo-Scholastic framework, music is often taught as a *discipline of knowledge*. Music history and theory are especially taught to university music majors as part of their *discipline*, not for the enhancement of their appreciation. Moreover, select "background information" from those disciplines, in boiled-down or simplified form, is said to be needed by *all* appreciative audiences to 'properly' contemplate musical values. "Listening lessons" in schools feature "Great works." In Texas, competitions are held for students to identify themes in contests of musical memory—apparently under the dubious assumption that the process of memorizing themes leads to appreciation.

Classroom music thus often features "activities" intended to promote learning concepts about musical form, melody, harmony, timbre, and musical terms (sonata, symphony, development, etc.)—just as with Idealism. Therefore, it is not surprising that a blend of Idealism and Realism often sustains Neo-Scholasticism despite their typically contradictory conclusions—rationalism vs. empiricism, analytic vs. synthetic knowledge—and implications.

It is not an overstatement to claim that this untidy blend of contradictory philosophy is the bedrock of schooling in many countries today. They may be old in their sources, but they are contemporary in making public schooling an extremely conservative and rigid social institution that stands in the way of schooling as a progressive and vital force in contemporary life.

Closing Perspectives

In general, the three traditional philosophies—Idealism, Realism, and Neo-Scholasticism—all share a usually abstract, "merely academic," and detached approach to schooling, as well as other traits. For all three, questions about reality, truth, and beauty are not questions at all! They are eternal and unchanging claims that exist independently of and, therefore, logically prior to the experience and needs of particular students. The personal detachment and irrelevance of such facts and information for students are in part a direct result of the intellectual, metaphysical, and rational claims of all three traditional philosophies.

This impersonal and inert status of traditional curriculums results in the typical inability of music educators to model or otherwise demonstrate the actual or even potential relevance of such studies for musicing outside of school and for adult life. Such learning, then, is not only abstractly received from outside the lifeworlds and needs of individual students but also, for most, lacks any foreseeable consequences of its actual relevance in life—regardless of any short-term interest in a class or rehearsal! The *direct instruction* required to teach such abstractions (e.g., lecture, drill, textbook reading, demonstrations, scripted activities, memorization, tests, "it goes this way" rote instruction) is likewise a motivational liability in comparison to the "hands-on," "learning by doing," *indirect instruction* of newer philosophies (e.g., Progressivism, Existentialism, and Progressivism, covered next).

Music curriculum predicated on one or any combination of these traditional philosophies falls prey to similar problems, particularly in general music and other classroom instruction such as music theory. And the influence of these philosophies is largely ignored or downplayed in general music classes in favor of "teaching concepts." In ensembles, the focus is usually on the next concert, not on long-lasting skills, attitudes, and values that enable individual graduates to continue to perform or to listen with discernment.

There is, as well, a shared realization in contemporary philosophical circles that aesthetic assumptions associated with Idealism, Realism, and Neo-Scholasticism are irrelevant to the actual practices and pleasures of music and confuse more than enlighten thinking about the 'real world' of musicing. "It would be hard to think of a subject more neurotically self-doubting than aesthetics. Claims that the subject is irrelevant, muddled and misunderstood have been a persistent theme, not only of recent, that is to say, post-war [II] writers, but from the very start of the subject. Alas, these claims have all too frequently been justified" (Proudfoot 1988, 831; see also 856).

Traditional aesthetic assumptions have also ignored the influence of the major 20th-century philosopher Ludwig Wittgenstein. His *Lectures on Aesthetics* begins: "The subject (Aesthetics) is very big and entirely misunderstood as far as I can see" (Wittgenstein 1966, 1). Moreover, "it is not only difficult to describe what appreciation consists in, but impossible. To describe what it consists in, we would have to describe the whole environment" (7)—because, as will be seen, music is a *social praxis*, and thus, the entire human environment has a bearing on its use and pleasures. Accordingly, the environments in which music and the arts are appreciated are, Wittgenstein points out, so "enormously complicated" that words referring to aesthetic ideas and criteria have negligible importance in typical circumstances (2; see also 11). "We don't," he cautions, "start from certain words" describing aesthetic qualities or concepts, "but from certain occasions or activities" (3)—namely from authentic musical praxes, from musicing.

Nonetheless, much of musical training in higher education uncritically accepts major aesthetic premises; form and analysis studies are examples.[13] However, also consider the curricular premises of "music theory" (i.e., taught as fact, such as perfect intervals), music history (as purportedly needed to perform in style), and much of the unspoken criteria that ensemble directors impose on students (e.g., all decisions about phrasing, dynamics, and tempi). In fact, despite the presumed aesthetic assumptions of musical value and meaning (whether formalist or expressionist), musicians rarely use aesthetic terminology, and like most people they find aesthetic theorizing *an*esthetic to the brain.

The need mentioned by Wittgenstein to get back to the unique requirements—"occasions or activities"—or praxes of music-making as they exist in particular conditions of situatedness, as we shall later establish, is among the influences of 20th-century philosophical theories on curriculum, and collectively of a praxical orientation to curriculum for music education.

3
19th and 20th Century Philosophical Foundations of Curriculum

Preliminary Considerations

More recent Existential and Phenomenological epistemology[1] and Pragmatism have decidedly more positive implications for curriculum than the three traditional philosophies discussed in the previous chapter.[2] They avoid the dullness of "merely academic" instruction in favor of recognizing student interests, needs, and differences. These more recent philosophies, unfortunately, face an uphill contest against the earlier described traditional philosophies. Their challenges to traditional curriculum models thus require resilience, courage, and personal resolve from teachers who are often expected by old-timers to "fit in" to traditional curricular agendas (e.g., Basic-studies and Perennialism, in Chapter Five).[3] If you're going to resist, it helps to know the disputed grounds at stake.

These three more recent philosophies are the result of new developments in science, knowledge, and philosophy, and the resulting implications for change in traditional curriculum theory. With ongoing developments in the modern world have come new responsibilities for schools and new demands on both students and staff. They propose understandings that are focused on change and values that are dependent on differences of individual circumstances, meanings, and societies.

Existentialism, Phenomenology

From these two often entwined philosophical disciplines, curriculum favors an emphasis on the primacy of the individual's reflective consciousness over the one-size-fits-all template of traditional philosophies and the 'delivery' of subject matter said to be true, good, and beautiful for everyone (Chapter Two). Thus, claims for eternal and absolute truths are rejected. Instead, the important role played by each person's reflection on inner-life experience is stressed.

Accordingly, existentially aligned thinkers (and such music educators) strongly reject the doctrinaire and a priori frameworks of traditional philosophies covered in Chapter Two.

Phenomenology's influence on existentialism is seen in the focus on human *activity*[4] in the sociohistorical and cultural lifeworld rather than on a priori absolutes. Knowledge, in this view, is *culturally created* by individuals in interaction with the natural world and with members of society and its institutions. Such knowledge is *personally reflective*. It focuses on the process of conscious goal-directedness toward valued things and events of life, and thus on their shaping of our responses to them. This *intentionality* of perception and conception—its goal-directedness or what it is "about" or "for"—is also shared importantly with Pragmatism (as will be seen later in this chapter). It means that *the mind always directs attention toward some object of interest*, toward doing something with it or learning something from it. (Remember: The brain cannot *not* learn! It always seeks objects of interest for intentionality.[5]) Fostering musical intentionality on the part of students is essential to promoting learning. Mastery depends on a sequence of student-held goals (musical intentions) focused on improved musicing.

Phenomenology thereby accounts for knowledge of our intersubjective, shared world in terms of our unique consciousness of it and particularly reactions to the objects of our consciousness. Sociological phenomenology encompasses the lived, social world as we experience it. Important for schooling is that hands-on *practical* knowledge precedes propositional or *conceptual* knowledge (consult Piaget's stages of learning from concrete to formal). Knowledge "that" something is the case results first from active knowledge of "how" to experience, interact with, or reflect upon that thing. Concepts, therefore, are active, individual mind constructions from experience that arise and are seen "in action," in use.

Phenomenological thinking focuses on whatever is in consciousness, bracketing out influence of extraneous theories, presumptions, and other beliefs; it relies on direct, immediate, and unadulterated perception or conception, though the "social mind" can still be influential. Attending to an object or a 'doing' (praxis) in this way, one can gain insight into the process by which it develops in our consciousness over time. Such reflection is especially useful with music since it unfolds over time. But even visually scanning a painting has a temporal dimension that benefits from reflecting on such unfolding attention. This habitual activity of reflecting on our 'doings' involves a *heightened inner awareness of the structure of our consciousness* that, historically, took two applications in the growth of existentialism.

Christian existentialism

Existentialism is less a philosophy in the usual, systematic sense than a philosophical *disposition* of habitually reflecting on *existence* (as lived), and with the attentive and constant scrutiny of such reflections by the individual (*my* existence). The two formulations of existentialism both avoid any sense of being a doctrinaire "school" of thought.[6] Instead, the literature describes different ways of focusing on one's "existence" in constructing personal meanings of life.

One aspect is the Christian existentialism promulgated by the Danish philosopher-theologian Søren Kierkegaard, who many credit with being the 'father' of existentialism. Important to stress is that Kierkegaard and his Christian existentialism are included here not with the intent of preaching it as somehow superior to or critical of any reader's religious belief. Many people at first dismiss existentialism as ungodly. Thus, such necessary to stress that its origins are Christian, and these origins are pivotal to understanding existentialism and its relationship to Self and, in consequence, the relation of a teacher's Self to school curriculum. It is quite possible to be informed by existential premises and to be a thoughtfully committed Christian. Kierkegaard demonstrated that!

As the first existential thinker, Kierkegaard posed many of the most basic questions and issues of existentialism. Among them is a fervent concern with the primacy of phenomenological experience (i.e., inner Being-ness) over abstract speculations (e.g., those of Chapter Two), the importance of personal choice and commitment (over enforced belief and conduct), and the subjective relationship of the individual to Jesus Christ (that is the foundation of faith). His emphasis on inner Being and authentic faith was the essence of his existential philosophy and theology. It also was the source of his criticism of dogmatic, doctrinaire Christianity, especially when dictated by a state government or King (*viz.*, the Lutheran State Church of Denmark of his time). Instead, he was concerned mainly with the inner life of individuals as they experienced their choices—especially concerning religious faith and the personal consequences and responsibilities of their choices, for themselves and others.

He regarded "faith" as a principled "leap" by an individual into uncertainty, not as a taken-for-granted, firm conviction resulting from, for example, uncritically following the particular denomination into which one was born.

By ordinary definition, "faith" is a belief committed to in the absence of logical proof or empirical evidence. Were decisions of "faith" proven in advance by empirical evidence and certain verification, "faith" would be impossible or meaningless. Kierkegaard's "leap of faith" is an existential 'leap' to follow the teachings of the God-Man Jesus.

Oddly, this choice for Kierkegaard is existentially meaningful according to the believer's *absence of certainty*—the humble accepting of God despite the possibility that *faith* might be wrong! Fundamentally, then, if God appeared and performed miracles, adherents would be obliged to acknowledge His authority as an empirical truth—like a temporal world King—and, thus, faith would be negated by fact.

For Kierkegaard, the "leap of faith," then, is taken, held, and followed "faithfully" in the absence of any factual proof or certainty. Consequently, for Christian existentialism, the meaningfulness of faith is dependent on *critical reflection* that the possibility one's "leap" of faith into the unknown could be wrong; its meaningfulness is that, nonetheless, it is believed and followed.[7] Throughout history, many religious people have instead been so certain of their belief that they would kill to further or defend it. Terrorism confuses faith with fact. Such self-assurance in effect denies faith by its *belligerent certainty*! And in existential terms, such "inauthentic" behavior is a major source of religious bias and many other human conflicts (e.g., the certainty of believers of conspiracy theories on social media).

Faith in all avenues of life regarding truth and values is meaningful in the same way for existentialism: for example, faith in a marital partner's love and fidelity. This kind of faith recognizes that love is never achieved in finished form, once and for all times. Rather, it is a continuing process that promotes ongoing positive acts that further a lov*ing relationship*. If one's "faith" and actions in life are not conditioned by the *possibility of being wrong*, then "faith" has given way to closed-door, dogmatic, certain, and misplaced confidence. In consequence, "faith" is nullified into 'fact'—its contradiction.[8]

"Pascal's Wager" is the position advanced by French philosopher Blaise Pascal that whether or not to follow God's laws is a gamble. Living as though God exists is the best bet, he reasoned: one gives up minor concessions in worldly life rather than gambling on eternity in Hell. This challenge takes on major consequences for Kierkegaard. The *absurdity of life* is that no matter what we do, it ends in death! For existentialism, this absurdity recognizes the importance of the meanings we create in life daily through choices.

Such *meaning-making* adds to our integrity and existential *authenticity*—we act according to what we intuit and inwardly believe, not based on dogma or other external authorities. It means taking full responsibility for our choices (actions) and their results for us and others. Being *inauthentic* is uncritically following the trends and 'truths' of others or casting blame elsewhere than one's Self when things go amiss in life or love.

Twentieth-century novelist-philosopher Albert Camus offered a parable based on the Greek myth of Sisyphus to illustrate the existential dilemma or *angst* of both Christian and Humanistic existentialism. King Sisyphus was punished for eternity by the gods to roll a heavy rock up a steep hill, only to have it roll back before reaching the summit or to roll down the other side. This quandary offered only the choice of starting over again and again, and always doing so hopeful of final success. However, the *action ideals*[9] that guide a reflective life (e.g., good health, good friend, good spouse, good teacher) are similar ideals that cannot be reached once and for all times; no such single state of perfection exists. The rock is not perfectly poised for all time. Thus, such beneficial 'goods' require constant reflection on how successfully we are reaching for them.

This existential absurdity compares to life, where death is equally predictable as Sisyphus's failure in dealing with his fate. Meaning, in this existential tale, comes from accepting and surmounting life's struggles, entering the fray again and again. It is an ever-lasting struggle that can be done well and even energetically, however absurd in the long run (eventual death). Life's meaning is the value of just pushing onward and upward and doing it with integrity, no matter how life's forces resist. Pushing against those forces (e.g., as a teacher) is itself a source of meaning.

Of course, it is certainly possible to accept others' conclusions that affirm God and the religiously guided life. But for existentialism, unreflectively accepting received or imposed values, doctrines, and practices is *inauthentic*— an existential cop-out! That is how Christian existentialism is defined in comparison, for example, to blindly accepting the religion of your parents, or as dictated by a King or religious authority. Similarly, following friends and trends, fashions and fads of all kinds produces lemming-like group-think values, not existential *authenticity*. Coasting in life or love is therefore an abdication of actions and choices that challenge complacency and thereby engage meaning-making.

Moreover, and importantly, such existential leaps of faith bring on *anxiety* ("angst") about their results (e.g., "Should I gamble on this new job?"; "Should I marry him?") that only the future can resolve. Decisions about values are hypotheses to be tested by experience. Consequences of such an "existential leap"—whether in religion or in other life decisions (or on a changing continuum between them)—are suffered by or credited to the individual's choices when faced with life's uncertainties. Therefore, existentially, *meanings are made through choosing and reflecting on those choices, not found readymade*.

And one is existentially always self-aware of both the uncertainties in life and the consequences of authentically meaningful choices made in the face of those uncertainties.

Christian playwright-philosopher Gabriel Marcel denounced the dehumanizing effects of contemporary industrial society as hindering the possibilities for *authentic* and meaningfully chosen life values. The materialism and technology of modern society dictate all manner of unreflective acquiescence in living that prevents free existential choice about alternatives. People are limited to life patterns that are not choices: just dehumanizing alternatives to which they think they must be servile and submissive—to be popular, a sheep-like citizen. This "false consciousness" puts them in positions where they are treated as "things" on the "production line" of "free market" neoliberalism, for example, with no attention to acting on their authentic values; blind, in fact, to their false consciousness.

Schooling is often described, in this framework, as a 'factory line'—or, by students, as a prison—for the same reason. Students are "processed" as though impersonal "things" to be passed on in some methodical way for the next stage of processing. This kind of curriculum is antithetical to existentialist educators' emphasis on the role of leading students to create their own knowledge and meaning through their actions on and choices in the world. Some (often despite schooling) become alert to the coercive forces of society and "struggle" meaningfully as artists and "free thinkers" who authentically create their life agendas despite social pressures and other challenges.

Humanistic existentialism

Existentialism probably exists on a continuum from religious to not so religious to not at all religious and shifting places in between. Authentic actions seek no God to blame or praise. We are left only with the angst of living with the consequences of our choices.

Humanist existentialism often take literary form—novels, plays, and essays. Friedrich Nietzsche and Jean-Paul Sartre are typical examples. Albert Camus often denied being an existentialist but explored existential themes in his plays, essays, and novels (e.g., *The Plague, The Outsider [Stranger], Myth of Sisyphus*).

Humanistic existentialism focuses on the individual, often as contending against (or at least as not blindly subservient to) society—a society that collectively denies full humanity to individuals through the imposition of group-think economics, ethics, and values.[10] 'Truth', then, comes to depend on your perspective, which is always changing over time according to the circumstances you face. And the fact that personal perspectives get influenced or inherited from powerful others (families, communities, nations, politicians, religious leaders, etc.), leads—or existentially should—to critical concern about their sources ("Is it warranted or just someone's subjective opinion?") and validity ("Is it defensible?") and about their consequences for Self and others ("Are the likely results positive or negative, and for whom?).

This coexistence of the competing perspectives of others results, then, in a *perspectival account* of truth and reality (Nietzsche). For example, one person sees welfare as a redistribution of tax money to allegedly lazy people; another sees the same situation with compassion and charity for the poor. *Perspectivism* is the source of the difference: each decides from different bases of understanding—in this case, political, social, and often religious sources. 'Truth' for such political and religious followers, therefore, depends on accepting a priori and culturally contingent judgments (these critics have never been homeless or poor) that they uncritically bring to their judgment, usually unaware of the sources of their respective positions. There is no "objective truth," only positions more or less strongly defended by argument or contentious evidence. At the time of this writing, even truth gives way to "alternative facts" of political ideology.

Inauthenticity is reliance on a default position to fall back on when challenged: a lack of taking responsibility for judgment and casting blame elsewhere. "What about-ism," rather than answering a claim, blames the challenger: "What about the homeless who take welfare monies to buy booze?" they say, repeating talking points and "fake news" as though they're in possession of the statistical findings of social science. Their present circumstances typically define their valuing. "Why should I pay taxes for someone's kid to have a tuba to play in school?" Sociologically, people tend to agree with and defend their friends and neighbors (particularly their shared religious and political partialities). 'Truth' becomes borrowed life, on loan for individuals and people according to the narrow perspectives of their lives at any moment.

The values of a philosophically or scientifically informed position on beliefs and knowledge are constantly under challenge by new developments. Then perspectives found to be unsustainable are replaced. 'Truth', then, relies on the aggregate of relatively congenial perspectives where each resonates with others into an even stronger position. It's called "society"—which isn't the same as being "authentic" (e.g., Nazi Germany).

Existentially worrisome, then, is that many perspectives amount to positions that cannot survive criticism. While perspectives can and do differ, they are not all necessarily warranted or authentic; there often are criteria or options for adjudicating different perspectives. For example, in social democracies around the world, many needs of people (such as free education and health care) are met by a government-supported safety net that is willingly supported by taxpayers who also benefit. For *perspectivism*, however, "truthiness" is clouded by cultural and other concerns, for example, conspiracy theories about "welfare cheats." Truth and facts depend mostly on a pragmatic consensus, as in science and the jury system. Truth, goodness, and beauty, then, are at best one comprehensive perspective (at any moment) and most assuredly not, as in traditional philosophies (Chapter Two), absolute and eternal. The implications for a curriculum are considerable.

'Reality', for existentialism, is nothing more or less than our physical existence as a Self fully engaged in the world. Instead, "being-in-the-world" (i.e., the *Dasein* of Martin Heidegger)[11] is fully and authentically immersed in life: *a taking of full responsibility with no excuses*. We are thus entangled in dealings with other Beings but *unavoidably alone* in the angst of making and confronting life's decisions and their consequences for Self and others. Rather than accept that humankind shares a certain 'essence' of the types preached by traditional philosophy (e.g., that humans are, in essence, rational beings), for existential humanists, we are free beings born into—as Camus once put it—the "benign indifference of the universe."[12] We find ourselves "being there" (existing) in a world that has no intrinsic meaning except what we make of life's choices.

Thus, we are born into a lifelong inevitability for acting and making choices that create our *particular essence*. What we "are" in life, then, is the sum of our ongoing actions, our *self-actualization*. We are rightfully and anxiously aware of being responsible for every "leap of faith" on which we act. Hence, against traditional philosophies that define a human's essence (Being) as given by the circumstances of birth (e.g., Original Sin, gender, blond, homely, and rich), we have instead been "thrown" by chance into a particular world of socially existing structures and meanings to contend with (racism, sexism, language) and creatively confront for the better (if we so choose).

Thus, existentialists contend that *existence* (being born into a world of chances for choices) *precedes essence* (what you make of your Self through those choices). In this indifferent universe, our Being (alive) means that we have the challenge of creating our own authentic Self through our choices and actions. Consequentially, who "I" am is the creator of my own life's meanings. Given the ever-new choices we make daily in living an authentic life, the dynamism of this process of Self-creation, means that who we "are" is not a matter simply of "Being" (alive). It is an unending unfolding of "Becoming." This "coming into Being" (full "aliveness") is, at any moment, an always uncompleted evolution of creating personhood and Self in response to life's unending offerings. It confronts life's challenges and opportunities for transforming one's Self and creating life's meanings.

In practice, then, the existential mind is concerned with observing one's inwardly 'felt' subjectivity, the phenomenology of lived experience as consciously reflected on when resisting control from any outside authority or agency. Existentially oriented thinkers, therefore, are "engaged" with life, lived enthusiastically through personal *meaning-making* rather than focused on detached, speculative metaphysics or blindly accepted, "pre-fab" social and religious meanings that "program" or "predetermine" certain choices of living. In the existential view, meaning is not received readymade or found. Rather, it is actualized or actively constructed through the choices for action available to each individual. The individual is the focus, not the crowd (e.g., fellow music teachers).

The individual, as engaged with the world, is central to the existential concern with 'reality'. Existentialism accepts that the things in our world of experience (tables, trees, etc.) exist. But as with pragmatic or internal realism, it rejects the common-sense claim that the things of the world exist irrespective of our mental images and understanding of them based on personal and sociocultural experience. The world, *as we come to know it*, is always dependent on our ongoing images and understanding of it. For existential innovator Friedrich Nietzsche, for example, the everyday objects of our daily lives are in effect *constructions* (Remhof 2018). They come into *our* existence—create *our* world of experience—according to the various human practices (praxes) by which we interact and experience them. As a result, these objects get their reality as constructed by our actions with or on them. Nietzsche's *constructivism*, then, is closely related to the *pragmatic Realism* explained earlier and later, and it stresses the role of social praxes on our understanding of the tangible world, what it has to offer as potential meanings (choices).[13]

Just as the reality of the material world as experienced is socially constructed, so then is our knowledge of that world—whether through science or, more commonly, through experiences with that world as chronicled by social history and passed on by tradition, especially language. Socially constructed things and happenings often have words that allow us to refer to them in our social dealings (some, however, are *tacit knowledge,* nonverbal; Polanyi 1962). However, just as the world as we know it is rooted in constructivism (from our engagements with it), students' experiences of it are needed for their constructions of knowledge derived from it. They need the chance to create their personal worlds of Being and Becoming.

These worlds include a host of 'things' to be known that are not material. For example, the word "balance" is meaningless without the experiences that in-form [sic] (i.e., *in*wardly give *form* to) its praxis. Telling a beginner who is learning to ride a bicycle or to ski to "Keep your balance" makes little "sense" (compare to "Stay in tune!"). Notice too how the word "sense"—the sentient knowledge of *aisthesis*—figures as a metaphor in descriptions of understanding: make sense, common sense, sensible, "I *see* what you mean," "I *hear* what you're saying," etc.

Of considerable importance to existential thinking is the construct known as "Self" that is the unity of our otherwise diverse inputs. The Self we 'are' (at any moment) is the unified merger of mental inputs. *Self-actualization*, existentially speaking, is truly a matter of *Self-creation*, an ongoing action (praxis) of constantly bringing-Self-into-Being-and-ever-Becoming by and through coordinating or connecting the input of our choices and decisions and (importantly) personal reflection on them and their consequences for Self and others.

Such self-creative *agency*—the action of constructing an evolving *personhood*—first of all (a) involves actions that *reveal our values to ourselves and others.* If we are abundantly self-reflective, our natural or spontaneous choices in significant situations often reveal our values to our Self (What value reveals itself to me and others when I make a choice?). Importantly, then, our (overt) actions and choices are seen as reflecting our (covert) values, not infrequently those we didn't know we had. (Ever feel the need to burst out in opposition to something you'd not thought much about?) This is the opposite of deciding on values, then acting on them. Instead, existentially, we act and reflect and thus discover our values. Try reflecting on the implied values of your chosen actions for a day. What do our words, choices, and actions reveal about our values? Such reflection, done daily, is to live existentially.

Secondly, (b) my choices and public actions serve as *models* for others to consider. "I" publicly model who I "am" as "my Self" through the actions and choices that I regularly expose to others. My Self or personhood is my collective choices and actions, as understood by a particular *public* ("He's a torrent of positive energy"). The public varies, and a Self can be adjusted accordingly (e.g., "daughter" to one's mother rather than to one's mother-in-law). An educator, for example, has a public of students and peers in schools but also has a public of a family, community members, religious membership, scouts, student athletes, and endless other publics. Each has its own requirements, and keeping a balance between the social roles we "play" can be a challenge (e.g., consistency as a teacher) or a mistake (e.g., the factory "boss" who continues bossing at home).

Through our actions and words (and especially our judgments of others), we are "coming out" to those around us as to who we 'really' are! This coming out has nothing to do with sexual orientation. Hiding who we "are" is futile; eventually, we "come out" whether intending to or not: we are seen by others as egotistical, needing praise all the time, or as saints or narcissists. We think we're admirable, though our actions eventually betray us to others (e.g., two or three years into teaching, seven years into marriage). However, given the role of teacher, parent, church elder, etc., notable inconsistency in our values and actions becomes evidence of an unstable, inauthentic^Self and therefore as being unpredictable in unproductive ways.

Who we "are," then, is always *demonstrated in action* to others. Whether others see us as kind, overbearing, patient, condescending, intelligent, or dogmatic is *read* by others (especially students) from our actions. What we think of as our private Self is really on constant display in our actions. Existentially, *we are the actors of our Self-created scripts*; those social roles we act out (parent, daughter, student) function as scripts.[14] When those scripts become predictably troublesome to others in a socially constituted environment, we risk becoming seen as a "type" playing a socially discrepant or abnormal "role" we don't recognize in our Self ("She's on an ego trip"; "He's a narcissist"). Being a "type," of course, is a problem with the social role of "teacher" and how the public, the students, and the institution of schooling see that role ("He sees students as enemies"; "She's strict but fair").

Humanistic Psychology and Existential Theory

Humanistic psychology has been a correlate of existential philosophy due to its central concern with the creation of a healthy and well-functioning Self (Regelski 1973). It parallels existential themes about functional and dysfunctional Selves. Leading humanistic psychologist Abraham Maslow (1962/2011) posited a *hierarchy of needs* to be met in producing a functional Self. While some doubt whether his theory was scientifically reliable, its concepts and terms provide a very useful *model*[15] for describing the growth of the Self. He described a pyramid-like hierarchy of the human "needs" that shape the Self (Figure 3.1).

At the bottom levels, most broadly basic, plentiful, and common are "Deficiency Needs" (D-needs): needs that are fundamental to being alive, healthy, of a settled mind, and able to deal pragmatically with the world. Any lack of fulfilled D-needs results in deficiencies in meeting higher needs. D-needs involve physiological needs (food, shelter, sleep), nurturance from

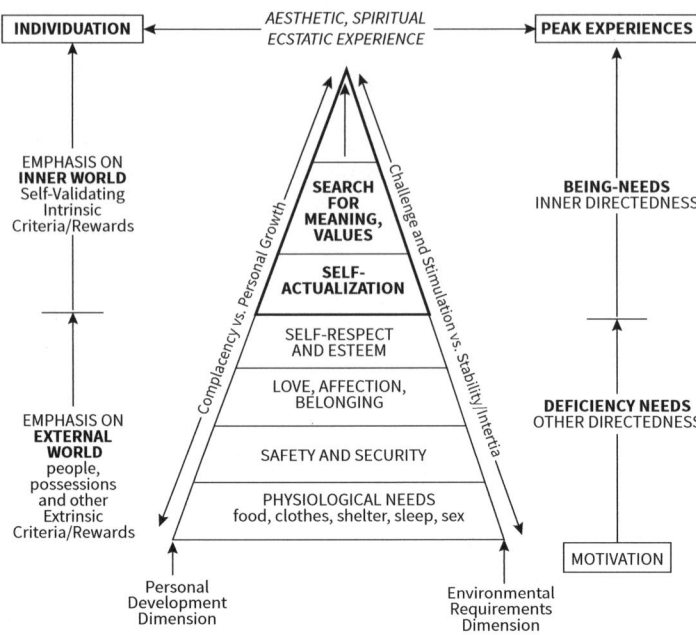

Figure 3.1 What Maslow called "aesthetic" is "aisthesic" since peak experiences that are aisthesic (i.e., involve intense aisthesis as described earlier) don't carry all the negative baggage claimed for speculative aesthetics.

others (safety and security), a sense of belonging, and approval from others (especially parents and peer acceptance).[16]

These needs, of course, are not always productively met by some families, communities, or societies; for example, some students come to school hungry. School breakfast and lunch programs are society's answer. But compensatory programs are not as simple for students who experience parental abuse and lack of nurturing support (love, encouragement, and positive models) at home, or who have difficult peer relations at school for dressing contrary to local adolescent styles (due to parental poverty) or being newcomers to the community or country.

Unless or until these D-needs are satisfied, these students have a reduced chance of successfully making their way in school or the world. Children from such home environments often repeat the model for their children. If beatings and other physical maltreatments were typical in their childhood, the same is likely to be the case with their children. In most cases, D-needs depend on "significant others" (parents, relatives, teachers, friends, community leaders, etc.) for their fulfillment. They are crucial to the young person's developing sense of Self, and if unmet in early life, they can complicate adult life too.

Such sources of fulfillment are deemed "outer" (compared to "inner") or "other-directed" due to their dependence on others. They are, nonetheless, important and pivotal to the evolving sense of Self. Nevertheless, some people (especially children and adolescents) can become neurotically dependent on others for their D-needs. They always ask for (i.e., need) praise or attention ("Look at me" on a swing set, etc.). But D-need "safety" refers not only to *physical* well-being—a mounting problem with school shootings and crime-ridden neighborhoods. "Safety" also means feeling *mentally* comfortable and accepted by peers and teachers in school. Students who, for whatever reasons, feel psychologically uncomfortable in school or a class are lacking this developmental need. Bullying is a widespread result. But so is a feeling of incompetence, either in comparison to classmates or if frequently implied by the teacher.

Going one by one down an ensemble section to reveal (i.e., embarrass) the student playing a wrong note or who is out of tune can jeopardize a feeling of safety. Some also become dependent on rewards and congratulations from others ("How did I do?" always asked after a sports match), leading to a condition of *other-directed dependence*. Attention-grabbing show-offs of any age often have unresolved D-needs for recognition.

A sense of belonging is, then, very important, as is shown especially in pre- through late adolescence with the D-need for positive peer group affiliations. Belonging to a gang or any *cohort*[17] can outweigh almost all other criteria, even sometimes the law in the case of gangs. Self-respect also often depends on how well a student is functioning *according to school standards* (including the hidden curriculum). Being recognized (by peers or by teacher comments) as "dumb" or "slow" or "abnormal" or "different" in some important respect (e.g., transsexualism) is, then, a curse to be endured: adolescent suicide is often the result of incapacity for suffering such circumstances. The opposite treatment is a platform for successful self-actualizing.

If intensified by the teacher (e.g., publicly posting grades or a posted roster of "winners" and "losers" in seating auditions) playing "favorites" (or being unduly critical of a particular student), the consequences can typically be very negative for the developing adolescent Self. D-needs are focused on and satisfied by the external world and *other-directedness*. Others—parents, teachers, friends, classmates—are the source of "extrinsic rewards." Experiences are "positive" only according to what *others* value and judge to be good (e.g., prizes, competition victories, public awards, sports recognition), and *intrinsic benefits* or *rewards* get snuffed out—prevented!—when extrinsic rewards heralded by the school and "significant others" are uppermost in mind.

D-needs that go unmet in early stages of life (especially adolescence) can lead to "unfinished business": to obsessive states of mind that remain unresolved and continually irritating or nagging fulfillment ("I have no good friends"); to unfulfilled needs or frailties that are often all too readily noticed by others (e.g., "bullied students"); to obsessively craving (needing) good grades (or first-chair status);[18] to exhibiting an athletic superhero persona; to "acting out" when facing public failure, shame, or ridicule; to being overly cautious to not make mistakes and thus often not even trying or easily giving up; to needing attention that may be met by being an attention-grabbing nuisance and unruly in class—being good only at being bad! Such unfinished business can, unfortunately, linger into adulthood, where the unmet needs can become neuroses. It may be that the most serious problems faced by adults stem from such unfinished business: unreasonable outbursts of temper, cozying up to superiors, or being an office recluse, a troublemaker, or—all of the above and more—an "asshole" (see James 2013, a serious philosophical study).

The development for most individuals who have, for whatever reason or source, had their D-needs met well enough[19] is the self-actualization by which a young person begins to create a healthy sense of Self-respect. They reflect on prospects for life beyond D-needs and attend more often to being-values. B-needs are "Being needs," existentially self-actualizing values. They heighten the experiences of being alive and lead to the pride of self-accomplishment. They contribute to a sense of Being and Becoming, both more human and an ever-growing socially competent Self. They are students' personal *action ideals* that are never perfectly met once and for all times, but always confront ever-new situations and challenges (e.g., best friend, reliable accompanist, successful student, conscientious worker).

B-needs are *inner-directed*, not other or outer-directed, as are D-needs. They are, then, increasingly *self-directed* (existentially authentic), not by the demands of parents, peers, or educators but by their developing values and awareness of interests and needs. B-needs promote *peak experiences*. These involve the summits of euphoria, exhilaration arising with music, art, and religion.

Peak experiences are the most intense experiences of Being (existence) and resulting peak experience *individuation* ("I did it!") that can be aspired to by humans fully engaged with life, and therefore the most "alive." Sex is also among Maslow's peak experiences, though not just sexual gratification. It is the sexual communion of Oneness-of-Being-together-in-love that is a peak experience. When thus existentially "authentic," it arises from love and is a peak experience confirming and fulfilling love.

Being "alive"—living fully—for the existentially inclined is much more than merely existing—more than going along on the routine treadmill of life.

"Aliveness" seeks out and promotes peak experiences that confirm one's Being and are Self-induced for their authentic intrinsic benefits (e.g., practicing to realize ever-greater musical peak experiences, not to win). Actions (praxis) in the existential mode of Being involve not only just being alive but also being fully engaged with life—seeking all it has to offer.

The source of B-needs is intrinsic. They are sought for themselves alone, even though others may take part in their accomplishment. They are also intrinsic in the sense that they arise in conjunction with the present circumstances (age, student, etc.) and are thereby relevant at that stage or for those circumstances.

In comparison, D-needs are responsive to external sources. They are other-directed and arise as expectations directed by significant others (or generalized others, in the case of groups, such as other adolescents, or the cohort known as "the faculty room"). They expect extrinsic rewards in the form of grades, stickers, praise, social reinforcement, winning (a competition or award), etc. D-needs only change over life. Where once a parent or teacher demanded certain outcomes, in adult life it is the boss, minister, husband or wife, school administrator, studio teacher, ensemble director, etc. They continue to nag at the other-directed person until confronted (by negative experiences, therapy, critical feedback from friends, etc.).

Two responsibilities are at stake with inner-directed B-needs: (a) the never-ending phenomenological *self-reflections* that are defining of a Self always coming into Being, along with a heightened awareness and concern for consequences of that creation[20]—such a Self evolves an increasingly self-directed agency, and (b) the mindfulness of *modeling* actions that demonstrate the values others can take notice of and adopt (e.g., being patient and polite when others are enraged and out of control, being a reliable friend, regularly having practiced the band part, and being a productive leader). Learning, valuing, and meaning, then, are all highly individual results of personal *agency*—of one's choices and actions. Honesty, charity, and love, for example, are learned that way—as processes connected with action, such as *loving* and *giving* of one's authentic Self.

Existentialism, phenomenology, and the music curriculum

The existential dynamics of D-needs and B-needs for students are important and consequential effects of schooling and curriculum. Instead of being *the* authority about the true, good, and beautiful (as with the traditional philosophies), the instructor with an existential orientation helps students explore questions and options of value, use, importance, and relevance, and the choices they entail. Students are not treated as widgets on an assembly line, subject to the one-size-fits-all 'delivery lessons', activities, and repertory year after year. They are "persons" deserving of being treated as individuals. Their *personhood* needs to be "drawn" out through their choices, not forced on them.

Existentially inclined music educators first guide students to aspire to musical goals commensurate with the type of class (ensembles, composition, general music, etc.). They tempt (or prime) students via conditions that are intrinsically motivating—*musically* so, beyond just amusing "fun" activities. Second, they facilitate or help students reach and reflect on those self-set goals.

Thus, they are not *authoritarian*, as is typical with the three traditional philosophies where teachers drive or impel students according to personally dictated curricular directions and values. Existentially oriented teachers, instead, are *authoritative*: their authority does not come from the label or formal role of "teacher."[21] They are recognized and authoritative in helping lead students to realize their own (but teacher-encouraged) goals. After being "turned on" to certain personal musical goals (say, 'mastering' their first tune), students are then led by steps to realizing ever-new *musical* goals—not just D-needs provided as rewards and extrinsic incentives, but actual musical goals: playing a new tune, learning a new key, and the satisfaction and pride of accomplishment at their level. Teachers who make a recording of each 'finished' piece on a student's MP3 file understand the relationship between the satisfaction of accomplishment and pride (*viz.*, proudly sharing it with parents and grandparents—the musical equivalent of refrigerator door art class displays). At every level, promoting musical peak experiences should be the intention of ongoing instruction.[22]

Students' existential development as a Self (i.e., personhood) is no less important than acquiring the musical content or skills at stake. In what way or to what degree will they experience a peak experience, an inner recognition of their musical achievement? That "I did it" and "I'm proud and personally rewarded musically by my accomplishment" is an existential focus on the inner life of the student's "course" (curriculum) of musical growth. Personhood that identifies with musicing ("I am a musician") promotes lifelong involvement with music.

We have already seen what in phenomenology is called "intentionality"—the *goal-directedness* that an action is about or tries to bring about. In "action theory" an "action" (doing something with an end in mind) is distinguished from mere "behavior" or "routine" (like reading the sports news first). This "aboutness" of intentionality needs to be mainly musical, the end-in-sight or goal-of-the-moment to achieve something musical and meaningful. Otherwise students' intentionality will only be about following directions (and some won't do that).[23]

The intentionality merely to have fun is naturally promoted by musical activities: music *is* fun—though not like playground fun and games. But students who seek only occasional fun often do not keep up with the practicing needed to extend that interest. Or they stop and start again and again for mistakes while 'practicing' to no musical growth purpose—seeking to experience the musical whole—no matter how often interrupted for corrections. Their only goal is the end! For the same reasons, they usually practice too fast for their current technique. It even may be that practicing is not always fun (nor is weight training needed in various sports), but done with intentionality (i.e., with to-be-achieved *musical* ends-in-sight), it is meaningful and eventually rewarded as "good time" (explained later). But unless students have in mind musical progress in addition to the "fun activity," any benefits will be gone when the students leave the classroom or rehearsal. The risk is that such activities become only a musical "recess" from the academic stultification of other classes.

Without this intentionality (or ATTITUDE DIMENSION, described in more detail in the Chapter Six discussion of a praxis-based curriculum), student efforts will be responsive only to *extrinsic,* other-directed motivation and D-needs (e.g., avoiding being scolded for not practicing; challenges for chairs in instrumental ensembles; awards or grades at competitions), not authentic, *intrinsically musical*, B-need motivation.[24] That involves the personal intentionality needed to aspire to and reach new *musical* goals, not just to get an approving response by the teacher, a gold star, sticker, or membership in the "210 club" (i.e., 30 minutes of practice, seven days a week, posted publicly as recognition for "good students").[25] As should be clear, students who follow such extrinsic motivations are just filling time, not prevailing over musical needs and problems.

Schools that force-feed values (musical and otherwise) to students and repress their uniqueness (despite giving "lip service" to individualism) are seen by an existential framework as outright harmful. First, by imposing meaning as ready-made ("It goes like this"; "Don't breathe there"), they *prevent* students from self-actualizing and thereby from personal *meaning-making* in action. Second, such other-directedness quickly teaches students that learning is something (extrinsic) schools and teachers do *to* you, not something you participate in and do (intrinsically) with intentionality for *your own sake*—the way most students master computer skills and sports on their own. An existential paradigm fits especially well into an educational philosophy that addresses the students' affective development and, consequently, on the central importance of Self-actualization and ongoing *recreation* (i.e., re-creation) through such actions as making and listening to music as adults (Regelski 1973). Re-creation (a Becoming or ongoing, renewed sense of Self), then, is the condition of beneficial recreation, not just mindless expenditures of mental or physical action. Art is to this extent a praxis by which people define themselves.

Existentially inspired instructors respect the individuality of each student. One-size-fits-all 'delivery methods' and "pre-fab" materials do not address such differences, neither as important to each learner nor as central to the learning process. "Pre-fab" materials that serve such delivery methods at the very least need to be adjusted, qualified, and crafted to students' differences. The curriculum, thus, is flexible and always open to change. For example, a university piano student, uninspired with the assigned literature, asked for greater choice. The professor agreed and, not surprisingly, the student's choices of literature were always the best prepared and most suitable for recital performances. And, as a bonus, the personally chosen literature—ironically called by the professor "recreation pieces"—were always more technically demanding than the usual assignments.

The affective—feelingful, valuing—dimension of students' B-needs, then, is a central concern and is ignored at risk of instead submitting students to uniformity and "discipline," both offered for their own sake. Readers must by now be aware that this *technical drill for its own sake is off-putting* to students, especially younger students who chose to study "music." They often vote with their feet—and quit.[26] Whatever the outcomes for the few who remain, this is not overall a pragmatic result for those who give up study.

Historically, phenomenology has a long interest in music. Early phenomenologists were centrally concerned to study, explain, or describe in phenomenological terms, for example, how we hear melody, experience musical time, and recognize a "work" even though no performance is the same (or when a tune is in a different key). As mentioned previously, a first consideration is that both music and the individual exist in the lifeworld (praxes) of a community, or music-world (e.g., of 'jazzers'), and its sociohistorical shaping forces. Things like art and events like music have meaning for us within a cultural and socially constructed *horizon*—a horizon beyond which learners at first cannot see, but that expands as new worlds of musicing are opened for them to reach. This sense of being situated in a culture and its music is the inescapable existential condition in which we live, and it affects our lifeworld.

A second consideration is that "the music" is not "the score." Scores (depending on era and composer) are always *indeterminate* to an important degree. The many unaccounted-for gaps get resolved in praxis by the performer's choices. This indeterminacy has, of course, been given a high focus in aleatory and stochastic music of recent times. But it also holds great interest with the standard repertory as we focus on how the indeterminate gaps in the score (e.g., tempi, phrasing, accents, fermatas, and rubato) get resolved in a particular performance. When it comes to a familiar "work," as listeners we attend with interest to familiar details and especially to the creative handling of un-notated variables.

Music is, of course, a consequentially important social praxis and experience, uniting diverse listeners with the community of composers, performers, and audiences across history. Even practicing or playing alone is fundamentally a sociohistorical activity. And, unlike the traditional contemplative ideal of traditional aesthetics,[27] music is inherently an embodied experience, a "minding" of the "body" through music—music as felt, not just heard—and is an affirmation of the full existential Self.

We turn now to the philosophy of Pragmatism that has important implications for curriculum, some of which it shares with existentialism and phenomenology.

Pragmatism

Pragmatism is an American-born philosophy (C. S. Peirce 1839–1914; John Dewey 1859–1952; William James 1842–1910, George Herbert Mead 1863–1931). It is critical of traditional philosophies (Chapter Two) for their emphasis on a priori absolutes and essentialism. Pragmatists (especially Dewey) have sought to "reconstruct" philosophical thinking by restoring it to ethical, political, and social relevance.[28] For Pragmatism, 'reality' is ever-changing with experience and history. It arises in *transaction*s with the things and goings-on of our lifeworld. Knowledge is rooted in tangible experience: we act in and on our lifeworld, and then observe the actual consequences that we then judge to be 'real' or 'valuable'. These consequences determine our conceptions of 'reality'.

Such consequences are also the *meanings* of our actions. Thus, rather than passively receiving inert, predigested knowledge according to *transmission* theories (i.e., Idealism, Realism, Neo-Scholasticism), we actively explore the world around us and thereby *transform* ourselves and it in certain ways. Our actions consequentially have a constructive effect on our shared world.

Accordingly, our lifeworld itself is dynamic and pluralistic. Even science gives only a temporary understanding of how the universe works and it is constantly updated and extended.

Pragmatism and *praxis* (described in Chapter Four) share a root meaning in the Latin root *pragma*, or concrete reality. For praxis, the focus is on "action" (its typical English translation); for Pragmatism, the etymology refers to "acts of doing." Action is also concerned with *agency*: "agents" are those who act to accomplish certain results (e.g., we are the agents of our own decisions in life). *Change agents* foster change, progress, new praxes, and new cultural lifeworlds and musical horizons. In pragmatic curriculum theory, educators should be change agents focused on changing the lives of students through music and, consequently, expanding the horizons of their future lifeworlds—what they can see ahead of them that beckons their interest enough to fulfill it musically.

A key representative of Pragmatism, especially regarding education and schooling, is John Dewey. For Dewey, Pragmatism goes well beyond the vernacular meaning of "practical," or "practicable." He writes that much "so-called practical activity is not practical. . . . That is, it either achieves nothing or it achieves its ends automatically, without care, attention, or involvement." Thus, for Dewey, beyond the usual utilitarian notion of practicality, "there lie those courses of action [praxes] in which through *successive deeds* there runs a *sense of growing meaning conserved and accumulating toward an end that is felt as accomplishment of a process*" (Dewey 1934/1980, 38–40, italics added). Accordingly, Dewey defines *an* experience as the basis of **authentic praxis** (a) where one acts to fulfill tangible "ends-in-view" (Dewey's term for intentionality), (b) where their *meaning* is the realization ("consummation") of those ends, and (c) where successive experiences are cumulative and progressive (learning).

"*An* experience" for Dewey is characterized by the key mindfulness or intelligent and reflective guidance of actions directed toward meeting a valued need or overcoming a meaningful problem; that is, ends-in-view are what action is about, intended to bring about or to bring to fruition. In other words, *an* experience meets the conditions of *intentionality* addressed earlier regarding phenomenology. Without such intentions (valued ends) in mind, efforts are random, pointless, and futile and don't accumulate into a functionally holistic body of learning or progress. Much of our behavior (as distinguished from *action*) consists of habits and routines that are mindless in comparison with *an* experience that is guided by intentionality.

However, our intentions often meet with obstacles that prevent them from being immediately fulfilled. This blocking of fulfillment stimulates

> (1) An obstacle to our intentionality (to our anticipated end(s)-in-view) of the moment is thus regarded as a *problem* to be overcome.
> (2) Recognizing a problem, we thoughtfully analyze the sources and conditions of the problem.
> (3) Then we search from our assimilated prior learning for potential resolutions of the problem. These serve as *hypotheses* to be experimented with in solving the problem. (Pragmatism is thus sometimes known as *experimentalism*). Resolutions can also can be new solutions to be accommodated to our fund of prior knowledge.
> (4) From these options (of #3) one *hypothesis* is chosen as most likely to solve the problem.
> (5) Then we act on it (i.e., experiment with it) as being most potentially instrumental (necessary, useful, causative) in overcoming the problem (Pragmatism is thus also known as *instrumentalism*).

Figure 3.2 Pragmatic mindfulness leads to mindful habits.

musical mindfulness (e.g., focused and determined thinking) for overcoming the problem that involves five stages or steps (Figure 3.2).

For example, an orchestra or band student has (or should have) an *aural image* in mind of how the new piece or part should sound.

1. The teacher must, first, promote this *audiation* ('hearing' in the inner ear[29]) or else the student has no idea of mistakes, of how it "goes."
2. "The problem" is *the student* independently recognizing that something played wrong is a mistake (compared to the initially audiated aural image). The student then *analyzes* what went wrong (wrong fingering, position, register).
3. Then, the student *hypothesizes* (reasons) what can be done to correct it (e.g., consults a fingering chart, tries random correction, or asks a neighbor).[30]

   Abductive reasoning is a principle of pragmatism. It describes logical inferences that start from one or more observations (e.g., of wrong notes), then "infers" the simplest and most likely explanation for the observations (e.g., wrong fingering). When such reasoning results in an apt solution to a problem (e.g., corrected fingering), a repertory of such conclusions (corrections) accumulates as *assimilated habits* that serve to resolve new but similar situations. Such pragmatic habits are not to be confused with mindless routines and behaviors. Slight differences between situations can result in *accommodation,* where a previous habit is updated and its accommodated form added to the repertory of mindful problem solving options.
4. What is judged to be the most likely *hypothesis is chosen.*
5. Then it is *experimented* with (enacted) as the anticipated solution.

This experimental result still needs reflection on whether stages 4 and 5 LEAD to consummation (fulfillment) of the original aural image (of intentionality, ends-in-view) before proceeding, or *acting adaptively* by reconsidering stages 3 and 4, as a basis for corrective action (stage 5). Practicing thus relies heavily on the initial aural image and the intentionality for getting it right.[31]

Following this sequence of cognitive steps (that often occur quite quickly, especially as *habitual skill* is acquired), it is possible to judge whether or not the *observable* result satisfies the intended goal. The hypothesis that succeeds in fulfilling intentionality is true or good (as qualified by that problem, or one very similar to it in the future). When an experimental action (stage 5) does *not* overcome a blocked intention, consideration of one of the other hypotheses generated at stage 3 becomes the basis for corrective testing (stage 5 again), and so on until reaching consummation of the aural intention.

Pragmatism also shares or overlaps several traits with existentialism and phenomenology. While it shares with Realism a disdain for Idealist aesthetics and corresponding respect instead for concrete experience, it otherwise has little in common with traditional Realist philosophies. *Pragmatic Realism*[32] agrees with naive Realism that the physical world is causally independent of the mind. However, it further qualifies that the world *as we know it*—its diversity into classifications, distinctions, labels, categories, species, colors, textures, and the like (tiny bonsai and massive redwoods are both "trees")—is the result of the functioning of the *social mind* in *transaction* with the (given) physical world or scientific experiments with it. Therefore, while the physical world exists independently of our thoughts, for us it exists and is known only through our transactions with it, our experiences in or of it, including experiences of ourselves as bodies acting in and on the natural world. Indeed, the experiential world ('reality') of residents of the Arctic is thus very different than that of people whose native experience is limited to tropical islands.

Pragmatists argue that there is no way of confirming the various claims of the three traditional philosophies concerning "ultimate" reality, value, truth, goodness, and beauty. What people can and do regard as 'real' and value or respect, according to Pragmatism, arises from their own down-to-earth experience. Values, including those in music, are therefore relative to individuals in varying ways—according to the range and specific conditions of the situations they experience. And they are pluralistic—meaning that different values exist because the experience of life is not everywhere uniform.

Values are not, however, wildly subjective the way some personal beliefs may tend to be. Rather, values are confirmed, demonstrated, and warranted by pragmatic experience that, in turn, is governed by situated or governing conditions that lead to experience in the first place. Beliefs that cannot be *dis*confirmed fail the scientific criterion of *falsificationism*: the belief that all swans are white is disconfirmed (falsified) by observing a black or gray swan. Personal beliefs that can be disconfirmed by experience are false. (*Verificationism* needs to survey all the swans in the world to confirm its claim about swans all being white.)

Fundamentally, then, for Pragmatism the truth, value, or goodness of any proposition (or action, thing, method, principle, concept, etc.)—for example, music—can be seen only in the tangible consequences that result from its situated use. This appeal to "practical bearings" or consequences is stated more precisely in the "pragmatic maxim" of Charles S. Peirce, the 'father' of Pragmatism: "Consider what effects, that might conceivably have practical bearings, we conceive the object of our concept to have. Then, our conception of the object of these effects is the whole of our conception of the object" (Peirce 1931/1958). In other words, acknowledging what practical differences the object of a concept's application (musicing) will have for praxis is its meaning—that is, the notable *difference it makes* in use. Moreover, when observing the difference made, its meaning (and usefulness) is clear to both student and teacher.

Meaning and value are, therefore, *naturalized* (Popp 1998; Väkevä 2000; Määttänen 2015). "Philosophical naturalism denies all immaterial entities that are supposed to have some effect on the material world. . . . It follows from naturalism that the mind is necessarily embodied. The living body exists as a part of nature, which makes life possible" (Määttänen 2015, 11). Thus, meaning and value are understood in terms of *overt* (empirical) consequences of (often covert) intentional actions, not in cerebral terms or otherwise presumed to be metaphysical, as is claimed for traditional hypotheses of *covert* aesthetic experience.[33]

Consequently, the world presents experience with a vast resource of possibilities for action (praxis). We always have choices to make, however important, between alternatives constantly facing us. This choosing, at every step, is a process of evaluating anticipated outcomes in terms of our current needs and desires (intentionality, ends-in-view). Pending our understanding of the world at any given moment, values are *already present in the world*!! We experience them as options afforded us by our world view, and our thoughtful actions are (or should be) those of mindfully valued choices.

Life offers a range of possible actions—called *affordances*—and we choose from them to consummate our current intentionality. When camping, then, a "rock" *affords* use as a "hammer" for driving in tent pegs; string bows tapping on music stands *afford* a range of rhythmic effects; "scat" singing *affords* vocal jazz improvisation without words. Music, then, offers a range of affordances according to the needs and goals of the moment. Barber's *Adagio for Strings* affords listening in the original string quartet version, in many different orchestral arrangements, in choral and wind instrumental arrangements, as the background music in the war film *Platoon,* or for funerals. The result, for Dewey's Pragmatism, then, is a *cultural naturalism* that echoes the focus in sociological phenomenology on the *social reality of the tangible cultural environment that governs an individual's transactions and opportunities for action within it.*

'Good music' is a matter of the value of the needs or use in question (e.g., religion, dancing, contemplation, weddings, funerals, patriotism, critical listening, mood management, and parties). Such social needs create different musics, to begin with! The demands of a worthy social need that brings about the creation or choice of its distinct music are then the criteria of the 'goodness' of that music—including concerts. Each type of music, then, has different goodness at stake, with its unique criteria of goodness or worth. Love songs, therefore, have different criteria of goodness than, say, marches; "easy listening" choices have different criteria than, say, 'classical' concert music.

Criteria of value in art and music too are subjected to the pragmatic criterion rather than metaphysical pronouncements of "goodness" by aestheticians, or claims by teachers and other experts. Therefore, questions of musical goodness, worth, or value take two (usually interacting) dimensions. First, "art is good which is good of its kind" (Dixon 1995, 53). Importantly, then, *music is good relative to its types*, such as jazz or the Romantic repertory, Taiko or Gamelan musics, and so on. Questions of quality or value, therefore, cannot be judged along a single hierarchy of worthiness with 'chamber music' at the top. Rather, the 'classical' Eurocentric repertoire "is not a quality of, but a kind of art" (Dixon 1995, 6; see also 44) and represents only one "highly peculiar 'taste'" (57)—at least in comparison to all musics in the world—a relatively esoteric "taste" among an infinite diversity of musics from which people typically choose a variety of preferences.

Second, *music is good as governed by the social conditions it is "good for."* These conditions across cultures explain the relevance of music shared by different cultures. Therefore, the goodness or value of any music is in part, but importantly, determined by the particular situations in which it is central—which is to say *the social affordances that brought it into being* and that promote its *recurring use.* It is indisputable that the many social occasions in life that typically involve music feature musics that are composed, arranged, or selected to be "good for" certain social needs at stake. 'Classical' music performed for a wedding, for example, even if by trained artists, is not concert music but is "good for" the religious and matrimonial meanings involved.

Those in attendance do not turn around and look at the musicians in the choir loft behind them; they remain focused on the bridal couple. (Here, the semiotics of space may come into play depending on where the musicians are in the architectural space.) Music for dancing may also be "good for" 'just listening', as well, but that is not its primary reason for existing.

In sum, (1) intentionality (a personal valued musical end-in-view), (2) its consummation in action (or not), and (3) the distinction of *an* experience are all vitally important to music educators, to music curriculum, and to daily planning. Without these three key ingredients of Pragmatism, students in schools will continue *to* experience music in classroom and rehearsal halls. But if such experiences lack intentionality in action, they make no valued and lasting contribution to their lives. Despite years in music classes and ensembles, instruction will have failed to make a *lasting difference* in the lives of most graduates. Further application of Pragmatism to music education curriculum is also discussed later concerning Progressive education. But first, Pragmatism's theory of art and music gets to the important matter of understanding what musical experience *is*, and how and why it differs from typical clichés about music education parading as aesthetic education.

Pragmatism and "artful living" through music

Dewey's Pragmatism regarding *Art as Experience* (1934/1980)—that is, art as *an* experience—criticizes and avoids analyzing art and music in terms of any of the *intellectualism* of conventional aesthetic criteria focused on contemplation. First of all, Dewey denies that most experience even requires coming *to know* something from it. Instead, many "things are objects to be treated, used, acted upon and with, enjoyed and endured, even more than things to be known" (Dewey 1925/1989, 21: i.e., they are objects of praxis). In this connection, then, aesthetic claims that music provides *cognition* of the inner, subjective life—that is, that aestheticized feeling is *intellectually known in symbolic form* rather than "felt" in an embodied sense—splendidly qualify for Dewey's condemnation of "intellectualism."

Similarly, the claim that appreciation requires "understanding" music also fails Dewey's pragmatic objection to connoisseurship criteria. Dewey's concept of *an* experience is thus contrary to and a corrective of conventional aesthetics. Attempts to call upon Dewey in support of aesthetic premises for music education (Reimer 2003; Westerlund 2003) are philosophically naïve and contradicted by Dewey's anti-intellectualist view of art as *an* experience, premises that he sought to "reconstruct" for theorizing about the arts.

Moreover, when applied to the arts, intellectualism is, in effect, *an*esthetic. It reduces a musical experience not to its felt qualities but to cerebral abstractions (for example, the 'elements' of music: melody, harmony, rhythm, form, and timbre)—technical terms (development, motif, etc.) and the like. Consequently, Dewey focuses instead on the praxical or instrumental benefits of the arts that result in or as a *consummatory* (fulfilling) experience. Art and music, then, are "instrumental"; that is, they are *means* for reaching the *ends* of artistically heightened experience for the life well lived—that is, for "artful living."

Dewey does refer to "esthetic" [sic] experiences. But in his theory of art as experience, these are down-to-earth and direct perceptual experiences in the "emotional" and directly "felt" sense he referred to in his theory of emotion as *affect quale*. In the philosophy of mind, the immediately felt, phenomenal character of a mental event is its *quale* (plural: *qualia*). Dewey used the term "affect *quale*" (or sometimes just "affect") to refer to such embodied feeling states.[34] For Dewey, then, *emotion* is not a state of mind that merely reacts to an external stimulus. "It is the 'attunement' [of the mind] to the situation" (Alexander 1987, 137)—a holistic submission to the experience that binds Self and world through the event. Such an emotion is in suspension (or in suspense) while *an* experience is anticipating its consummation and thus is present in some degree from the first. Emotions then take on an *intentional* quality relative to the consummatory satisfactions anticipated by intentionality.

Intentionality can also be negative, and thus its consummation involves avoiding a negative experience. Thus, students with the intentionality of avoiding the director's wrath when mistakes happen practice for unmusical (extrinsic) reasons. A lenient and compassionate director avoids this musically extrinsic intentionality and instead promotes the possibility of musically intrinsic intentionality to motivate practicing.

In contrast to conventional aesthetic theory, for Dewey, the antithesis of the esthetic is not practicality or sociality, but what he called "the humdrum." For Dewey, *all* nonroutine, intentional activities—arts based or not!—have an emotional component (a greater or lesser "wow" factor, depending on the experience). It follows, then, that *an* experience of *any* kind is consummated in some out-of-the-ordinary, heightened "esthetic" [sic] quality. As a result, Dewey laments the separation of art from everyday life by "art for art's sake" aestheticians who advocate the merely contemplative character of the art experience.[35] Instead, he stresses the important role of esthetic experience in everyday processes of living. As with sociologists and anthropologists of art (and proponents of so-called "everyday aesthetics," e.g., Light & Smith 2005; Mandoki 2007), Dewey, therefore, sees the nature and value of the arts as "immediate enhancements of the experience of living" (Dewey 1934/1980, 30). Everything from gardening to home décor, the attractiveness of food served to setting an attractive dinner table all qualify. The Japanese, for example, are well respected for stressing the "artfulness" of everyday living (Saito 2007).

Dewey stresses too that the practical, emotional, and intellectual are inseparable in *an* experience: (1) "emotional" or felt qualities bind "an experience" with holistic unity; (2) the "intellectual" aspect "simply acknowledges that the experience has meaning"; and (3) the "'practical' indicates that the organism is interacting with events and objects which surround it" (Dewey 1934/1980, 55) rather than engaging in pure, for-its-own-sake contemplation. Life, then, is best lived artfully every day, not just in rare moments of leisure time contemplation (although those are important too).

Importantly, when "practical" is defined pragmatically, even a concert is practical. It involves not just the auditing of the performance, but also all the experiential *qualia* of the total sociocultural event. For example, many visual and social aspects are missing from recordings: that is, the spatial semiotics of the concert venue (e.g., a jazz concert heard in a church), the conductor, the bodily deportment of performers and soloists, attire, other audience members, their deportment, clapping, postconcert commentary, etc. Christopher Small (1998) coined what he calls "musicking" to stress the experience of the *entire socially situated praxis*, not just the sounds of the moment.[36] Musicing, as a verb form, stresses the "doing," not "music" simply as a static noun. The same is the case when "love" (as a noun for mental state one is 'in') is more fruitfully understood as "loving"—as loving actions.

Regarding what is conventionally called "the music," however, Dewey stresses the special and "direct emotional expression" of sound (Dewey 1934/1980, 238)—its ability to directly trigger or agitate internal "commotion" (237). In contrast, a typical failing of conventional aesthetics that is insufficiently noted (or admitted by proponents) is overlooking the differences of the artistic medium. The philosopher who originally gave aesthetics its name, Alexander Baumgarten (1714–1762),[37] speculated entirely about poetry, but his attempt at an aesthetic theory subsequently was indiscriminately applied to all the arts by subsequent thinkers. As a result, for conventional aesthetic ideology, so-called aesthetic experience per se is essentially disembodied; it is *incorporeal* and *intellectual*. This claim is a primary reason for audiences sitting as still as at a funeral and not moving to the music. It is also why some have called concert music "ear candy" and why aesthetes have denounced the physical 'chills' (frissons) that people wrongly think are "aesthetic" responses.

Consequently, in the larger picture of schooling, any artistic medium for supposedly getting students to have—at all, or improved—'aesthetic responses' can be rationalized as equally benefiting students. Visual art education, poetry, and literature, for example, can claim to meet "aesthetic education" premises in curriculum documents (and are a lot less expensive!). In consequence, the special and significant qualities of *sound* itself got overlooked—an oversight that Dewey's Pragmatism does not make due to its naturalist and embodied account of perception and cognition.

Dewey is also critical of negative comparisons between 'ordinary listeners' and connoisseurship claims. He points out, on the one hand, that "the appeal of music—of certain grades—is much more widespread and much more *independent of special cultivation*, than that of any other art" (1934/1980, 238, italics added), although he allows that the result may sometimes lapse into emotional excess. "On the other side," he caustically observes of the taste for 'classy' music, "there are types of music, those most prized by connoisseurs, that demand special training to be perceived and enjoyed, and its devotees form a cult, so that *their* art is the most esoteric of all arts" (238, italics original). The connection between "High Culture" (with a capital "C") and "cult" is thus inescapable.

Philosopher Immanuel Kant's (1724–1804) theory of "free beauty" (i.e., as unburdened by concepts or thoughts that refer to the physical world, like words and worldly uses),[38] was institutionalized by subsequent philosophers and aestheticians in the *cult*ivation of 'fine art'. The *aesthetic theory of art* is the product of dualistic conceptions that humans are detached from nature and can relate to each other only through reason. It has resulted in the problematic and paradoxical nature of subsequent aesthetic theorizing.

> Aesthetic experience seems paradoxical and problematic to Kant for it is neither cognitive nor ethical. It struggles to be consumed under our cognitive judgments, but its objectivity, universality, and necessity turn out to involve subjectivity, particularity, and contingency. Art seems to appeal to human desire, but only in a strange disinterested manner. The work of art marks the random occasion for many to enjoy the abstract harmony of his own faculties. (Alexander 1987, 189)

This dualism resulted in the theory of art's autonomy from life—known by musical aesthetes as "absolute music"—music as thus being "for its own sake."

Theorizing the autonomy of art has persisted to this day among analytic aestheticians. Given such separation of mind, body, and culture (with a lowercase "c," as in anthropology and sociology, not as in highbrow "Culture"), the ideal of 'pure art' was espoused. However, "the ideal of 'art for arts' sake would be unintelligible to most human cultures throughout history. This was an attitude generated in the nineteenth century under the rising influence of an industrial bourgeois society" (Alexander 1987, 190) where, by being useless or impractical and not necessary to living, art's main use was to show off the wealth and prestige of the bourgeoisie aspiring to 'classy' aristocratic status. This cultural history of the rise of aesthetic theorizing demonstrates the *social origins of aesthetic theory itself* in the growth of the new 19th-century upper middle class.

Subsequently, museums and concert halls became "special locations for the new social class with money and free time to carry on the practices of the contemplation of what was called disinterested pure beauty." Yet, the *spatial semiotics* of such places are part of the "system of meanings with which we orient ourselves to the environment, how we experience it" (Määttänen 2017, 5). Thus, meaning is not literally 'in' the work of art but 'of' *an* experience of art *in* such places.[39] Instead, for Dewey, "the ideal of art for art's sake is only possible when art has ceased to play a direct and vital role in organized community life; it is, in other words, a symptomatic response to a disorganized society which cannot grasp itself as an aesthetic project" (Alexander 1987, 190).[40]

Pragmatism and the music curriculum

Dewey's theory of art as (an) experience is surely more applicable to the needs of music education and schooling than fanciful and false claims for enhancing students' "aesthetic responsiveness." It is useful to remember, however, that when removing music from its normal socially situated conditions to the school classroom, it takes on a different "use" or purpose in schools, and thus, its meanings are attuned to this different social milieu. The situated circumstances of any musicing in part determine its meaning. Thus, school music (with the possible exception of concerts), in consequence, is a unique form of musicing! It is educative and, as such, intended to benefit the growing social minds of students.

It can't be repeated enough that it is all-important to pragmatic learning that *music students must have an intention—an aural, musical goal or value—in mind as the basis for meaningfully productive musicing*. The ample pleasures of music are a source of intentionality and a reward, but the undertaking is educational. In music education, then, intentionality should be *musical,* not *extrinsic* to music (e.g., getting a gold star, winning a seating competition, earning praise, avoiding scolding). Education based on pragmatic "problem solving" is predicated on the earlier described sequence of five stages of musical thinking (see inside back cover): posing a musical problem the students will value solving and then "scaffolding" (i.e., systematically structuring into progressive steps)[41] the experience according to the remaining four pragmatic stages are required.

In distinction with *an* experience, *to* experience refers to experiences that you just undergo without an intention, goal, or plan; attentiveness; care; or thoughtfulness—at best, a lot of mindless habits (Which foot goes first climbing stairs or into your pants? Are your dominant hand, eye, and foot the same?). *To* experience walking into a tree at night or falling on the ice are also examples; no end-in-view beyond avoidance has been accomplished that further enriches the good life.[42] This latter kind of disconnected moments of experience is too often involved with musical activities and performances that, *to students*, have no primary, long-term *musical* end or growth in mind beyond obeying the teacher's present directions for the next concert.

Hence, random and fragmented musical *activities* are properly distinguished for educational purposes from *actions* (praxes) guided by students' mindful musicing and their disposition (intention) to learn and grow musically. Merely "going along" with a lesson or rehearsal plan does not fulfill the intentionality condition of "trying to" learn and improve *musically* to overcoming current limitations. At best, "going along" follows the intuited intentionality of crowd dynamics or autocratic leadership.

Many general music teachers believe, for example, that an "activity" supposed "to experience the concept of melody" is valid and valuable. But, first of all, that is *the teacher's* goal for the musical goings-on to follow, not necessarily the students' intentionality. At most, then, "to experience" will be at stake, not "an experience." Even if students dutifully follow the teacher's directions, they will not usually have that in mind as *an* experience from which they seek to grow musically. They didn't enter the classroom having intentionality for learning the concept of "melody" or "steady beat."

Teachers often mistake concepts as abstract words or terms ("melody," "development," "form," "tone color") that need to be "filled" with *experience*. This is a major philosophical and psychological misunderstanding. Concepts are personal inductions (generalizations) from past experiences and are seen only at work in enabling further experience.[43] A student who sings or recognizes a Christmas carol already has "the concept of melody," and the term adds little beyond future communicating verbally about melodies (e.g., in a listening lesson, "how many times is the melody repeated?").

"Teaching concepts" via the "activities approach" is a contradiction of all recent curricular philosophies—as though the concepts said to be at stake are a priori abstractions (from Mars) to be transmitted to students. Teaching the 'doing' (praxis) as *an* experience (i.e., with intentionality) is the proper objective! In other words, concepts are cognitive constructs of individuals and vary according to the musical intentionality at stake. They are not transmitted from the teacher's mind (or a book) but are *enacted* through and as praxis—by doing, having *an* experience as guided by intentionality.

To experience a teacher-'delivered' lesson, then, lacks students' intentionality, and therefore the key conditions of *an* experience are missing. The goings-on, however much fun, will be fragmentary and fail to result in a meaningful and cumulative consummation of the active process of learning. Similarly, in ensembles, the fulfilling of members' own musical intentionality (personal goals) needs to be at stake lest the experience be no more than *to* experience their part of the score (according to the director's musical intentionality), not *an* experience that leads to enriching their *independent musicianship* for the future. Consider, for example, the growth of independent musicianship of the second trombone player, not just the overall performance. Students' motives, then, in the overall performance may well be musical as directed: "Hold the fermata longer"; "Don't breathe there."[44] But such directions are followed without the intentionality of growing musically for the future—"Why not breathe there?" "What musical difference does it make?" And if the students don't know or can't tell, what purpose is served? Only the concert result? Not a growing foundation for independent musicing?

Accordingly, for music education, pragmatic actions are those concrete actions thoughtfully oriented to reaching musical ends (musical intentionality)—more precisely, Dewey's term *"ends-in-view"* that are individual students' valued *musical goal(s) for the moment* (in class or rehearsal) that guide their actions and experiences. Importantly, for Dewey, such ends-in-view are not once-and-for-all, long-term finalities (e.g., giving a concert).[45] The *consummatory* stage of short-term ends-in-view (successful stage 5, solving the immediate problem; see back cover) Dewey held produces *mindful habits* that cumulatively and thoughtfully address the demands and possibilities of new situations. Ends-in-view do grow over time with skill. At first, then, learning the fingering for a new pitch is an end-in-view, and eventually performing the entire passage or tune is the end-in-view, and so on up a ladder of increasing complexity (and musical rewards).

Dewey's unusual term "consummatory" means that the action *consummates* (successfully accomplishes with a rewarding sense) the anticipated possibilities (affordances) *an* experience offers, resulting in the sense of satisfaction, fulfillment, and often rewarding growth ("Wow! That was awesome."). However, these pleasures need not wait in consciousness for the completion of their consummation. "It [the consummation] is anticipated throughout and is recurrently savored with special intensity" (Dewey 1934/1980, 55) from the beginning to the end of *an* experience. Consider the plotting and "intentionality" of an upcoming first date that fill the time (counting the days) until the event. Christopher Small includes anticipation of a concert as part of its musicking (his spelling)—the point at which musical intentions seek fulfillment by buying a ticket and attending.[46]

There is, therefore, a rewarding *sense of accomplishment* in *an* experience that fulfills a present musical end-in-view when overcoming the limiting problems. Achieving today's musical end-in-view is also a stepping stone to ("learning *readiness*" for) its possible relevance for tomorrow's ends-in-view—those that usually are more advanced or sequentially developmental. Achievement of past ends-in-view creates a fund of past musical experiences (successes *and* failures) that serve as possible hypotheses in stage 3 of pragmatic problem solving.[47]

When, under conditions of *an* experience, student problem solving has involved a natural sequence of connected stages of learning, then past experiences (facts, information, concepts, skills, learned habits assimilated along the way) serve in effect as 'maps' among the alternative 'means' or hypotheses for guiding future musical decisions and actions in ever-new situations. Thus, the "doing" in "learning-by-doing" associated with Dewey's educational Pragmatism (and Progressivism, covered later) is praxis (action) guided by musical intentionality; and an instance of being "done" successfully is the consummation (rewarding effect) of that musical end-in-view.

Dewey's pragmatic view was that school is not a *preparation* for life but already a *part* of life. Students directly engage with stepping stones to a life of Being and Becoming, full time—even in their play. They are already engaged in school life with embryonic versions of what they will encounter in adult life. Accordingly, students need *choices* to make that will be the basis for the musical intentionality guiding their school experiences. Moreover, in a world without the absolutes proposed by traditional curricular philosophies (Chapter Two), schooling puts democracy into action. Thus, teachers are leaders, guides, or facilitators, not autocrats. They are authoritative in helping students reach students' felt needs, not authoritarian in dictating either those needs or how the world 'really' is—even the world of music.

In a rapidly changing world and music world, not even teachers or other adults can foretell future needs. "In such a world, the last thing a teacher needs to give her pupils is more information. They already have too much of it. Instead, people need the ability to make sense of information, to tell the difference between what is important and what is unimportant, and above all to combine many bits of information into a broad picture of the world." This means

> schools should switch to teaching 'the four Cs'—critical thinking, communication, collaboration and creativity. More broadly, schools should downplay technical skills and emphasise general purpose life skills. Most important of all will be the ability to deal with change, to learn new things, and to preserve your balance in unfamiliar situations. . . . If someone describes to you the world of the mid twenty-first century and it sounds like science fiction, it is probably false. But then if somebody describes to you the world of the mid twenty-first century and it *doesn't* sound like science fiction—it is certainly false. (Harari 2018, 263, italics original)

Today's educators are the products of a different age, lifeworld, and training, and often lack the pedagogical up-to-datedness to help students deal with a world of transformation and uncertainty (this may also be true of some collegiate instructors). Along with existentialism and phenomenology, Pragmatism is geared to the world of today and tomorrow—to inevitable change—not to abstract and illusory, a priori 'truths' from the distant past.

In a shared spirit of Pragmatism and Existentialism, some educationists have made a useful distinction between "lead" teachers and "push" teachers. The former are like a scout leader who proposes interesting destinations for a hike, then who leads, facilitates, structures, draws, or scaffolds getting to such new (at least to students) destinations, and whose proposal and plan ended up being consummated and appreciated by the scouts, and from which they learn—in other words, a teacher who seizes upon students' interests and leads them to relevant consummations. The "push" teacher, however, shoves students in the directions in which the teacher wants them to go. This prodding predictably leads to recalcitrant behavior. The "discipline" preached by scholasticism falls by the wayside with them. Some more compliant students (under the threat of the hidden curriculum) may obediently "go along" with the teacher. But without musical intentionality, being "good students" results in no effective musicianship for adulthood.

In avoiding rebellious stand-offs with students, pragmatically oriented music educators focus on a "child centered" rather than a "subject matter"-centered or "banking" curriculum (more on this with "Progressivism" in Chapter Five). The latter presumes to "fill" students with valuable subject matter information "about" music believed to be "banked" for future use (dubiously, since it serves only for tests of recall). Child-centeredness does not dictate to the student according to values from the (instructor's) past, but in terms of the student's present or potential ends-in-view (those to which they can be led), and with lifelong benefits in mind for a changing world.

A pragmatic curriculum, then, is *put into action (praxis)*, not just "covered" with lessons that lead (culminate) nowhere. It is a selection of experiences, guided by students' intentionality, each experience of which (a) culminates in a consummatory (fulfilling) moment when savoring successful learning, (b) contributes to the fund of past learning (assimilated as past consummations—stage 3), and (c) promotes future applications by students, especially as adults. *Lifelong learning is the curricular goal and the criterion for curricular integrity and success.*

Action Learning (explained more in the next chapter) is a version of Pragmatism. Action Learning for music brings models of musicing from the 'real life' musical world outside of school into the curriculum, thus preparing students to engage musically with what is already commonly available in life today (e.g., in their communities, maybe jigs and reels of square dance musics, maybe new popular styles, maybe steel drums or harmonica). Yet it also focuses on *change agency*, what a contemporary music curriculum can newly promote in the community that will allow students to incorporate music into their lives, now and as adults.

Take, for example, the typical pedagogical focus on large ensembles. They are entertaining for school concerts and as evidence of students' practicing. But they are difficult to organize for adult participation in later life.[48] Where they do exist, rehearsals and performances are difficult to schedule into busy adult lives. School chamber groupings (of various musics) provide more practicable models for continuing musical enjoyment by adults (duets, quartets, transpositions for typical combinations of instruments, piano students learning to accompany soloists, etc.). Accompanied solos enrich the instrumentalist's musical pleasures and musicianship by providing the other half of "the music" while helping pianists who study privately learn how to accompany (which for most is more likely in adult life than is a virtuosic career).

Double or triple chamber groupings have two or three students per part and largely rehearse on their own with periodic coaching from the teacher. They avoid the misleading averaging effect of large numbers, which always sound better than individuals in the large ensemble, and they put full musical responsibility on the two or three people on a part, for example, a triple trio (SSSAAABBB) based on SAB choral literature. Chamber groups can easily augment a large ensemble curriculum. They can perform for the ensemble (who become their audience) during scheduled rehearsal periods (thereby furthering listening experiences for the other ensemble members)[49] and in concerts. Small schools without enough string players for an orchestra should start and accommodate string students in duets, trios, and quartets. Failing to do so is an professional ethical lapse.

Such chamber groupings will promote the likelihood of students continuing their musicing after graduation. They readily engage in all of the four Cs just mentioned: critical thinking, communication, collaboration, and creativity. Becoming competent with computer software in various musical endeavors also provides a foundation for lifelong engagement with the rapidly evolving technologies for musicing. With such new pedagogies, teachers are flexible, no longer rely on old paradigms, and accommodatingly prepare students for the musical worlds of today and tomorrow.

In sum, in a rapidly changing world, the rejection of a priori absolutes and an emphasis on the diversity of musics and musical experiences characterize a pragmatic philosophy of curriculum. In aspiring to be fully pragmatic, a music curriculum also profits from many lessons of existentialism and phenomenology since both are fundamentally concerned with the qualities of an experience as reflected on in personal terms, and with the creation of a musical Self that can successfully partake of a rapidly changing world of music. Music education has failed if it doesn't promote pragmatic results that, in some degree, musically fulfill students' Being needs and develop the potential all people have for musicing.

4
Contemporary Perspectives for Curriculum Theory

Preliminary Basics of Praxis and Practice Theory

Praxis and practice theory together span the centuries from Ancient Greece until our day, with Pragmatism (arising in the early 20th century) being a close relative and Practice Theory a new social philosophy. In recent years praxis has attracted considerable notice in music education circles as an antidote for the speculations of "music education as aesthetic education" (MEAE) and the pragmatic irrelevance of traditional curricular offerings in music education.

Praxis, as already mentioned, shares its root (*pragma*) with Pragmatism in referring to "right action" or "consummated action." Given its origins in Aristotle's writings, it might be thought to be among the traditional theories. But it has had active continuing presence in many aspects of human life over the years (e.g., religion, political philosophy), and most musicing in the Western world was praxis until the mid-18th century. Then, the invention of aesthetic theory and its association with the social aspirations of the rising bourgeoisie, the institutionalization of public concert subscriptions, music criticism, and (of course) most formal music education propelled elitist aesthetics into prominence based on its social pretentions for promoting 'classy' music and 'fine art'.

However, the contemporary relevance and application of praxis and practice theory[1] to music and music education was newly recognized in 1991 when *music as praxis* was reasserted and stipulated that music education should encompass *all* musics, not just those approved by aesthetes (Alperson 1991).[2] Soon after, the first book appeared by David Elliott that advanced praxis as a philosophical theory for music education curriculum.[3] Since then, the term and its range of ideas have become well known and more and more confirmed in contemporary music education theorizing. The term "praxis" gained currency in Aristotle's *Nicomachean Ethics*—named after his son and student *Nicomachus*. Contemporary meaning and reference to the term praxis (and adjectives, "praxial," "praxical") in today's music education relies on Aristotle's ideas about knowledge and ethical behavior (Dunne 1993). These ideas are altogether distinct from his Realism discussed in Chapter One. Not surprisingly, Aristotle regarded thinking as an activity of intelligence (*dianoia*). He then categorized knowledge (*epistēme*) into three types, *theoria, technē*, and *praxis,* each with distinct traits.

Theoria

Theoria referred to knowledge and understanding of "eternal (Ideal) forms" (as per Platonic Idealism) that, in Ancient Greece, was studied and learned for contemplation, and was appreciated on its own. Examples are the theoretical studies of Pythagoras concerning the overtone series of vibrating strings, but also the beauty of the "Golden Mean" (or "Ratio"—3:2; also relevant to the overtone series), and early geometry and astronomy. It was put to use mainly as contemplation. It implied a process of "looking upon," "seeing," or "examining" that the Ancient Greeks called *theorein*. This contemplative "seeing," in turn, implied 'speculation' (i.e., in*spec*tion; today's "theorizing"), musing, and insight of an immaterial and strictly intellectual nature that was therefore not concerned with practical matters.[4] Instead, it involved an object, topic, or subject of alluring interest or reputed importance—called *thauma*— that warranted study and contemplation because it stimulated thinking and brought about a sense of wonderment (i.e., the illuminating pleasure of becoming aware of new knowledge).[5]

The idea of a "*spect*ator" or "*spect*acle" is also part of the 'seeing' of *theorein,* and the idea of *theasthai* came about, the basic premise of "*thea*ter." Not surprisingly, then, Greek dramas (usually tragedy) were entertainment for educated Greeks. However, the Greeks understood "art" *not* in today's sense; rather, what they called *ars* referred to any practiced skill. "Beauty" was the result of any skilled action—including, for example, in athletics (a "beautiful" play in football, as we might say)—and any activity engaged in *excellent making* (*poiēsis*).

The Greek term *aisthesis* referred only to knowledge gained through the senses (sentient knowing) rather than through reason, not to 'beauty' as we know it. And what was then called "music" was mainly an intoned chant-like speech (somewhat like Gregorian chant). Greek musical instruments included strings, winds, and percussion. Aristotle mentions a "flute" in connection with *technē* (see later).

Theorim and *theasthai* together provide the root of our modern term "theory." In sum, then, theoria implies speculative knowledge studied, organized, and contemplated for admiration and enlightenment. It was decidedly intellectual, autonomous, universal, pure, and absolute, and thus said to be timeless and unchanging—fitting closely with Idealism cultivated by Plato. Theoria was not conceived or experienced with any practical, utilitarian, or functional intentions in mind.

However, some theoria had a side benefit of practical application (e.g., geometry for building; anatomy for medicine). But when contemplated simply for the sake of knowing, it was not basic to the daily conduct of life—other than filling the time of the intelligentsia. Indeed, just the opposite: it cultivated the life of the mind, the *vita contemplativa*[6] (*contemplative life*) in the leisure of rich, learned, and intellectual free men—women and slaves being otherwise engaged.

Aristotle had studied in Plato's famous Academy (hence the "academic" study of ideas). However, Aristotle differed with Plato's Idealism by emphasizing the value of *aisthesis*, sentient knowledge gained from the tangible "things" of experience. In the modern age, of course, theory takes the form of what, for example, is variously called basic, fundamental, or pure research. And, as in the Aristotelian tradition of theoria, the contemplation and creation of such theoretical knowledge are often described in terms of simplicity and elegance as 'beauty' (Glynn 2013). However, countless generations of students have described such knowledge as "merely academic," or "that's fine in theory but what about in use," comments that are ignorant of Plato's Academy and Idealism.

However, *applied aspects of theory*, then, can be useful in bringing about practical results. Such "spin-offs" of theoretical advances in science are quite common in modern life. Rather than appealing simply only to the pleasures of the *vita contemplativa*, the 'beauty' of *applied theoria* is also a matter of its usefulness in serving certain pragmatic ends. The contribution of philosophies explored in this book to curriculum theory is an example.

Technē

Aristotle also distinguished *technē* and *praxis* as two distinct types of *practical knowledge*. They differ according to the ends they serve and the processes by which such knowledge is created and used. Furthermore, technē of a relevant kind often supports praxical knowledge; applied theoria supports both technē and praxis.

Technē is the knowledge needed for 'making', 'producing', or 'crafting' objects or other tangibly useful results (Dunne 1993). This active form of technē Aristotle called *poiēsis*—in English, "excellent making." **Note:** This 'making' involves (a) artifacts and other tangible results (b) whose value a society accepts as being 'good', necessary, or useful. Furthermore, (c) such traditional 'goods' are generally standardized according to their typical use and (d) thus take traditionally accepted forms and (e) depend on a standardized and traditionally 'practiced' (skillfully applied) knowledge base (e.g., materials and design). For example, traditionally determined types of functionality standardized the making of baskets or ceramic pots.

"Learning by doing," as with Pragmatism, builds over time both the *applied theory* and the *practical skills* (artisanship) for "excellent making." When making an error (e.g., a board cut too short), nothing is lost except time to start over; what is learned is only knowledge for avoiding what went wrong (e.g., "measure twice, cut once"). Technē, of course, is responsible to clients and customers. But originality occurred only within the range of accepted functions (e.g., a commission for wine goblets).

In Ancient Greece, then, *poiēsis* implied *technological* or *technicist* excellence and a fund of *techniques* practiced through "hands on" learning by *technicians* or artisans. Hence, the knowledge involved—both physical and cognitive skills—is usually acquired through *observational learning* (i.e., social behaviorism). Innovation and creativity are not at stake and not usually considered unless newly improved ends become conventional. The use-value of technē is *separable* from the process involved in producing it: the process itself has little or no value or interest to users—if they like the wine goblets. Such competency is often *impersonal*; others could do as well.

Hence, *technē* **itself** *is not individuating*![7] It doesn't distinguish one's knowledge, personal competencies, or existential personhood (Self) from competent others. It is undertaken to "get the job done." The acquisition of such learning typically involves *apprenticeship*—the learning that results from observing the modeling and other direct instruction of a skilled master. This knowledge also often requires 'rudimentary' theories that are 'basic' to producing results—for example, physics needed by an electrician, properties of clay by a ceramist, or the overtone series to brass players.

Technē also requires *supervisory oversight*—understanding needed for controlling and managing the execution of the process in action. This is *action feedback*—feedback that functions in the way of a servo-mechanism, such as a thermostat constantly adjusting temperature according to preset standards. The action feedback in the praxis of music relies on an aural image of how the music is intended to go (end-in-view). Technē also incorporates *learning feedback*: criteria and diagnostic skills for evaluating a result after completing the action and, when needed, for making procedural adjustments intended to produce a corrected or improved result. Note: This opportunity to undo a bad job or poor result is *not* available with praxis where people's welfare is at stake!

Since both action and learning feedback are central to musicing, the basic "technical" knowledge required for producing music of any kind is technē: the practiced psychomotor skills and cognitive skills called "musicianship." This is perfectly clear when musicians themselves refer to their acquisition of foundational knowledge and skill as their *training*. And it is also clear that the most basic "applied" knowledge in music, namely private studio lessons, is typically almost entirely a matter of apprenticeship.

The "technical" dimension of all *musicianship training*—its technē—involves a standard and traditional body of knowledge that is literally "practiced" in bringing about certain predictable conditions that are the common "standards" or prerequisites of any musical action.[8] However, the *musicianship* resulting from practiced technique and technical knowledge is a necessary but not a sufficient condition of praxis. Therefore, musicians commonly accept an important difference between "playing" an instrument technically well (i.e., technē) and "making music" well (i.e., praxis).[9]

Accordingly, the standard, predictable results for which technē exists can usually be described in advance or at least recognized intersubjectively as criteria of evaluation. In music, then, such craft-like technical mastery is distinguished from matters of 'artistry' and 'musicality' that are not standard. Rather, these aspects entail important matters of personal style, interpretation, and insight that are individuating for the performer and each performance, and highly valued by listeners. Such matters of "quality control" or standards of *technical accountability* in fields such as music, medicine, or teaching are standards of technē.[10]

In sum, technē is a matter of *instrumental* (pragmatic) and *operational* knowledge and skill used in achieving the most efficient methods of reaching standard results widely accepted as being 'good'. Technē does not question the validity or value of the ends served by such knowledge. Such questions are, in Aristotle's tradition, a matter of praxis.

Praxis

The active form of knowledge for praxis is governed by *virtuous* or *excellent* 'doing' called *phronēsis*—an *ethical* criterion that calls upon knowledge for achieving 'right results'.[11] Thus, unlike technē, praxis is centrally concerned with the diagnostic and rational knowledge of both 'good' means *and* 'good' ends-in-view, both chosen as 'right results' for *people*. While technē involves technical knowledge needed to achieve customary practical ends with things, the ends of praxis vary according to the *people* to be served. Phronēsis denotes the capacity of an agent (e.g., doctor, lawyer, therapist) for bringing about the 'goods' that are correct or 'right' *in or for a given situation* person, group, etc.

Praxis not only (a) requires knowledge of effective means for achieving such goods but also (b) involves the *ethical discernment* for making *warranted* and *prudent* judgments that effectively *diagnose* the 'goodness' of such ends and goals in the first place (e.g., medicine or pastoral counseling).

Such ends become, then, the criteria for 'right results'. Praxis thus involves *setting goals* for action (praxis) that are "good for" the people affected by that situated praxis—in education, the students (situated in school). Importantly, such 'good' or 'right results' are *not reproducible* like wine goblets are. What are 'good' or 'right results' vary considerably from one person or human situation to another and over time.

There are, then, no singular or "standard" instances of praxical results! Think about that! The "standards" involved are *standards of care* (phronēsis). For example, in medicine, "malpractice" (i.e., "malpraxis") is an ethical matter of whether or not the physician observed accepted standards of care (criterion: Hippocratic Oath, "First, do no harm"). These are *ethical* criteria involving phronēsis, not the standardized techniques of technē and 'delivery methods'.

As a result, *any praxis that fails to bring about 'right results' under pertinent considerations of phronēsis cannot be undone*! In such situations, the agent (e.g., the instructor) can't just start over as though nothing had happened. A failed result becomes a newly relevant hurdle to be overcome. For example, a doctor's mistaken diagnosis brings the patient back even sicker and perhaps with new doubts about her competence.[12] Attempts to improve on a failed lesson in a classroom or ensemble are complicated by the failure of the

---

(1) Knowledge for diagnosing what *ought* to be done concerning the needs (values) at stake (the problem)

(2) Knowledge needed to carefully *choose* the actions most likely to reach the 'right results' (problem solving) for (1)

(3) Knowledge required to *supervise* the actions as they unfold (i.e., action feedback) guided by (1)

(4) Planning how to *evaluate* the 'goodness' (excellence) of results in terms of the individual or group served; i.e., learning feedback regarding (1)

Compare these four intellectual criteria to the *four secondary values* in Figure 4.2 p.86 that facilitate these criteria

---

Figure 4.1 Phronēsis involves *four intellectual criteria* for the agent (i.e., teacher).

previous lesson. Subsequent changes are, therefore, altogether more difficult (or at least different) than would otherwise be the case.

These criteria, plus the organization of knowledge for future praxis, put a very strong obligation on *standards of care*. Thus, 'right action' (successful praxis) amounts to 'right results' judged in terms of particular situations and individuals—e.g., *this* fifth-grade class or student. Choosing new literature for students requires diagnosing their *readiness*—the present ability needed before new learning—and the interest and advanced degree of the next challenge.[13] All such judgments are provisional: other choices may be needed—especially in the future.

As noted earlier, curricular 'action ideals' are not 'idealistic' in the sense of being utopian, once-and-for-all perfect. Rather, they envision 'ideal' ends (pragmatic ends-in-view) that have no single, perfect, or one-time, final result. There is no perfect or ideal state of physical health; it matters whether you're 8 or 80 and depends on symptoms. Accordingly, perhaps excepting virtuosi, there is no ideal state of musical 'health', at whatever age.

Such rationally and ethically determined regulative or action ideals for curriculum and instruction, then, cannot take the same form for all people, places, and times: obviously, 'right results' vary considerably according to the specifics of situatedness. Hence, the 'right action' of praxis is not susceptible to standardized, formulaic, prescriptive, or 'delivery methods'.[14]

Praxical knowledge

Praxical knowledge depends in part on general guidance derived from *applied theoria*. These principles are the premises for making judgments and diagnoses and by which 'right action' is guided by action feedback in its doing phase. They also serve as the basis for adapting action to the requirements of ever-changing particulars (e.g., next year's fifth graders). So, while competent practitioners may use somewhat different "methods," the underlying theoretical premises informing the praxis of individuals are most typically held in common (e.g., competent electricians). They are, as explained earlier, an assumed part of the 'basic training' that exists to be put into action as praxis when applied to the particulars governed by phronesis—for example, functional knowledge of age-group cognitive abilities and development (developmental psychology); findings from educational psychology (Piaget and Vygotsky and related details); and, hopefully now, curriculum theory—especially Existentialism, Pragmatism, Praxis, and a spoonful of relevant Critical Theory and Postmodern thinking (covered later).

These principles or insights are not just matters of book learning, direct instruction, lecture, or observational learning. Accordingly, *reflective action on past praxis* develops 'applied' and 'operational' instructional tools. This is the proper sense for references to "professional practice." Professional praxis is not simply the "practicing" of technē roughly comparable to practicing the use of standard carpentry tools (teacher: "Today we'll practice hammering"). The "practice" that develops professional practice (knowledge *for* praxis) *is* knowledge *from* praxis—learning through doing! It presumes that foundational theory (meta-knowledge) supports praxis in terms of the particulars of each human situation. Praxis always involves ongoing "rehearsal," not once-and-for-all-times 'delivery' of "pre-fab" lessons.

Dealing successfully with always-changing particulars contributes new knowledge and skill to the practitioner. Such *praxical knowledge*, then, is generated by the experiences of praxis itself (successes *and* failures). As a result, individual praxis is very personal, individuating, self-actualizing, and idiosyncratic. While two practitioners may have similar theoretical and technical training (e.g., two surgeons), the application of these 'basics' will nonetheless be unique because the situations and requirements they face will necessarily be different. Consider, for example, a physician who practices general medicine in an inner city and another who works in a rural community; or consider the differences faced by educators in those same two contrasting settings. There is no recipe-like template that can ever apply to all.

"It works" claims for one-size-fits-all methods are clearly misleading or advertising hoopla to sell materials or books or promote workshop attendance. Instead, praxis inevitably exhibits a considerable degree of *personal style* and other individuating qualities. It involves heightened consciousness of an individuated Self that is a condition of pursuing the satisfaction of one's "life work" in comparison to the impersonal results and alienating conformity of many "jobs." It is, therefore, a condition of the *vita activa* or 'active life', a life of action (praxis) where personal agency contributes to the meanings and values of the "life well lived."

The individuating consequences of musical agency also characterize all forms of amateur, recreational, and avocational musicing. Such *freely undertaken action* (as opposed to praxis undertaken for pay) is perhaps the purest and most satisfying type of praxis. The meanings and values of amateuring stem from and reward the "love" that is the meaning of the Latin word *amat* at the heart of the word *amat*eur.[15] An amateur, properly speaking then, is a lover—a doer for love, not simply for pay.[16]

It is an important trait of praxis that its results depend on far *more* than the kind of intersubjective accounts that can be "passed around" as verbal, propositional, formal knowledge. In short, the fact that *praxical results are unrepeatable* in their specifics is both the source of the challenge facing any praxis and the source of the pleasure and rewards for the practitioner. Stating the results of praxis in advance can rarely (if ever) be done in the form of logical criteria or detailed, formal standards (national or otherwise). Teaching musically requires musical judgment that is appropriate to the age groups and individuals involved, and the musicing at stake.

However, the 'right results' are usually pragmatically obvious to both the agent *and* those served, because the action ideals are rationally obvious and overtly discernible (e.g., when the patient's health recovers, and when the student musician's initial frustration gives way to the joys of successful musicing). As is the case with both theoria and technē, excellent results of praxis may be called "beautiful." But for praxis, such superlatives are expressions of heartfelt, personalized, and individuating reflections on the 'right results'.

Ethics of school music as praxis

As mentioned previously, praxis depends on the conditions of phronēsis that amount to the important *ethical obligation* to be 'care-full' [*sic*]. Aside from some instances of physical harm (e.g., assigning a student to a vocal part that harms the voice, beginning clarinetists not using a neck strap,[17] and poor acoustics that damage normal hearing), "harm" in music teaching is often attitudinal, psychological—for example, seating competitions for instrumental ensembles that lead all but the winner to feel like "losers," singling a student out in a rehearsal or class in an embarrassing way, or noticeably favoring certain students over others.

But perhaps the most common "harm" is "turning students off" to music instruction and thus to the musics experienced there, and the kind of ensemble directing that leads large numbers of elementary and middle school students to quit so that high school groups consist of the survivors, with the "cream of the crap"[18] having been discouraged and thinned out earlier. The ethical criterion of phronēsis is a major and distinguishing difference of praxis from references to "practice." Except in some professions (medicine, law) where "praxis" (in the ethical sense) is called "practice" (e.g., a doctor's "practice"), a "practice" is usually a repeated, automatic habit with no ethical criterion.[19]

In consequence, praxis is centrally concerned with the ethical criterion of producing the 'right results'. And such 'right results' are judged in terms of the particular benefits to the well-being (*eudaimonia*) of those for whom the action is undertaken—in teaching, the well-being of students. Praxis understood as 'right' or '*virtuous* action'—*eupraxis*—first of all depends on the need to be *prudent, caring, wise,* and *far-sighted* in bringing about 'right results'.

> (a) the *acquisition of knowledge* needed to make effective decisions; musical knowledge plus developmental and educational psychology and curriculum theory
> (b) the *ability to judge* or diagnose what is 'right' and just for all who will be affected
> (c) the *understanding* needed to analyze all the relevant variables at stake
> (d) *the ingenuity or versatility* to competently handle the always unique situations presented by the unique differences of individuals
>
> * "Secondary" meaning that they facilitate the four intellectual criteria of Figure 4.1 p. 82

Figure 4.2 Aristotle's four *secondary* (i.e., intellectual) values.

Unlike in theology, "virtue" in Aristotle's philosophy was not "moral" behavior but the *excellence of praxical results*: 'right results' are evidence of excellent praxis. *Dyspraxia* is the failure to achieve 'excellent' or 'right results'—a failure of the professional 'due responsibility' to observe ethical *standards of care*, thereby causing harm by being care-less [sic].

Phronēsis is the active form of the knowledge that serves praxis. This *practical excellence* requires, first of all, *caring* for those served[20] and, secondly, being prudent or care-full in decisions and actions that affect their well-being. Phronēsis and its *primary ethic of care* rely on Aristotle's *secondary* or intellectual virtues (Figure 4.2).[21]

Considered from the perspective of ethics, then, instruction should properly be praxis, not standardized, routinized, recipe-like 'delivery' methods, but rather, a professional and *ethical 'doing'* that exists and is 'practiced' to serve the needs of students.

Duty Ethics

In philosophy, there are three 'schools' of ethics: deontological (or duty) ethics, consequentialist ethics, and virtue ethics.

In teaching, *duty* ethics focus on general professional teaching responsibilities. They are rooted in the concept of "rights" (e.g., 'natural rights', civil rights, animal rights) and the rights of those the profession serves (e.g., patient rights, student rights, animal rights).

The most important consideration of duty ethics is that music educators have a *duty to provide the service for which their profession exists*: discernibly advancing the musical well-being of students.

1. First, instruction should benefit the *individuals* served, not the teacher or 'music programs' as ends-in-themselves. Too often, students end up

serving *the program* rather than the program being the pragmatic totality of serving their individual musical needs.
2. Already mentioned is the duty to "first do no harm." Not improving skills central to a student's musical well-being can rise to the level of harm by, in effect, leaving students musically 'handicapped'.[22]
3. The *right of students to be safe*—from embarrassment, bullying, belittling, and threatening tactics that, given the volatile emotional life and self-concepts of adolescents, can have serious, long-term negative consequences.
4. The traditional *duty to be fair and just*. However, when instruction serves the needs of only an elite few, most students are denied—by competition and audition, or because the program does not offer anything of musical relevance to them, such as chamber music opportunities for string *players* in schools too small to have an orchestra.
5. *Beneficence toward the needy* is supposedly the 'calling' that attracts practitioners to a helping profession like teaching. This means that students' "needs" must be determined and then met, not dictated by one-size-fits-all curricula and 'delivery methods'. Without discernible benefits, instruction falls short of being ethical.
6. The *duty to allow and promote free expression*, a basic human right. Ensemble directors often dictate all musical and other ideas and choices. Freedom is promoted, instead, when students are offered *options* from which to choose and can give reasons (criteria) for their choices.[23]
7. Finally, one of Immanuel Kant's famous *categorical imperatives* (i.e., duties): "Act in such a way that you always treat humanity in your own person or the person of any other, never simply as a means, but always at the same time as an end." This duty is failed when music teachers *use* students as means to the ends of their 'programs',[24] or to the teacher's own musical ends and pleasures. Instead, students are the ends for which school music exists, and it is their musical benefits and satisfactions that are at stake.

Consequentialism

In school music, often duty ethics can be too general. Instead, *consequentialism* focuses on actual—notable and noteworthy—results (consequences) of instruction that have defined and observable criteria.

Consequentialism is the contemporary version of the *utilitarian* philosophy of Jeremy Bentham and John Stuart Mill. It introduced the concept of "utility" to ethical theory: for an action to be ethical, its *consequences should be useful*.

The "good" supposedly served by an educator's actions must be good in its *usefulness* for students, not just supposedly "good for" them on some vague or noble-sounding aesthetic claims or teacher say-so (e.g., "It's aesthetically good for you"). Thus, results also need to be *consequential*; they should *substantially* contribute to meeting a *significant* need and to a *functional degree* of usefulness.

Furthermore, for consequentialism, an ethical action is one that (a) produces "the greatest good for the greatest number" (as the axiom goes) and (b) is 'good' when more productive of happiness or pleasure or more preventive of unhappiness or discomfort than *disagreeable* or negative consequences such as boredom or aversion. In sum, school music is most ethical when it serves the greatest number of students in ways that are clearly "good for"—useful for—their present and future musical well-being and avoids unpleasant, unwanted consequences for all students. With these general traits in mind, consequentialism also has further criteria:

1. (a) First, consequentialism analyzes or diagnoses the potential for positive *and* negative consequences; (b) then it judges if the positives outweigh the negatives and (c) whether the musical well-being of the greatest number of students will be served. *Ethical responsibility requires special remedial efforts for struggling students.*
2. Concerning *curriculum*: What of all that could be taught has the most 'utility' for students' musical adult lives given the instructional circumstances, and what will benefit the largest number of students? Concerning *methods and materials*: Which are hypothesized to be most efficient and effective and best suited to reaching the most students? Concerning *assessment*: How will teaching and learning be evaluated? What will be evidence of success? How will the 'utility' of learning be judged?
3. Some instruction can result in negative consequences or lack usefulness. This rules out "no pain, no gain" pedagogies, the use of competitive strategies for ensemble seating that produce only one 'winner' and many 'losers', doing nothing about students who drop out, and other practices that typically result in unethical consequences for too many students.
4. Consequentialism focuses attention on *individual students*: not the needs of the 'program' or teacher or claims that all students have the same need—the excuse of one-size-fits-all methodolatry.
5. Consequentialism focuses especially on whether the benefits *promised* produced *tangible consequences* for the musical well-being of students and graduates. Results that are neither clear nor unmistakably consequential in the *musical* lives (choices, actions, capabilities, etc.) of students and society are evidence of the failure to fulfill the functional contribution promised by curriculum and failure to live up to ethical responsibilities of the profession.

Virtue Ethics

The third family of ethics is *virtue theories*. These focus on the personal ethical dispositions of an individual agent (i.e., a teacher). This "virtue" (excellence) is not a religious or moral status but is specifically qualified as attaining the 'right results' for students' well-being. Therefore, virtue theories reinforce criteria from both duty and consequentialist ethics, while making their unique contribution to *applied ethics for school music*.[25]

Virtue ethics arise notably in the writings of Aristotle and have had a strong influence on subsequent virtue theories.[26] Aristotle distinguished two kinds of personal virtue: *ethical* and *intellectual*. The four *intellectual* virtues were listed earlier in connection with the functional role played by phronēsis in praxis (p. 86). The ethical virtues describe dispositions, 12 in all, of the *ethical person* (exact terms differ according to the translation):

- Courage
- Restraint
- Generosity
- Dignity
- High-mindedness (honorable behavior)
- Proper ambition
- Patience
- Truthfulness
- Wittiness
- Friendliness
- Modesty
- Righteous indignation

It is useful to consider in practical terms what each requires: for example, "proper ambition" rather than promoting an educator's personal glory: "I've got the best band in the state." Importantly, all occupy the "golden mean" (middle) between two vices: for example, "courage" is the mean between rashness and cowardice, "modesty" the balance between shyness and shamelessness.

Virtue ethics accordingly depend on personal dispositions and the developed "know-how" of the earlier listed four secondary virtues of phronēsis. Virtue ethics also draws upon at least six criteria from duty ethics and consequentialism. And through the ethical character and disposition of the instructor, they collectively lead to an *applied ethics* of teaching as praxis.

1. Virtue ethics focus on individual students. The 'rightness' or 'goodness' of results is a matter of their needs, not those of the school, the 'program', or the teacher. When students' individual musical and educational needs get subverted to the greater good (or glory) of the ensemble (or director), the ensemble may appear to thrive but is not ethically benefiting its members for future musicing outside of the school ensemble.
2. Diagnostic excellence (virtue) entails diagnosing individual student needs, not force-fitting all students into lock-step 'delivery methods' that ignore differences between students. However, Aristotle's virtue ethic exceeds consequentialism by stressing the responsibility for instructors to remain up-to-date—and the versatility of meeting students' differing needs', for example, through new technology.
3. Virtue ethics exceed the "good intentions" of duty ethics. 'Right results' judge whether the teacher has shown ethical "due care." If children cannot match pitch after K-6 years of "singing activities," then "due care" has not been observed. The responsibility is to promote 'right results', not just "go through the motions" of offering "fun" activities that lead to no discernible progress or growth.
4. Furthermore, 'right results' need to be consequential (as with consequentialism) and should make a significant and lasting *musical* difference in the lives of students that ethically justifies the time, effort, and expense of instruction. 'Right results' should be 'functional', then, and congruent with the 'utility' criterion of consequentialism.
5. Aristotle taught that virtue (excellence) involves the "precision" that is proper to a particular endeavor. He wrote, "a carpenter and a geometer investigate the right angle in different ways; the former does so in so far as the right angle is useful for his work, while the latter inquires what it is or what sort of thing it is. . . . We must act in the same way, then, in all other matters as well" (Aristotle 1998, 14). The aims of school music students are significantly different than those of university and conservatory students. Importantly, then, curricular criteria and expectations of school music should differ from collegiate criteria. Music in the general education of *all* students involves a different kind of "precision," namely one serving the students' future musical needs as amateurs.

    When school music is taught to protect music from students (i.e., musicianism), all ethics have been thrown out the window.
6. Finally, *virtue is observed in contrast with its absence*. Where instruction is always 'good enough', there can be no real virtue. Worse, there can be no praxical knowledge developed: real professional growth (phronēsis)

depends on acknowledging mistakes and learning to avoid future mistakes.

The virtue of praxis

Praxis is virtuous because phronēsis serves unmistakably ethical and useful ends. The *functional excellence* of praxis—its ethical value or excellence in the function it performs—entails actions that cope with change and human variability. 'Right results' therefore require the virtue of the inner and underlying rational and ethical disposition of the instructor to produce 'right' or 'good results'. Thus, the intellectual virtue of praxis

1. draws upon aspects of *technical competence* of technē (musicianship) and
2. applied *theoria* (educational psychology, philosophy, ethics, and curriculum theory)
3. in pursuit of 'good results' for *individual or groups* that the praxis intends to serve.

These lead to the good life of teaching as a life of good teaching (Regelski 2012b).

With technē, methodolatry, and 'delivery methods', there is little credit or reward to the existential Self of the agent whose results are not unlike those of another technically competent individual. The virtue (excellence) of praxis, then, takes the form of its involvement with and commitment to serving the needs of *people*, not simply producing 'things'. 'Things' may well be involved (e.g., the house designed by an architect), but praxis requires that such results (including non-'things' such as musical results) unmistakably serve the needs of the humans whom they are to benefit. Consequentially, the architect whose building is beautiful but dysfunctional, and the musicians whose music is ill-suited to the criteria of the social situation, are engaged in malpraxis.[27] Both the knowledge and the 'doing' of praxis are extremely personal and individuating and amount to a *personal style* that is reinforcing and defining of Self in important ways.

The satisfactions involved in such 'doings' are not just personal but existentially self-actualizing and produce "optimal experience" or "flow" (Csikszentmihalyi 1990). With music, then, praxis theory, agreeing with

Pragmatism and contemporary *practice theory* (Bourdieu 1990; Schatzki et al. 2001), rejects conjectural accounts of aesthetic essences and metaphysical claims of beauty, meaning, and value in music in absolute terms. In particular, the idea that musical "works" are autonomous—what social theorist Bourdieu criticizes as the "pure gaze" of "absolute music" (Bourdieu 1993, 215–266)[28]— is thoroughly debunked by social philosophy.

For praxis theory (and ethnomusicology and sociology of music—e.g., Rice 2014; Martin 1996)—musical *meaning* and *value* do not inhere simply in the acoustical arrangement of sounds, nor can they merely be analyzed from the score (where there is one). Musicing always entails interaction with the sociocultural conditions governing and eliciting the sounds and the situated social praxes that condition it and that, in part, it helps shape (Regelski 2016a).

Music as a social praxis

Sociality is human interaction through institutions, life patterns, language, and other traditional social structures. Humans are intensely social beings— especially through language and music! Music, then, is inescapably social. Society and culture do not just influence music. Rather, music is a consequence of the interaction between people and sounds socially called "music" in connection with a social praxis. In sum, music (a) stimulates and conditions sociality (b) at the same time that it is a product of sociality.

Musical meaning, then, is not *in* the sounds or their relationships, but is in the *interaction* of such sounds with the sociocultural structures, contexts, uses, and other governing particulars of musical situatedness that brought them into being to begin with and that occasions their use for a present instance. They were socially determined to begin with, and reused according to ongoing social needs. The social dimension of music is, therefore, importantly determining of music's meaning, and music is importantly determining of human sociality (Regelski 2016b). Societies are distinguished not only by language, then, but also, importantly, through the musics each has evolved.[29]

In this give and take, music's social functionality is somewhat parallel to spoken language. Both are creative *of*, at the same time they are created *by*, sociality. And they share the fact that in neither do sounds inherently signify fixed meanings. There is nothing about the sound of the word "pain" that is homologous with the experience of pain. Meanings associated with the sounds of music, like the sounds of words, similarly depend on a variety of social and cultural associations.[30] They are governed by the situations in which they are used and evolve.

For instance, a Bach chorale as part of a church service has a different meaning and value than that same score performed on the secular concert stage in Bach's *St. Matthew Passion*. In the same manner, a secular love song used in a wedding ceremony takes on religious and ceremonial meaning, and "gospel" song easily became "soul" music when the words were secularized. And in 1999, the Vatican allowed hula music and dance for the Catholic liturgy in Hawaii. The meanings of words and expressions evolve and change according to usage chronicled in good etymological dictionaries. So do the meanings of music change, even "classics" of the past that respond to ever-new sensibilities and interpretations, new life situations and experiences of listeners, and even new technology.[31]

However, musical sounds are not suited to just any meaning. Sounds and their embodiment in perception have certain material conditions. And the range of meanings that arise from the sociality of music alleviates 'silly' relativism where "anything goes." The range of possible states of human awareness and meanings is flexible but finite. Marching to a lullaby is absurd.

Sounds created for a social praxis, then, become "musical sounds" (i.e., **"music"**) *in terms of that praxis*. Read that again! The sounds themselves "make special" (Dissanayake 1992, 1990) and more meaningful a social praxis at the same time that the sounds are made special (into "music") by the praxis.[32] The relationship is thereby totally reciprocal, and no distinction between internal-external, intrinsic-extrinsic, and inherent-delineated meanings and values can be valid. Because traditional aesthetic accounts rely on the first term of such dichotomies to the exclusion or denigration of the opposite quality, they fail to account fully for and thereby falsify the down-to-earth holistic values of all kinds of musics and musical experiences.[33] Praxis theories instead stress all manner of down-to-earth musical 'doings' that bring about 'right results'.

To begin with, the very existence of an unlimited variety of kinds, types, styles, and genres of music in the world is in itself conclusive evidence that musicing is as varied as the human sociality that leads to so many musics. Furthermore, at best, aesthetic theory is historically situated to the 18th century and is false to modern musical life. And, at worst, this aesthetic theory was, even in its heyday, an artificial and mediocre philosophy that served the ideological interests of the intelligentsia in the upper middle class and their attempts to be 'classy' in conspicuous demonstration of 'good or 'refined' taste and social "distinction."[34]

An unfortunate consequence of the 'high class' influence of the aesthetic orthodoxy has been the notable decline in amateur and recreational music-making of all kinds that it created. Middle-class homes used to have pianos, and *Hausmusic* was a common family and group entertainment. Being that such musicing falls short of aesthetic standards, CDs (and TV) have replaced it. And most citizens are not musically skilled (or interested) enough to make music at home. School music should change that.

Secondly, praxis theory points out that all kinds, types, and genres of music are "good for" an unimaginable diversity of 'good results'. All kinds of praxical roles for musicing fall within the range of praxis theory. The overwhelming preponderance of music in the world is clearly made for an unending diversity of life's social values—"the indigenous, unhomogenized, uncalculated sound of a culture becoming itself in the streets, bars, gyms, churches and back porches of the real world" (singer/composer Ani DiFranco, quoted in Farley 1999).

But, in this connection, "absolute" music and the "pure gaze" of 'aesthetic distance' either (a) denies or deprecates the social value of such music or (b) attempts to tear such music from its *originating* social roots to exhibit it solely for contemplation. Attempts to apply 18th-century aesthetic criteria to, for example, world and multicultural musics result in colonialism and exploitation by Eurocentric aesthetic theory that misappropriates and misrepresents the music and devalues its authentic musical meanings engaged only in situ by its practitioners.[35]

In sum, then, praxis theory accounts fully for all kinds and uses of music and finds musical value in the constituting sociality of music and the functional importance of music for social structures that govern collective and individual consciousness. It addresses "concert music" (of all kinds) presented for just listening as inescapably imbued with sociality and as a discrete praxis of its own that is no more or less important than other kinds of musical 'doing'—despite 'classy' pretensions. But praxis theory redresses the imbalance aesthetic orthodoxy has promulgated on behalf of 'just listening' and particularly reasserts the importance of musical agency through various kinds of performance, composing, and other types of musicing (e.g., collecting CDs, making playlists for listening devices to accompany aerobics, and exercise workouts).[36]

Furthermore, whether just listening in concert situations or at home, praxis theory accounts for and points to the value of all kinds of music in terms of the "good time" thereby created. Good time is literally "worthwhile" to both its sociality and its individuating benefits and other meanings and uses. "Worthwhile" time (as the British hyphenation makes clear) is "valued (worth the) time (while)." In contrast to time we "kill," "pass," "waste," or "spend," the "good time" of musical praxis promotes a variety of socially structured meanings in which the social mind participates in a way that is self-defining and self-enhancing.[37]

In particular, then, praxis and practice theory provide support for all kinds of amateur and recreational benefits of music (Regelski 2007) that are denied aesthetic value or validity by the aesthetic ideology. Playing jazz in a local club, the artistry of many country fiddlers and banjo pickers, garage bands of aspiring musicians, or folk guitarists and untutored music-making of all kinds, such as community ensembles, church choirs, Christmas caroling, and the like—each has a place and personal, social, and musical value in the praxical account. In its social breadth and relevance, music education merges with a community musicing, and all forms deserve consideration for curriculum planning. Moreover, audience listening expands its appreciation in praxical accounts to forms and types of listening where music is an essential part of social practices such as religion, weddings, ceremonies, dancing, mood enhancement, and the like.

Music does not just "accompany" sociality in a minor role (obviously so even including concert music). Music is (a) intrinsic to and defining of the social value-structure at hand while at the same time (b) that the sociality entailed is intrinsic to and defining of the "music" and its meaning and value. Consider weddings without the music chosen by the couple; church worship without its music; patriotic events without patriotic music; a birthday without singing the standard well wishes; a parade without its marching bands; even the background music carefully chosen for

> **Classical music?**
>
> **What about classical music?**
> Be clear: **listening** (to whatever type of music, in whatever setting—in concert, at home, with earphones) **is its own praxis**. **Listenership** has its own "good for" (listening entertainment) and in live performance has its own especial bounteous social interests. It has its own musicianship demands. Concert audience listening to such music, for example, presents completely different musical demands than for concert audiences of other musics: jazz in clubs, popular forms in auditoriums. *Praxis theory makes no judgment about the music*, other than it is all saturated with **sociality**.
>
> Yet many people either don't connect with the kinds of sociality associated with the classical repertory, can't afford it, savor it only in rare moments of leisure time, or are excluded from such concerts by rural living. Accomplished performance of band and wind ensemble literature is mainly available only in university towns and centers (and concerts of military bands). Yet local school music students often don't willingly attend these usually free concerts. Nonetheless, the band 'program' rules the roost in many schools, especially where marching band for American football half-time shows are a major adolescent social activity (also college half-time displays) and a reason given for school music: to *'elevate'* musical taste. **It isn't working.**

a dinner or cocktail party. Don't forget the music accompanying TV and films, and its essential role in the experience of viewing: for example, the music for the film *Jaws* (also performed in concert and on CD by the Boston Pops orchestra).

An accompaniment is usually half of "the music." Schubert's *Der Erlkönig* simply isn't "the music" without its piano accompaniment, and the piano accompaniments of Beethoven's violin sonatas rival his piano sonatas in difficulty and musical depth. Elton John's piano accompaniments likewise are an essential part of "the music" as are the vocal 'accompaniments' ("Voicestra") to the singing of Bobby McFerrin. The music of a social praxis, then, is just as central to the meanings and experience of the praxis as accompaniments are to solo literature.

In the praxical account, then, music is of and for the down-to-earth conditions of everyday life well lived in terms of the "good time" thereby created for the "good life." It is not above life in some intellectually or cerebrally abstract, disembodied, "pure gaze," or other-worldly realm of metaphysical ideals or "expressions" that supposedly exist for their own sake. Rather, for praxis, music's meaning and value are in and for action and human agency, for creating or enjoying musical sociality. Consequently, music creates "good time" (as explained above) for everyday people and everyday life. And praxis theory is altogether more down to earth as a pragmatic foundation for the decisions guiding curriculum for music education.

Action Learning

Brief emphasis should expand upon the earlier-mentioned pragmatic curricular purposes of *Action Learning* (Regelski 1998). This curricular model relies on musicing *modeled*[38] from real life outside of school for inclusion as part of the school music curriculum. Musicing drawn from the local musical life of a community (or country) is, first of all, keenly noted by students, their parents, administrators, and taxpayers in general. This notability supports claims to the relevance of teaching music in schools and to the relevance of the musics taught. Musicing not connected in some way with students' everyday lives will often be more difficult for engaging their musical interests. Musics foreign to their lives are at first like a foreign language. On the other hand, the uniqueness of some musics can be the first attraction, for example, steel drum praxis also promoting percussionists in ensembles.

Action Learning is, in effect, an *apprenticeship* leading from school to adult musicing. Schools that offer hand bell choirs often promote their use in local church services (where they are part of the service, not just musical diversion). And, in general, school learning put into praxis outside of and after graduation from school will become a permanent source for the "good life" contributed by music. Such an apprenticeship also draws on social learning theory, with its emphasis on observational learning: for example, a demonstration of a chord fingering on the guitar, new strums, etc., learned from any competent player—teacher or not.

The "action" of Action Learning, however, is important to qualify. It is synonymous with the criterion of "*an* experience" of Pragmatism. "Action theory" in several disciplines is concerned with the goal-oriented *intentionality* that guides an agent's actions. *Action*, then, is not mindless but instead is always focused on desired ends. In other words, there needs to be the guiding mindfulness of the intentionality of ends-in-view.

"Action" is also the English translation given to the Latin *praxis*. Likewise, it stresses "agency," the actions needed to bring about desired ends. Therefore, Action Learning reinforces praxis theory and is centrally concerned with musicing and all the knowledge and skills that make such musical 'doings' rewarding. Also important is musicianship typical to a particular kind of musicing (e.g., steel bands): it both arises from the demands of social praxis and contributes to the agency of that praxis.

The key to Action Learning, then, is the relevance of the intentionality of students' values. The musicing at stake is drawn from recognizable sources in the community (or media) that spark students' first interests (intentionality) and validate the goal of subsequent musicianship gains. Also vital is that students can judge for themselves that what they are learning has an important place in the world, not just in the school. And, finally, school learning can be extended to other music praxes—folk chords get expanded into jazz chords—thereby extending its value over time and through use. A functional degree of *independent musicianship* is the goal of teacher and student alike: the ability to engage in familiar or appealing musicing without assistance—except for input sought for going onto advanced levels (new chords, changing meters, alternate fingerings, capo use, typical transpositions, etc.). Motivated students (even as adults) will access YouTube and other Internet sources in search of new skills.

In this, however, *general musicianship* learned through locally common musics, but that applies to several kinds of praxis, is most mutually reinforcing. It promotes what educational psychology calls *transfer of learning* where the musicianship learned (assimilated) in connection with one praxis applies to another (is accommodated) as well, thereby reinforcing each praxis.[39] Musicianship gained with a particular praxis (e.g., its harmonic language and rhythms) can add to musicianship applicable to another praxis.

On the other hand, learning that has little or no potential for transfer of learning is likely to be effective only for the original (e.g., harmonica). And lacking occasions for a praxis out of school (e.g., Orff arrangements), transfer of learning is minimal, even nonexistent. The knowledge or skill of such lessons goes unapplied in 'real' musical terms and usually forgotten over time through a lack of meaningful use. Instruction in some originally attractive musical praxis (rhythm bands), then, can be a dead end upon the conclusion of the lesson or once the student graduates.[40]

The same result, of course, is often the case with performance ensembles where the next concert was always the goal. Upon graduation, there are no more concerts, and no likelihood for the second trombones or tuba players to continue musicing. The same can be true for musical praxis that depends on expensive or otherwise hard-to-acquire musical means. For example, individuals typically cannot usually afford a collection of steel drums for practicing (the musical skills can, however, be practiced and enjoyed with electronic drum sets). But, when the skills and knowledge learned in school via that medium can be "transferred" to other also enjoyable musical practices, the value of that transferable learning goes up (e.g., percussion ensembles and sections).

Postmodernity

Postmodernity[41] is the most recent collection of ideas applied by its devotees to curriculum theory in music. It is not a systematic philosophy, but somewhat of an attitude or disposition toward "unpacking" questions of truth, knowledge, value, reality, and freedom from traditional notions—all of which are regularly implicated in curriculum design. It gained notice (and ample criticism from some philosophers and intellectuals) during the latter years of the 20th century. As the term suggests, it follows in time what many scholars in various disciplines have called "Modernity." However, it is not just a sequel to Modernity but mainly a response and an assertive reaction against it. As a result, some of the key features associated with Modernity first need clarification.

Modern*ity*

Modernity itself is a highly contested notion. Some experts identify it as early as with the demise of feudalism and the rise of capitalism in the Renaissance

(c. 14th to 17th centuries), and with the onset of political institutions, such as the beginnings of today's nation-states. It is associated with urbanization, industrialization (the Industrial Revolution [c. 1760–1780]), secularization, bureaucratization, and the economic, military, social, and cultural domination of the nation-state.

Other scholars identify Modernity's main flowering with the 17- to 18th-century European "Age of Enlightenment" that led the way to many new developments in thinking and society. Still others view it as less an era than as a constellation of ideas, beliefs, values, and socioeconomic developments that arise at different times in developing societies as they become more "modern." In any case, an attempt to pinpoint the quintessence of Modernity is, at best, only suggestive of several traits associated with different phases in the world of contemporary thought.

By the late 17th to early 18th century, the importance of reason, empiricism, religious diversity, secularism, and individualism was solidly established. With the rise of the individual as a result of Renaissance humanism came the modern idea of romantic love. Among the traits associated with the Enlightenment, nature was turned from a source of intrinsic (God-given) meaning and value into an object for rational (scientific) inquiry. The resulting development of the *scientific method* was a major outcome of these attempts to rationalize the natural world. Science as an instrument of human reason led to the increasing rejection of superstition and religious dogma.

Modernity envisioned the world discovered by scientific knowledge as a machine, with scientific laws operating somewhat like mechanical laws. Knowledge of those laws as 'certain' truths gave the (misleading) impression of *control* over nature. In consequence, *knowledge became a form of power*. Moderns also believed that reason provided individuals with power for controlling their destiny, and thus that humanity as a whole could evolve from lower to higher, more civilized forms through the rational and scientific organization of society. Along with the new *empirical sciences*, then, were the beginnings of the *social sciences* by which personal and social conduct could be studied and understood.

Together these changes promoted a strong belief in *progress*. Rational and empirical knowledge of the world resulted in the progressive rejection of religious world-views and led to the secularization of the lifeworld. Knowledge, when *divorced* from traditional religious sources, enabled not only worldly control and power but also empirical 'certainty' that trumped faith. Scientific understanding, then, was at once a *mirror* believed to reflect reality and at the same time a *lamp* that cast its light on the heretofore unobserved recesses of reality (thus "Enlightenment").

The scientific method supposedly produced 'objective' and 'neutral' learning. A hallmark of science, then as now, was the ability to replicate an experiment; replication gave evidence of 'objective' validity. Offshoots of Modernity are scientific technologies that end up influencing nonscientific life that enriched life in many ways.

Modernity also led to wars and weapons of mass destruction. Like canaries in a coal mine, the arts were especially attuned to these and other failed promises of Modernity.

Modern*ism*

Modernism refers to a cultural movement in literature, art, architecture, and music noted for its rejection of the taken-for-granted Modernity of bourgeois 19th-century ('classy') society at the height of Romanticism. It consisted of a jumble of "isms" (e.g., Impressionism, Abstract Expressionism, Dadaism, Futurism, Symbolism, Cubism, and Conceptualism) and an exploration of the deeper, sometimes pathological recesses of the mind from Jung's and Freud's studies of the unconscious. Each movement sought to redefine "art" and, often, to deny the quasi-sanctified and commodified status of art that had flowered with Romanticism's aesthetics. Today, the term "Postmodernism" has been generalized beyond the arts and to Postmodernity in general—much to the muddle of an already confused account.

Modernism's critique (in the arts) of Modernity's false claims about social progress set in motion a confrontation with conventional sensibilities and methods of artistic creation and tastes. More than just nonconformity, modernists reacted with active hostility to what they regarded as the superficial role of the arts in bourgeois society (late 18th to 19th century), especially the canon of "Great Works" sanctioned by "establishment" cognoscenti. The arts had already become evidence of wealth and social standing—symbols for modernists of decadence. Thus, many artists of the time progressively sought to shock bourgeois tastes. Failure of artists to attack the elite 'artworld' was a liability to their careers.

Postmodernity and modernist art and music

Ironically, despite Modernist confrontation with the elite tastemakers of the 19th-century "establishment" (i.e., elite academies of art and music, juries, exhibitions), today's "modern[ist] art" has continued to be the playground of the ultra-rich, with visual artists commanding vast sums of money. It is no longer a statement against excesses of capitalist commodification of art; finding buyers and galleries is ever-more a preoccupation of artists. However, their opposition to Modernity's tastes came to be accepted by the Establishment as "avant-garde"—new, bold, and appealing to newly reorganized social tastes and wealthy society (e.g., collector Peggy Guggenheim, a rich, bohemian socialite, advanced the reputations of many unknown artists who today are world-famous). Some scholars conclude that these developments signaled the end of Enlightenment Modernity; with the advent of postmodernism, then, it seems everything is up for grabs in the marketplace of arts and ideas.

Many artists in the 20th and into the 21st century did continue to take stands opposing the socially elevated quasi-spiritual status of 'fine art' among the rich and cognoscenti. Among the most notable were the "ready-mades" of Marcel Duchamp (e.g., a urinal entitled "Fountain" signed and exhibited as museum 'art'), John Cage's 4'33" (of silence observed by a concert audience), Conceptualism (where the artist takes credit for the idea despite its execution by factory workers), etc. (Figure 4.3).

One such "anti-art" statement attracted world news in October 2018 when a painting ("Balloon Girl") by the notorious artist "Banksy" (a pseudonym), after its winning auction bid for $1.4 million, started to self-destruct in front of the bidders via a shredder the artist had built into its frame. It jammed

Figure 4.3 Public art, SUNY, Fredonia, NY.
"Tin men." William King. Factory construction. Courtesy, SUNY Fredonia NY.

halfway through, however, and added considerable commercial value to what remains of the original.

Numerous commentators have time and again declared the end of art; yet what is still called "art" and what previously had been "crafts" (ceramics, photography, weaving materials and design, etc.) have newly been given museum status. "Installations" in major galleries are usually one-time events, removed and replaced with another: the permanence of art as a repository of history gets rejected. The question, then, "What is art?" is answered by a form of Pragmatic Realism (described earlier); the question gets submitted to the elite "artworld" of society (galleries, museums, buyers, connoisseurs, reviewers, aestheticians, critics, art historians, etc.) for its definition—a matter, unsurprisingly, of labeling. Contrary to aesthetic claims, then, sociologically, what the elite 'artworld' defines as art is art!

Most modern forms of music (post-Webern) have rejected tonal music. While they have some dedicated admirers, it seems fair to conclude that most have not caught on with audiences or collectors as tonal music had. Most symphony orchestras continue with a major dose of the standard repertory, only occasionally offering new compositions, sometimes commissioned works.

The social ends of art continue to be served by the results of the postmodern open-arms ethos. The false authority of "high" over "low" art is targeted by postmodernism focused on ridding art of its elitist aesthetic meta-narrative. As a consequence, an alliance has arisen with popular culture (e.g., "pop art," cross-over musics). On the other hand, rather than catering to populist accessibility, some artists and composers have sought to challenge or startle their audiences, with sometimes unsettling results.

Postmodern pluralism has largely rid music of conventions like tonality, formalism, and even serialism. Composers have invented completely new musical 'languages', sometimes for each new composition[42] or series of related works. Many new works use invented notation in escaping the limitations of traditional notation and organization, and explore *schizophonia*—the separation of sounds and their electroacoustic reproduction and distribution (e.g., see R. Murray Schafer).

However, these new musical languages *deconstruct* conventional expectations (i.e., critically identify and analyze traditional categories and meanings): for example, chance (stochastic) and aleatory music, indeterminism, collage quotations, electronic-computer-based sound, algorithm controls, minimalism, postminimalism, process music, and soundscapes. Opera and vocal music reveal some of postmodernity's ambivalence about texts but mainly still adhere to narratives (e.g., minimalist John Adams).

Audiences who have a taste for postmodern musics usually find listening to be challenged (or enriched?) by the lack of traditional, conventional formal markers for following along. They are to be just carried along with the changing music.

Postmodernist composers exhibit either an intentional rejection of conventional premises of aesthetic theory (a hallowed *meta-narrative*[43] of Modernity) or a complete disregard for such speculations. An ethos of "anything goes," ordered-disorder, is a typical result. Each work represents a potential new friend that you may get to know better in time.[44] However, in most cases, the "autonomy" of a work for at least a concert audience is assumed.[45] Nonetheless, postmodern musics move with ease from the concert stage to other cross-over spaces and places, and new roles involving audience response and input are growing in frequency.

Postmodern tendencies

Given the elusiveness of Modernity and the slighting of it first by Modernism and now by Postmodernism as an all-inclusive idea (and label), it should be easy to realize that Postmodernism is not easy to understand—or for some to accept. Some have seen it as a revolt against Modernity, others as a critical history of the themes and traditional beliefs of Modernity. Some see Modernism as simply an unfinished project that leads to its negation by Modernity itself (or as Postmodernism). Postmodern discourse (or theory) is therefore not the purview of only philosophers; it arises from a wide range of scholarship and literature contending with troubling issues of contemporary existence. In the U.S., it has often found a home in university English/literature departments (despite its many French roots and psychoanalytic theories).

The commonly taken-for-granted meta-narratives of Modernity are emphatically opposed, critiqued, and rejected by Postmodernism. As briefly noted earlier, *meta-narratives* are all-embracing historical systems, accounts, assumptions, and uncritical indulgences that *legitimate a status quo* by which dominant social and ideological groups control other groups. One theme of Modernity had been its championing of reason and science—for example, the dual meta-narratives of *scientism* and *positivism*.[46] Hence, even the status of "facts" and "truth" comes to be doubted by postmoderns.

Aesthetic theorizing has also been a meta-narrative of Modernity that has clumsily attempted to legitimate the cognoscenti's bourgeois, high-class, and elite conception of art and artistic meaning and value. Postmodern references to "aesthetics" in art and life are oriented instead to the original meaning of "aisthesis" (i.e., as sentience); to the aestheticization of everyday life (i.e., heightened sensibilities of daily life); to the "de-aestheticization of art" (i.e., of the aesthetic meta-narrative); and to "the aesthetic regime" and "politics of the aesthetic" (i.e., critiques of the institutionalized borders separating the arts—from each other and life) (Rancière 2009a, 2009b). The "free market" of capitalism is another meta-narrative that legitimates the socioeconomic power of the "haves" over "have-nots" (or as capitalists prefer, the "makers" over "takers"). *Religious belief* is another major meta-narrative legitimating powerful control over people's lives through religious doctrine.

Earlier philosophies (e.g., empiricism, skepticism, naturalism) and physics had already dismissed a world of causality (i.e., a world that is devoid of cause-and-effect linkages). And philosopher Immanuel Kant satisfactorily denied that we can ever get to ideal knowledge of the "thing-in-itself" (i.e., 'reality' that is independent of mind; "noumenon," a quasi-metaphysical essence, akin to Idealism's 'ideal forms'). We are consequently left only with knowledge of the "phenomenon" via perception (sensibility, aisthesis), not any 'ideal form' behind it. Causality is a taken-for-granted intuition that is so ingrained in humans that it is built into many languages.[47] But seeking causes for any given effect often leads to an infinite regression of a multiplicity of contributory conditions, never arriving at "the" cause (e.g., of poverty or of a war).

"Both/and" reasoning of postmodernism replaces "either/or" binaries, hence resisting any certitude—an effect also of the "uncertainty principle" in physics.[48] Without 'truth' as a foundation for our beliefs, we only have language by which we subjectively construct our 'inner world' models (the "internal reality" of Pragmatism) for dealing with the world 'out there' (including others in it) that we can never know directly.

The same fate applies to claims for universal principles of human nature, objective reality, factuality, facticity,[49] reason, progress, beauty, etc. All such claims to universal and timeless relevance and application get rejected as meta-narratives (e.g., the a priori claims of Idealism, Realism, and Neo-Scholasticism). The result is that in the postfactual world of postmodernism, there is simply no access to 'reality' on which to ground belief except language, and our language-created world is plural, existing in each mind differently. Physicist Steven Hawking dismisses two theories about 'reality' and affirms "Pragmatic Realism":

> One is the 'realist' viewpoint of classical science based on the belief that a real, external world exists, a world that can be measured and analyzed—that is the same for every observer who studies it. The other is what Hawking calls the 'anti-realist' viewpoint. This viewpoint is so insistent on confining itself to empirical knowledge

gleaned through experiment and observation that it has little use for theory and ends up self-destructing with the notion that because anything we learn is filtered through our brains, we can't really count on there *being* such a thing as empirical knowledge.... "Our perception—and hence the observations upon which our theories are based—is not direct, but rather is shaped by a kind of lens, the interpretive structure of our human brain." That goes for everyday experience, he says, not just in science. (Ferguson 2017, 422, italics original)[50]

Therefore, as has been seen with Pragmatism, while the physical world causally exists apart from the human mind, *pragmatic* (internal) reality arises from interactions of a mind with the physical and social world to which we append (or learn to associate) words as labels—about distinctions (adjectives), qualities (adverbs), thingness (nouns), actions (verbs), categories, etc. We, therefore, know the world only through our language-aided (or obscuring) experiences of building our mental models of it.[51]

Knowledge, as *constructivism* in cognitive psychology has found, is aided in part through language that divides the world into linguistic boxes. These categories are influenced by the mind's prior experiences, perceptions, understanding (cultural and personal), feelings, beliefs etc., of each person, and filtered through language—or language is the result of the brain's filtering of the external world. In other words, knowledge is always subjective and provisional. It is provisional because it involves a temporal dimension that varies over intervals with fluctuating inputs of subjectivity, new worlds of experience (e.g., travel, learning a new language, and prior categories of understanding). Thus do we construct the particular world we know (have mental models for) and inhabit! Leave it, and we experience some degree of "culture shock"—a 'reality' check.

Such world-making is predicated at first on categories of understanding (models) derived from (imposed by?) the words, syntax, and other symbols of an existing language; cultural givens (music, art, food, institutions, and habits); manners of sociability (bowing, shaking hands, generational traditions); social habits and values (clothing, work, play); institutions (schools, banks, police, money, traditional gender roles); taken-for-granted beliefs and traditions of a culture (national folklore and history, religion); and much more. Accordingly, there is no place in a Neo-Pragmatist, Postmodernist world for otherworldly aesthetic meta-narratives.[52]

We are thus born into a world of the local or family language culture. The structure of that inherited language itself first shapes the course of our cognitive development. Concepts of time and space develop at different times for children according to their native language context, and the vocabulary of a language influences the world as they come to experience it.⁵³ Then, in school, that world is expanded (i.e., new words for new learning) and attention given to overlooked details (still in the local language—unless a child become bilingual), and finally we go into and through adult life in terms of ever-new language-mediated situations (e.g., professional terminology, technical language used on the job, regional jargon, and countries visited or lived in). Language is also always expanding, sometimes by borrowing from other languages (e.g., canoe, sauna, pronto, and repertoire).

Furthermore, given the presence of "the Other" in *our* world and *their* equally self-constructed worlds of understanding (see note 49, this chapter), the unavoidable sociocultural differences between groups take on a relevance beyond the narrow experiences (and mental models) of any individual Self. Sensitivity to the worlds of "the Other" (gender, ethnicity, economic and social status, race, sexual identity, politics, religion, etc.) thus presents challenges because *their world ("internal reality") is different than ours*—sometimes significantly so. In addition to communication problems, then, there are the attitudes and values exhibited to and by social groups. For example, unlike those holding social power, the choices of the disadvantaged are limited. Realization by society of the significant variables that govern a socioeconomically impoverished world-view should promote compassionate understanding rather than ideological stigmatizing, and instead, steps should be taken for combating such social inequity.

Postmodernists are, as a result, typically distinguished by their concern with socioeconomic class, class struggle, and related themes of institutional power, justice, equality, and freedom. The meta-narratives of such struggles are targets for deconstruction. This process provides potential bases for change agency to overcome the lack of human opportunities for those stigmatized in a hierarchical society predicated on inequitable socioeconomic and cultural class rankings. Acknowledging such conditions without taking corrective actions leaves us (and society) with a distorted world-view that will be dysfunctional in the presence of such class-based disorders. Actively contending against such disorders allows us to avoid falling into accepting or aggravating the social power dynamics involved. Instead of enslavement by prevailing social class hierarchies, the "us vs. them" stance of fascism (i.e., native-born 'purity' vs. 'immigrant's otherness', and ingrained class-based consciousness), postmoderns honor, commend, and support *cultural pluralism* for its enrichment of everyone's life.⁵⁴ Do you like pizza or tacos?

With language a foundation for world construction, postmodernists seek to *transform language* in restorative and progressive directions. They adopt discourse that uncovers and 'unpacks' whatever is manipulative or distorting of important sectors of life hidden in 'packages' of meta-narratives and taken-for-granted traditions and assumptions. For example, the discourses of feminism or racism reveal the disguised domination of power and control over women and minorities of much everyday language ("them" as Others). The discourses of postmodernism are more than the merely softening effects of "politically correct" language; they are, instead, a language that intentionally bypasses or *critically interrogates* taken-for-granted meta-narratives (about minorities, immigrants, etc.)—for example, how the use of *power-laden discourse* defines and discredits 'abnormality' in ways that demean the lifeworlds of LGBTQ+ individuals by portraying them as a threat to the meta-narratives of 'normality' that critics rely on in their narrowly biased world-views.

A consequence of this inventiveness is postmodern discourse often loaded with unfamiliar concepts, dazzling displays of acrobatic syntax, and novel language, and investing new meanings in old words or subjecting them to exaggeratedly careful interrogation. "Common sense" concepts are decentered—where there is no Self, only a core of ideas, values, and tendencies orbiting around the words "I," "me," "self," "my," etc. Common sense 'direct' reality is shattered or fragmented, and dualisms 'unpacked' or deconstructed.

Given the fact that European thinkers are among the leading postmodernists, vagaries of translations abound. And playing with word meanings adds to the sense of bewilderment some readers face when encountering postmodern texts. For postmodernism, the meaning of a text is a joint creation of the encounter of a reader with the words of the author, playing together with meanings. There is no "given" meaning, only a duet with the author.

There is undeniably a sense in which postmodernism is a victim of its language games as it "interrogates," "unpacks," "decenters," "deconstructs," identifies, analyzes, and critiques "metanarratives" and posits "*différance*," "the Other," "hyperreality," "archiwriting," "de-realization," and a lot more that has taken many books to explain and many more to clarify or defend. It is ever in danger of becoming its own meta-narrative, one notably lacking consistency between theorists. It is not unfair to say that it has a bias of its own against conventional "language games" about 'reality'.

According to Wittgenstein (1953/2017), with language games (postmodern or otherwise), words are like moves in a game with rules interwoven and related by "family resemblances" between different kinds of wordplay—for example, the similarity affecting all aesthetic discourse and musical terminology. A word in one context has a different meaning than the same word in a different context: "You're playing games with me" (interpersonal relationships) vs. "The games children play" (childhood observations). However, often the language games proposed by a given postmodern theorist are stated without condition (despite uniform antagonism toward "absolutes"); they are their own word game. Thus, postmodern theory only challenges such wordplay (e.g., gendered language) but often adds its own word games that need to be mastered to 'understand' claims made.

Similiar games hold for music as a "text" that is played. "The" meaning of any text (including music) is therefore rejected (which is good news for those facing true/false tests). Language is so central to dealings with 'reality' that it is not a personal "interpretation" of a text or music that is involved, but a unique creation as reader or listener encounters author and composer. The playing of music is obviously different than the playing of sports; a family resemblance between the two senses of "play" is at stake—an important one, if the sense of 'play' (*homo ludens*: mankind as playful, maker of games) gives way to the tedium of drill. And such word games tremendously complicate both the learning of a new language and translations between languages.

These dynamics also sometimes erupt in conversational exchanges. Kingsbury (1988) demonstrated how the five divisions of a major U.S. conservatory related to the word "music" differently through the word games of their specialties. And simple exchanges—as between, say, director and student—can become loaded with word games of power and control. Much classroom and rehearsal discourse convey the absolute power of the teacher/director: in rehearsals, "*I* want X" (vs. "**Let's** try X—let *us* see the difference"). Note too the power play, "Who can be quiet enough to be chosen to play the drum?"—a word game just dripping with authority.

Postmodernity and the music curriculum

Some educational critics and philosophers consider the so-called "postmodern turn" as a theoretical dead end that excessively stresses the quirks and word play of all language and is otherwise vague concerning actual social and transformative change (e.g., Hill et al. 1999; Norris 1990). Typical criticisms focus on traits of postmodernism that pose challenges if applied to schooling. For example, its denial of universal truths admits only personal perspectives filtered through a lens or kaleidoscope of race, class, gender, and social and economic variables. This leads to the "Rashomon Effect," named after a classic film in which director Akira Kurosawa portrays a murder in four contradictory, self-serving versions. Consequently, where truth is so relative as to represent only one person's *perspectivism*, the 'content' of curriculum—what is included in instruction—is at least imperiled.[55]

As far as the 'traditional' focus of schooling on the metanarratives of the past, postmodernism critiques a Eurocentric reading of Western history and culture (e.g., of the "Great Works" of 'fine art', literature, music, aesthetic theories, and male artists and composers) that have served only to promote racism, sexism, capitalism, colonialism, and Enlightenment concepts of reason and progress. Deconstruction's wariness of language leads to its abundant use of jargon and gymnastic prose and syntax suggestive of U.S. politics (2019) about "alternative facts." It also points to the unreliability of language, where 'truth' is no longer the result of reason or researching and judging evidence, but a futile and foolish denial of 'fidelity' that eventually sabotages communication.

Therefore, postmodernists seem to be inclined to stating 'positions', often supposedly supported by details of their personal lives,[56] and are often cynical about the relevance of traditional humanistic learning and its claims to authoritative learning. But they stand vulnerable to having postulated their own metanarrative, which is nonetheless suspicious of its self-indulgent claims to authority and unable to unseat the supposed hypocrisies it claims to debunk. Thus, it contests social justice, inequality, musical programming, race, feminism, LBGTQ+, and even ecological issues in music education.

Metanarratives "deconstructed" and the transformation of schools

However, postmodernism's opposition to meta-narratives that legitimate the privileges of dominant social groups does alert us to the *social construction of knowledge* and the various institutional sources by which *power* is exerted through language and music (e.g., some hip-hop). Schools, as agencies of knowledge distribution, are among the institutions most directly implicated. They can abet such dynamics of power in ways that too often, if taken for granted, go unnoticed (e.g., more than ample attention to male and white composers and less to women and those of color).

In particular, public schooling deals centrally with the many metanarratives of middle-class values and priorities, unfamiliar to students whose families are poor, and often are put on display by students whose families are wealthy (designer clothing, their own cars, owning first-class instruments, etc.). Students from the precariat[57] and even further underclasses, then, are expected to toe the line in school that is unfamiliar to them at home and not easily coped with in school.

The norms and concerns (e.g., dinner time talk) of their family life are also typically disconnected from those of their schooling. Home life can contradict the values and norms of schools and vice versa. Such students' parents, for example, were also sometimes at academic risk in their school days and their expectations for their children's education may not be forward-looking. Teachers, in conferences with parents, hear too often "Well, I wasn't good at math either," as though math competence is genetic.

Middle- and upper-class families, in contrast, support their children's schools and teachers and work diligently to pass on the privileges they have to their children. They also have resources to augment schooling: taking the children to concerts and museums, owning diverse CD collections, travel experiences, costs of organized sports ("soccer moms"), and private tutoring (music, dance, language lessons, etc.). Their children more often own their musical instruments, for example,[58] and get plenty of parental support (e.g., encouraging practicing, attending school concerts—not just dropping their children off, parent-teacher conferences, parent-teacher associations, etc.).

These parents are also likely to take for granted the advantages their children have in comparison to their disadvantaged classmates. And this class-based deportment is too often reflected via their children: their stylish and expensive clothes, owning personal computers and cell phones, their scholastic accomplishments, vacation tales, their popularity on social media, school behavior, etc. Postmodernists are not content with this inequality, and they work to overcome class inequities and maximize eventual economic benefits for students. As with Pragmatists and Existentialists, then, most Postmoderns aim to function as social change agents!

Schools are criticized for *social sorting* of students via grades, honor rolls, awards, AP courses, electives, "student of the month," newspaper listings (e.g., of music festival grades), career tracking (college vs. vocational), etc. If this process is noticed at all, it is only by parents of the middle and upper class, and by teachers at each level.[59] Students of lesser abilities or accomplishments, in contrast, are 'taught' by schooling itself—often via the hidden curriculum discussed earlier (e.g., publicly posting grades)—that they are 'poor' students.[60]

Teachers tacitly classify 'good' students as average (or less), above average, and exceptional—and, in music, as 'talented'. Weaker students are judged as lacking the drive to get ahead in school and the world and as satisfied just to get by and follow in the well-worn paths established by their parents and older siblings. Graduation for them is truly "commencement," but on a life track that challenges them socially and economically. Marriage, family, and (if lucky) wage laboring are the cards they are dealt.

Schooling, then, is largely geared to *preservation of the social and economic status quo* (middle class and above) and to what is uncritically (and conservatively) regarded as "social stability"—a norm, for example, upset by LGBTQ+ students. Pregnant teens, at least in the U.S., are also problems and are sometimes forced to homeschooling or separate schools. Hence, for Postmoderns, the school is often complicit in perpetuating and even initiating many of the negative dynamics that beset society: inequality, injustice, social class discord, economic exploitation, political polarization, racial tensions, women's rights, and religious intolerance, to mention a few.[61] Since knowledge is power, schools are centrally engaged in a monopoly over learning and the power that comes with it; and they have a massive influence on the present and future lives of school-age children—for example, entrance to college or the military.

With the Internet, however, this long-lasting domination of knowledge and its dissemination by schools is now compromised; today's students arrive at school with much more knowledge of the world (and musics) than previous generations. Among other effects, this has made schooling a site of social controversy, not stability![62] And schools have become "front lines" of many social pressures (drugs, gangs, bullying, social media abuse, racism, antitranssexualism, vaccination politics, religious controversy over teaching evolution or sex education, etc.).

Schools, by their very nature, serve all students and are sites of *plural perspectives* about values, religion, politics, ethnicity, gender, sexuality, etc. And the larger the school or community, the more potential there is for confrontations with "Others." As a result, schools are expected to acknowledge such diversity and rightfully stress equal opportunities and democratic communication where diverse perspectives are encouraged and heard. This, of course, is too often short-circuited for poor and immigrant children whose perspectives are perhaps the most in need of attention. Their unique needs and those of special needs and disabled children require different approaches than for most children.

What does school music education offer to students interested in, say, ethnic or folk instruments? Before World War II, the "school orchestra" used to consist of students playing whatever instruments they owned and could play. When, why, and how did music education become an enterprise of promoting school ensembles for their own sake and not cultivating or meeting the needs of those who already had an interest in an instrument, including vernacular instruments like accordion? Why they became so narrowly based on the musics of the upper social classes is questioned by postmodernists. Why can't students interested in strings be served in chamber groups of various sizes?

Where "popular" musics prevail (e.g., many European schools), how does music education keep up with the changing scene inherent to the recording industry? Keep up with what, we might ask? Capitalism and neo-liberalism? (Is "popular" itself a concept needing deconstruction? Recall the popularity of Hitler and Mussolini and their musical choices for their nations (*viz.*, Wagner and Verdi, respectively).

This traditional model of schooling is still often premised on the *transmission* of knowledge: Idealism, Realism, and Neo-Scholasticism are all predicated in their respective ways on preserving this veneration for lofty ideas, "Great Works," repeating standard scientific experiments, etc. And all are complicit in promoting meta-narratives and predigested knowledge as transmitted from teachers, other authorities, and texts. Students suffer through true/false, fill-in-the-blank, and multiple-choice tests; essay exams on "the" causes of the U.S. Civil War; and tests on a host of inert factoids in a variety of subject areas—all of this in a world where such information is easily and efficiently accessed on a computer or smartphone if and when needed.

A postmodern and critical perspective of schooling focuses instead on *transformation,* not on direct transmission of knowledge. First of all, students deserve the personally transforming effects of schooling that prepare them for the changing world outside of school and for productive futures. When this is not the case, students impatiently ask (or more patiently think), "Why do we have to study this stuff?" (Answer: "Because the curriculum says so," "It's educational," or "It's aesthetically good for you"). Student engagement with topics of study regularly reflects their rejection of its transformative potential. The "someday you'll see its importance" will never come for most.

Secondly, meta-narratives that sustain the power and control mechanisms and language of social power brokers (e.g., politicians, big business, chambers of commerce, NAfME leaders, union leaders, etc.) need to be exposed and resisted. This process, therefore, looks to transforming and reconstructing society along more egalitarian lines: for example, to make learning *emancipatory,* thereby freeing the individual from the dominance of controlling power interests and language games (especially "pre-fab" textbooks, worksheets, etc.). Whose values are at stake, for example, in choosing the musics to be studied and performed over those not included in the curriculum? Why is the diet of school music so often alienated from other musics, of which there are plenty?

Postmodern thinking works in many ways against the *hidden curriculum* detailed earlier: the unspoken, tacit power over students that underlies the institution of schooling itself. As already mentioned, critics argue that changing of class per bells, behavior and dress codes, respect for authorities, unhesitating following of orders, the 'assembly line' of subjects throughout each day, learning as "work" requiring steadfast dedication and responsibility (e.g., home*work*), sitting still and with attention to directions and lectures, etc., all have the effect of producing good, reliable *workers*—but not knowledge and skills that advance their capabilities as self-actualized persons.

What the curriculum does *not* include that may nonetheless be of interest to more than a few students is "learned" by them as being officially unimportant—"dissed"—according to the school (e.g., Puerto Rico's lively music scene or history in U.S. schools having a large Puerto Rican enrollment). Of course, the world of music outside of schools, to which students of all ages have more and more recorded access, is far more than what authorities typically include in school curriculum. Why? Because of the meta-narrative and ideology of MEAE as solidly promoted by many in the professoriate who live in cloistered worlds of 'classical' music—worlds into which they have been indoctrinated and, unaware, impose the same ideology on teachers-to-be.

Students who are not well suited to the middle-class values of schools are usually those most likely to run afoul of them. Their failures with the hidden curriculum are more likely to be of concern (to teachers, at least) than their progress with the standardized curriculum. In any case, regarding the often-unbending demands of the hidden curriculum, the social world of jobs and work has changed in recent years and requires new worker competencies. These include, for example, flexible applications of existing knowledge, openness to engage with the "information society" (particularly technology), willingness to engage and cooperate with the multiple perspectives of people in the workplace, and adaptability to the ever-new demands of a changing business world. The jobs of tomorrow are difficult to see and prepare for in the present.

Thus, we return to the original question of curriculum: What of all that can be included in a curriculum is most worth learning? And options for "most worth learning" rarely include student input. In fact, teachers, having been on the student end of institutional dynamics as students themselves, are often unaware of their dependence and harping on hidden curriculum criteria. Moreover, their training has often focused on the musical "classics." The question of "What of all that can be taught *can I teach*?" especially ends up too often limited in favor of the 'classy' musics of their university training. They, and their professors before them, confused 'classical music' with 'good music', when in truth, it is clearly only one *kind* of music in a world filled with other musics.

Moreover, given the knowledge explosion in recent decades, "delivery" of curriculum by schools relies more and more on "prepackaged" knowledge put together by educational publishers and adhered to slavishly by teachers. Such "pre-fab" knowledge assumes the transmission model already dismissed: that knowledge comes pre-formed from the past and is passed on to present-day students by teachers and prepackaged materials. This practice has led to what sociologists call the *de-professionalization,* the dumbing down, of teaching. Music textbooks and instrumental lesson series are examples in music education masquerading as a one-size-fits-all 'curriculum'—on to the next "canned" lesson simplifies planning.

The Internet now even offers lesson plans for sale to teachers that their sellers claim are proven to be "what works." Such "one-shot lessons" might be well received by students, but besides smooth 'delivery', what are such lessons imagined to benefit in the way of a well-considered curriculum? The 'delivery' of prepackaged lesson series further reduces teaching to a *technicism* (or technē) devoid of any claim to a *professional* praxis.

Once again it leads to prolific excuses of "I taught it to them; if they didn't learn it, it is their fault" (or blaming television, social media, unsupportive families, uncooperative administrators, and much, much more—but rarely the instructor). When children go astray, good parents wonder, "What did we do wrong?" and then puzzle how to remedy it. Teachers instead blithely award grades without concern for what *they* contributed to the failing result. Again, plenty of blame is being directed at every source other than the failures of instruction!

Postmodernists agree in practice with the cognitive theory of learning that knowledge is *constructed* from experiences with the physical world rather than discovered or directly transmitted intact. This was also a premise of Pragmatism—that 'reality' as we know it is internalized through meaningful experience with the tangible world. In a postmodern vision of schooling, this also includes interactions with the 'content' of instruction—though learning is focused on the "process" of construction, not on prescribed 'content' as such. And, again as with Pragmatism, knowledge is *provisional*; it evolves in connection with the challenges of ever-new situations and their accompanying "ends-in-view" (Dewey) or "Being needs" (existential psychology).

Each new situation is, in consequence, a "problem" to be solved by reliance on existing learning—*assimilating* it with each successful attempt. But when attempts based on past knowledge are not successful in dealing with a new situation, problems are solved by *accommodation*[63] with new creative attempts (for assimilation through ongoing successful use). Such knowledge is accordingly fragile and fallible as it is tested and grows and is corrected by ever-new problems set by the teacher (or in life).

In a sense, 'truth' is the compatibility between the concepts and knowledge of different individuals. Remember, the brain cannot not learn; it craves new experience! Fortunately, to a certain degree, the experiences of others can be conveyed through language—though, for postmodernity, language is not a reliable means of communication. Lectures are best followed by questions, discussion, and disputation. Hence, within limitations of accuracy, knowledge can to some degree be shared or developed.

However, the reinforcing effect of group knowledge can be constructive, as in religious congregations, or dangerous, as in neo-Nazi and white supremacy groups. Shared knowledge rooted in shared experience is the basis for institutional traditions, expectations, and communication. So agreement on what is 'real' (e.g., "money" is a social construction[64]) is always at stake. However, in today's pluralistic society, students are often exposed to the different traditions, expectations, and languages of classmates. Differences between a majority culture and minority cultures arise because students come to school with roots in different experiences and languages.

The differences of 'marginal' groups need to be taken into account in facilitating learning for all (which usually is slanted toward the 'realities' shared by the majority culture and focused on social assimilation: the "melting pot"), and in building the foundation for a sense of community that facilitates cooperation and mutual understanding in a society (and related capacities, such as work). But the majority culture too benefits from exposures to various minority values and traditions and profits from mutual respect among all members of a community or society.

Music Appreciation Reconsidered

Given all the philosophical options examined so far, old and new, it should be clear that instruction requires a functional level of philosophical, curricular thinking if it is to go beyond the mere delivery of stand-alone, "pre-fab" activities or solely looking to the next concert as its singular end[65]—in other words, if it is instead to result in learning that is functional, lasting, and transformative of individual students and society. Then, students will benefit from musical learning in making their musical choices from among the mounting complexity of musics and types of musicing they face outside of school.

The fact is that appreciation (of any kind) is evidence of what people choose to integrate into their usual lives (e.g., religion, clothing styles, foods, collecting stamps, ethnic musics, fast cars, habits, etc.). Music appreciation results from a rich exposure to and engagement with musics and musicing of many kinds—at least those of the local and technically mediated community. But also, ideally, appreciation amounts to the facilitating of lifelong musical habits and choices that also go beyond a local community. Ours is a time of considerable relocation, and an ability to tune in to the musicing in a new community is all the more helpful.

Schooling, in this view, is, therefore, among the most important institutional roles devised by society to advance knowledge and to promote living the "good life" beyond just being alive (other candidates are religion and government). But as society changes, so must schooling. As knowledge is increasingly available via information technology, successful instruction will focus instead on nurturing the kinds of deep-seated attitudes and values that will promote students' *use* of musical knowledge—attitudes and values regarding music and musicing. It will also attend to the worlds and values (musical and otherwise) of "the Other" with whom we share a community. An action ideal warranting lifelong engagement with music in music education predicated on lifelong and deep-seated musical values will in many ways join hands with "community music" education, with the school as its center.[66]

Musical learning, then, should not terminate with graduation. It should anticipate moving out of the school and into the community, where it will be shared and extended to and through others. Having in mind a *notable presence in the community of* what school learning should be is a useful general criterion to address daily in answering the question, "What of all that can be learned of music is most worth curricular inclusion?"

To pre- and beginning in-service teachers, that question also takes the form of, "What of all of music am *I musically prepared* to teach?" And that leads to, "What more than from my university music schooling do I *need* to **learn**?" Harmonica, ukulele, recorder, steel drums, guitar, composition software, arranging for school groups, sources of nonclassical musics, and much more are typically needed.

Music educators should consider themselves to be in a race to keep up with musics and musicing. Many "old time" teachers find it too easy to settle into a predictable and comforting 'delivery' routine pronounced to be "good" or "good enough" or "it works" at some point in their careers. Like music, however, instructors who are stimulating, diverse in their musical offerings and abilities, and progressive regarding youth, schools, schooling, and society will not only be notable in their success as teachers but also noticed in their communities. Be advised: Music is a major element that characterizes every culture. It is too important to be delivered like cold pizza.

5
Curriculum Models from Educational Theory

Preliminary Considerations

The traditional philosophies summarized in Chapter Two have, to some considerable degree, typically influenced schooling in the past and today's schools. They help understand much about why schools are as they are in every developed country. Idealism, Realism, and Neo-Scholasticism still dominate many aspects of schooling and curriculum.

The contemporary perspectives offered in Chapters Three and Four have been opposed by the entrenched impact of these ancient philosophical traditions. That entrenchment, it can be said, is among the reasons that schooling and teaching have so many habits and traditions that students are only in a position to object to—but of course, they don't or can't, other than to misbehave. Aware readers may well remember problems experienced in their school days that stem from these outdated philosophies.

Music has its own traditions and habits that often work against change, in particular, "aesthetic education" and its claims to somehow magically lead students to the supernatural benefits of being 'aesthetically educated'—whatever that means, and of course, neither students nor teachers can say. Conservatory-type teacher preparation imposes on pre-service students' truckloads of musical assumptions and aesthetic premises that are problematic even in higher education.[1] And the music covered in the formal teacher education program is typically limited, especially the many musical skills, beyond being able to play a graduation recital, needed to teach. Image the embarrassment of the pianist who, having taken his first job, was asked by surprise at the faculty welcoming banquet to play the *Star-Spangled Banner*—and couldn't because he had no score! This experience must have just been the beginning of his surprises in the classroom.

In addition to such burdensome baggage, new teachers in all subjects are usually overwhelmed by the staid "establishment," by the social and political forces in schools that work against a teacher as a true "professional." Unions protect teachers' working conditions, but at the same time, they protect the status quo of the accepted practices in a particular school (especially matters of the hidden curriculum) that newcomers must adopt—or else! Administrators have one eye on the budget, one eye on the board of education politics (or education ministry), one eye on the students, one eye on the union, and one eye on the staff—so, not enough eyes to see all of what is really going on.

It would be a grave omission not to mention in the present survey the various *educational theories influencing curriculum*: usually not philosophies but influential nonetheless, perhaps more influential than the often deep traditions of the traditional philosophies covered in earlier chapters. What follows, then, is another group of theories or models that have, over time, influenced the conduct and content of curriculum. Readers will recognize some from their school days.

Most have unstated and mistaken assumptions derived from the philosophies considered in Chapters One and Two. But those who follow these modes, styles, or types of organizing curriculum rarely understand or can defend the philosophical and practical implications of what so thoroughly guides their efforts. Some burn out and are gone (statistically they leave in the U.S. after only five years). Others "settle in" and are consumed with union protections of their role in the fiefdom of the school community.[2]

The following are some historical, educational models that continue to have a notable influence on schooling. Some are easy to fall into. Others require daring to be different—to valuing students more than preserving the school's routine status quo.

These models or modes (styles, types) of instruction are much more likely to get mentioned than the philosophies that often contribute to their differences. Some are influenced by more than one traditional, taken-for-granted philosophy, sometimes in conflict. Some are well known and have a somewhat developed reputation in the history of education; others go by various names. References to these models are often meaningless (e.g., to the public and for professional discourse) without connection to their related philosophies.

"Labeling" a curricular style adds little understanding. Nonetheless, it will be helpful to familiarize readers with some of the leading terms if only to help avoid falling into mindless sloganeering. Some of these labels will arise in dialogue with fellow educators who are not aware of the philosophical discernments to follow.

Basic-Studies/Essentialism

This model presumes to promote curricular studies claimed to be "basic" or "essential" in some undisclosed way. "Basic-studies" is probably the most frequently encountered label, at least as feedback from parents and politicians. These two groups get active when "Back to Basics" is cried from the rooftops. The idea of a "core curriculum" of school knowledge is currently a discordant issue in the second decade of the 21st century in the U.S. Such a need to "return" to basics assumes a "departure" from some hypothesized "basics" or "core" of knowledge. However, given the vacuity of "basics" as a designator, it is seldom clear what has been departed from and what status the shouters want returned.

At first, then, the idea of "basic" needs to be addressed. The term "basic" suggests a "base" or "foundation" upon which to build something. This meaning is quite clear when building a house: the base is a foundation for the rest of the structure to be built on it. When we discuss house building, however, we don't wonder what the house is *for*. But in curriculum theory, the reason "for" instruction is the key criterion. What is a basic-studies curriculum a foundation *for* building?

Basic-studies is apparently all about foundation building, but thought as to what to build on it is usually lacking or unconvincing. Some will loudly claim that it is to be the foundation for a "basic education" (whatever that is). This claim changes the basic metaphor from "foundations" to the idea of being educationally "necessary" (i.e., *essential*). But essential to what? We are left then with the unanswered question: What is basic education (studies, skills) basic (essential) *to*? The reply, as though one is stupid for asking, is that it is basic to "basic education," to be "basically well educated"—a circular definition.

What, however, does that mean in everyday terms? Having been exposed to knowledge of one's society or nation? Or the "basics" of Western civilization (in the case of the West) or of one's nation (who decides: for the "lies" of American history texts; Loewen 2018)? *Transmission* of various "facts" (or "factoids") deemed important (Why? Criteria? To what ends?) by the nameless authorities and to be passed on to the next generation? Students arrive at school with the functional "basics" of their spoken language, only to have it polished according to someone's idea of "refinement" (e.g., reading and traditional grammar and syntax vs., say, African-American vernacular English).[3]

In again considering "foundations" as a "base" for "building" a future, what and whose future? Can this one-size-fits-all foundation support the variety of futures that it pretends to serve? The future of the factory worker, IT specialist, clerk, at-home parent, police officer? That's how "basic" curriculums are typically promoted. Is there the supposed "base" that is "covered" in the required years of schooling, and then specialized studies are for fine-tuning? Or is that left for college and university? However, lo and behold, universities mandate "general/liberal" studies, basic to being a "generally well-educated" college graduate—whatever that means. What about, in any case, the non-college-bound graduates?

As for "back to basics," it seems that any curriculum and its pedagogy that violates traditionally approved teaching methods of the "three Rs (reading, 'riting, and 'rithmatic) fall afoul of that criterion. "New math," "phonics," or "whole language" are compared unfavorably to the traditional image someone important has in mind for the "basics"—never asking how the "basics" became basic and whether they should have been. When thinking clearly about the "basics" of living—the daily needs faced—we don't think in such terms. Where needed, children learn the "basics" of, say, using chopsticks by doing so until mastered. Many if not most of such basics (e.g., when and how low to bow in Japan or China) are taught by the family, relatives, or the community.

The "basics" claimed by schools as their groundings are illusions or fancies of educationist authorities who are in positions of power to impose their personally valued profiles of "basic" learning on schools, staff, and students. *They have decided that language arts, mathematics, history (national, world), and science should be the possession of everyone else, like them.* They have also decided to teach music (usually of whatever passes in a culture for "classics"), visual arts (finger-painting for children, art history, and studio art for older students), and literature (usually weighted toward "Great Works" or national notables). Some (European) countries deem it necessary to require two and three foreign languages, while others focus mainly on language arts for the national language (U.S.).

What explains these choices for curriculum? To readers of this book, there is an answer: the philosophies of Idealism, Realism, and Neo-Scholasticism. All subscribe to a diet of prescribed subject matter that is judged venerable and "basic" to one's social and cultural heritage and educated status. What is more, these philosophies, given their often abstruse a priori and abstract contentions, demand *discipline* rather than indulging or engaging students' interests. The a priori abstractions to which they are committed are not of immediate interest to most students of any age. Not surprisingly, most school days consist of an alternation between subjects devoted to the "essences" of these philosophies.

So elementary education promotes literacy and numeracy, plus usually boiled-down partisan history relative to national status (in the U.S., the Columbus and Thanksgiving myths; Loewen 2018) and the classical scientific findings but not the doing (praxis) of science or history. And secondary education (called "comprehensive," in some countries, a term that belies its claims to breadth) adds a lot of dedication and "hard work" for those not otherwise attracted to the complexities of a second language,[4] higher mathematics, chemistry, geometry, calculus, and physics.

So, "basic education" is basically Idealism and Realism as propelled by Neo-Scholasticism, which, if you've been paying attention, are basically contradictory about key details. While Idealism fuels much of language, literature, and history studies, Realism is the next-door neighbor that fills in the gaps of the "basic" needs for math and science. The 'truths' they aspire to teach are typically at odds: for Idealism, the 'truths' of ideas; for Realism, the 'truths' of empirical reality.[5]

Optional curriculum alternatives beyond required "basics" allow students to focus on occupational skills that prepare them for jobs (agriculture, secretarial skills) or personal interests (e.g., photography, psychology, a second language, music composition). But the existence of such electives is evidence that what is 'basic' knowledge for life has a hierarchy of levels that only some can reach, and after that schools address alternative "basics" of vocational preparation.[6] In today's world, "vocational skills" have exploded into IT, technological competence, mechanical engineering, robotics, and specializations that negate claims for a universal foundation of basics offered for all. In these offerings, language and computational skills relevant to the technical study are learned via the study itself.

Basic-studies is a deceptive game offered by defenders of Idealism, Realism, and Neo-Scholasticism, or by those who have themselves submitted to their stultifying limitations (e.g., teachers who perpetuate the basic-studies model). Ask yourself: What have the typical 'activities' of, say, general music classes been basic to in life? Should pitch matching and music reading be the criteria of an "essential" or basic education in music for typical citizens?

What have years of ensemble membership been a foundation for doing? If not lifelong musical amateuring, then what? It's a revealing truth that those who play self-taught instruments, or who were taught by a peer (or these days, by YouTube), continue to play in adulthood. Why? Their intentionality for learning carries over into continued amateuring, even gigs. But most ensemble graduates do not typically continue musicing. "Music is basic" is merely an advertising slogan.

Perennialism

Perennialism is committed to teaching the "great ideas" and "Great Works" of Western civilization (i.e., ignoring most of Indian, Islamic, Japanese, and Chinese cultures). Such learning is said to be *timeless* in its value. In use, Perennialism overlaps considerably with basic-studies and especially Neo-Scholasticism and adds little more. Its original format was a "liberal" education—one based on Greek and Latin, and the "Great Works" of Western literature, music, and art that, it claimed, liberated the mind, developed the faculty of reason, and promoted freedom and democracy.

However, as universal education became the norm, and the children of factory workers and farmers entered common schools, Greek and Latin became rare electives. Classical ideas of the past were condensed and, following basic-studies and essentialism, predigested in textbooks, and the originals rarely read. Study *about* the classical world replaced the direct study *of* it.

This strictly intellectual orientation owes much to Neo-Scholasticism's focus on the rational intellect that reveals timeless truths of reason to be passed on to succeeding generations. Being also rooted in Idealism and Realism, then, Perennialism is heavily engaged in the *transmission* of ready-made knowledge to learners rather than the *transformation* of either learners or the knowledge base. Perennialism rejects recent psychological findings that knowledge is personally constructed through experience. Its emphasis is on rote learning, drill, memorization, lecture, and written tests of recall. Activities that promote intellectual discipline are the only "active" learning addressed (e.g., debate and rhetoric, usually as a club). In general, this is probably not much different than what readers experience today in their "General Studies" requirements as university students, or experienced during their high school studies.

Perennialist education focuses on clear and rational thinking and excellent communication skills (especially writing), supposedly all the better to support a democratic nation. Schooling is not, for Perennialists, concerned with vocational futures and not even indirectly with preparing for adult jobs. Aside from reading, writing, and simple math, today's job skills are often apprenticeships—vocational training, job internships, and working one's way up the adult work ladder.

Perennialists believe that because all humans are rational (despite other evident differences) and since knowledge is 'true' based on the sages of the past, curriculum should be the same for everyone. The knowledge taught—what is most worth teaching—is guided by Perennialist and Neo-Scholastic criteria and needs to be taught to *all* students if people are to communicate about and improve their worlds. This model is self-evidently well suited as a "one size fits all" template for mass education.

Students' interests give way in favor of developing a 'disciplined mind' for living a rational life. Hence, "student centered" curriculums (e.g.,

Progressivism, covered later) that build on students' interests are rejected in favor of the primacy of often abstract subject matter. Language arts, mathematics, general science, world and national history, and the arts are typically addressed—though the latter are poor stepchildren to the other subjects and favor studying "about" the "Great Works" of literature and visual and musical arts.

Since Perennialists regard such traditional knowledge as a repository of learning that has "survived the test of time," its study is not viewed as being *of* life (i.e., what is going on in the contemporary world now, such as popular musics, social conflicts, and politics) but on vague ideas of rational preparation *for* life ("someday"). As a result, "Why do we have to learn this?" is answered with "Someday you'll need it!" or "It's good for you."

The focus on mental discipline, shared with Neo-Scholasticism, demonstrates that many students resist learning such knowledge for its own sake or because the teacher (or curriculum) says so. But it presents other difficulties. For one, the choice of "what is most worth learning" is still left to the subjective decisions of textbook publishers,[7] teachers, and higher authorities—who often differ. Which Shakespeare play to "cover": *Macbeth*, *Hamlet*, or *Othello* (with a Black Muslim [a Moor] the hero)?[8] Secondly, "covering" Shakespeare does not guarantee that the learning is effective or has value for life.

Perennialism is usually doomed to paper-and-pencil recall tests. At most, students may be expected to apply their understanding in writing assignments (e.g., comparing Shakespeare's *Othello* to Verdi's *Otello,* or pondering class conflict in *Romeo and Juliet*). The 'doings' of musicing often give way with Perennialism to mastery of information from history and theory *about* music.

It is more than likely that Perennialism and Basic-Studies/Essentialism are the dominant models in schools in the U.S. and around the world. Going beyond such tired traditions requires fresh thinking about why students' brains are not learning.

Progressivism

Progressivism was a historical and political movement in the late 19th to early 20th century in the U.S. that also influenced new thinking about curriculum. Progressivism as a sociopolitical movement is widely associated with Presidents Woodrow Wilson and Theodore Roosevelt and philosopher John Dewey. In politics it fostered democracy by opposing the power of monopolies and generally was focused on the social problems brought on by rapid industrialization and relocation of the poor—often Blacks—from the rural South to cities, especially in the North.

Its spirit of reaction to such precipitous and problematic 'social progress' and its advocacy of social welfare also reacted against traditional educational practices. Most of these were Basic-Studies/Essentialism and Perennialism/Neo-Scholasticism, teacher-directed/dominated subject matter and instruction, teacher use of punishment for student "discipline problems" (an offense against the neo-scholastic emphasis on school subjects as "disciplines"), textbook generalizations, lecture, memorization, and paper-and-pencil tests. A decided lack of concern for social reality also had divorced the school from students' lives. The influence of John Dewey's progressive education put a premium on pragmatic results to be put into lifelong praxis by students outside school.

Rather than passive learning by memorization, Progressivism focused on *active learning* by students. In Progressive classrooms, students are at least as mentally active as the teacher! Progressivism puts aside the "banking metaphor" where students' 'blank minds' (*tabula rasa*) are to be filled with valuable information and data and 'saved' for use "someday." In other words, the curriculum focuses not on the organization of subject matter (by the instructor and textbooks) but on drawing on, organizing, and scaffolding the natural pleasures of learning and students' questions about life as the focus of school learning.

Rather than being *authoritarian*, Progressive educators are *authoritative* in guiding, steering, advising, and facilitating students' learning. They don't repeat their learning to students; instead, they draw upon it to promote and expand students' learning. For Progressivism, "experience" is understood pragmatically as "*an* experience." A focus on student intentionality promotes tempting musical problems or key questions (even from students—real example: "Why is music fast?" rephrased for the age group as "What makes fast music fast"?)[9]

Neuropsychologist Robert Bilder summarizes the research in the field:

> "What is valuable for children is freedom where they are solving problems with no predictable answer. . . . When it is open-ended, they retain the curiosity to learn more things. And that is going to be essential for their futures." Children who are given an open-ended problem are more apt to explore a variety of relationships and patterns, unlike when they are given a toy with preset instructions or uses. "The 'thing' should not be dictating the activity. . . . The person dictates the activity." (Bilder 2019)[10]

The solving of such problems involves (a) the guidance of a *musical* "end-in-view" (intentionality) to be achieved, (b) generating several possible solutions, (c) experimenting with hypothesized solutions, (d) comparing those results with the initiating intentionality (end-in-view), and (e) acting adaptively if needed by recourse to alternative hypotheses. In sum, students learn actively by exploring their own musical and life interests and experimenting with self-generated potential solutions to musical problems (posed by the instructor or students[11]) they find attractive and motivating, and that henceforth guide their efforts at a solution.

The key to such "problem solving" is using students' natural interests in life and music as the basis for "learning by doing" (praxis). As to "What makes fast music fast?" consider an experiment: Each group [of five] will compose a sound composition in three sections of 10 seconds each, where one section is fast, and the other two sections slow, your choice. Use only sounds you can make in your seat." Compare, discuss, and do again with classroom instruments: no vocal sounds. This time only two sections: "the fast part is your feelings while running to see your favorite team play [don't name it to avoid controversy!]; the slow part is them losing and the music you compose sounds like you're *bored* or *upset*" (again, no vocal sounds). Listening to each: Could "bored" be distinguished from "upset"? Obviously this requires the "readiness" of having previous sound compositions done in class (see Regelski 2004, 109–133—or using computer composition software). Understandably, students will be 'turned on' to the possibility of the next lesson where their team wins: "The first or A section should be tense or worried sounding, awaiting the big play; the next or B section is celebrating the win."

Student groups who have cooperatively examined and hypothesized solutions (by drawing on their already forming concepts) have had *an* experience that will be relevant to their subsequent experiences with music (and class interest in how other groups solved the problem focuses their listening). "*To experience*," in contrast, does not result in functionally holistic *musical* learning for future praxis. Such an "activities approach" is typically seen in general music classrooms organized by teachers around a supposedly "active" approach to teaching (abstract) concepts or (inert) information, and in ensembles where the director gives all directions and makes all corrections. This "follow the leader" approach to teaching puts students in the role of lemmings who follow innocently but mindlessly. Whether in general music class or ensembles, the students respond like organ pipes to the organist-instructor. Any benefits are short-lived or may be momentarily fun in the sense of a release from boring 'academic' classes rather than a focus on the pleasures of musicing.

Beyond Dewey's pragmatic influence on "problem solving," "learning by doing," and the "project method," for Progressivist educators, classes are not an island set off from society (as is the case with Perennialism and Neo-Scholasticism). The "child centered" learning of Progressivism is related to the "whole child." The knowledge and skill students bring with them to school is acknowledged (e.g., fast-slow in music); if needed, "updated"; and added to until reaching a truly functional level (i.e., different musical effects of tempo; does fast music need to be loud). Furthermore, as was explained regarding Action Learning, the music curriculum consists of musical models and motivations drawn from the society at large, or that clearly (to students) can be savored as adults through one or more praxes.[12]

Importantly, with the school in a two-way relationship with society, giving and taking, curriculum and instruction are *democratic*. Students cannot become democratic adults if school is a repressive place. The classroom, then, is a place to model and prepare for the adult praxis of democracy. This kind of teaching puts an emphasis, for example, on shared decision making, including sharing teacher planning with students (i.e., with their interests in mind).

Furthermore, it privileges *cooperation* over competition. While the day-to-day life of adults can sometimes be based on meritocracy and the dynamics of social power-grabbing or climbing, schooling best insulates students from the ill-effects of such competition, save for situations reserved for it, such as sports, debate teams, and academic contests.[13] Progressive teachers focus, instead, on the kind of social relations that are otherwise typically democratic and forward-looking in adult life.

Competition has multiple liabilities as an instructional method. First of all, it is dependent on *extrinsic motivation* (existential D-needs)—the motivation to "win." When such motivation is no longer relevant, the student loses interest (i.e., no motivation, no intentionality). This is, by definition, typical after graduation, where such extrinsic motivations are absent. Accordingly, extrinsic motivation denies students the lasting benefits of *intrinsic* motivation (existential B-needs). Intrinsically motivated students practice because their musical satisfactions grow, not because of a grade or to avoid teacher (or parent) censure.

Most important, educationally, competition is a method where *all students except one fail* to reach their goals—in other words, all except the winner.[14] Instruction predicated on such massive failure is lacking ethical integrity as a teaching method: it gains no support from Duty, Consequentialism, or Virtue ethics. Worse: Fragile pre-adolescent and adolescent mental lives are in jeopardy from such failures—they even risk causing negative self-images. There is also no role for competition in *social learning theory*;[15] failure sometimes only motivates already high-achieving students, but their rewards still center on winning.

Cooperative learning, instead, is encouraged according to the psychological premise called "zone of proximal development" (ZPD)[16] advocated by Lev Vygotsky. Vygotsky, a contemporary of Piaget, expanded Piaget's *genetic constructivism* that saw learning as unfolding according to *biologically maturing stages* in individual learners, and progressing from "hands on" learning of a baby eventually to "minds on" learning of late adolescents. So we don't expect the very young to master trigonometry. But Piaget only later took some notice of students' progress over time from the *ego-centric* learning of lone individuals to learning from *socio-centric* interaction. Vygotsky took this one step more.

He saw instructional value in the social interactions of cooperative learning where the student gains assistance from a teacher or peer who has more competence. As any teacher knows, individual classes usually consist of students having a variety of skill sets. Therefore, Progressive teachers do not avoid cooperative learning among peers—for example, they often use the "project method" where students cooperate in completing a group task they all value (e.g., the earlier-described sound compositions). Accordingly, students who are more knowledgeable, skilled, or creative (for the learning at hand) are placed (carefully) in groups with other students of varying ability, yet all make a contribution: in the sound composition example given earlier, all would perform according to cooperative decisions. This is a perfect pedagogy for chamber musics!

Depending on the situation, some students might also become *peer tutors*—such as when, for example, a student who has already learned to play guitar tutors students who are beginners. The teacher too "scaffolds"[17] the efforts of students who cannot complete a learning task without the assistance of step-by-step guidance and does so until they can over time complete such tasks on their own. The situation is akin to an *apprenticeship* until *musical independence* progressively replaces the need for assistance. This notion of an apprenticeship is typical of praxis-based curricular theory and instruction and benefits from the ZPD theory of cooperative and social learning theory.

Progressivism *as an organized movement* lost some cohesion over the years, especially with the intervention of the social disruptions of two world wars and the Korean conflict, and the return to civilian life (and teaching) of many soldiers. Nonetheless, many of its most important ideas and action ideals have found a continuing relevance in the domain of curriculum and instruction methods, for example, the idea of "student government"; classroom seating that can be arranged for group work or in a circle (teacher too) where all are equally seen and heard; carpeting that allows for floor work; a de-emphasis of rote learning, memorization, and similar regressive traditions—all in favor of child-centered praxis. Both the ethical and practical side of Progressivism also embrace many of the previously mentioned positive traits of Existentialism, Action Learning, and Music and Music Education as Social Praxis, and even some aspects of Postmodernity.

Reconstructionism and Critical Theory

These two influences on schooling arose in the 1930s in between world wars. Both share an emphasis on teaching for social change or, put differently, on overcoming the social status quo class divisions that the traditional approaches to schooling were *reproducing*. In consequence, then, both are concerned with *transformation*, not *transmission*—two themes addressed several times already in connection with other philosophies, this time with an emphasis on social reconstruction. The three traditional philosophies—Idealism, Realism, and Neo-Scholasticism—along with Basic-Studies and Perennialism, were centrally concerned with transmission, not only of the existing status quo but also of predigested knowledge via textbooks and teacher talk: "advance organizers,"[18] directions, reviews, lectures, demonstrations, and summing up ("Today we learned . . ."). Existentialism and Progressivism, in contrast, were focused on the transformation of individual learners and not on transmitting knowledge as "information" sanctioned by authorities or texts.

Reconstructionism

Reconstructionism was a reaction to World War I and the Great Depression, and to resulting social discontent. It was concerned with *institutional power*—the power of curriculum for *reproduction of the social status quo* rather than *reconstruction* for greater social equality. Its subscribers proposed that the teaching profession should make its power felt on behalf of social change and empowerment, that schooling should become a major influence in the reconstruction or rebuilding of society along more socially equal lines. This called, in consequence, for innovation in society and in schools—the latter because virtually all citizens are impacted by schooling, not only in terms of knowledge but also in terms of social values (usually middle class).

Reconstructionism, like Progressivism, also emphasized *democratic principles* that would release students' creativity and intelligence from the strictures of traditional educational practice and thus creatively address society's many problems. Today, of course, the threats of global warming, nuclear warfare, political acrimony, rapid technological change that threatens jobs—all these and many more still confront society and, consequently, students graduating into such a world. Schools, however, generally avoid such controversial topics. As a result, students are not only often unprepared for the difficulties they'll find but also unlikely to take an active role in social change after 12 years of what amounts to an assembly-line model of education that only solidifies the troublesome status quo.

Traditional schooling may produce some workers, but its power structures fail to develop or release the critical appraisal of social changes needed to bring about a better life for workers and their families. Traditional schooling, in today's terms, regards topics like global warming, creation science, evolution, Civil War revisionism, genocide of Native Americans, dropping of the atom bomb, LGBTQ+ issues, and the like as too hot to handle. As an unfortunate result, students lack knowledge and perspectives for understanding the conflicts that continue to plague society.[19]

Critical Theory

Critical Theory shares this dual concern with power and critical thinking. It first arose with the so-called Frankfurt School (Germany) of social theory and philosophy.[20] It was not just a proponent of progressive reconstruction, but steadfastly resisted all manner of power and oppression in society and politics. Although its members (now into the second and third generations of followers) are idiosyncratic in their thinking, they tend to share a concern with the relationship between political and social power and knowledge.

While they understand "knowledge" to include all kinds of knowing, they are especially focused on institutionally *accepted knowledge* that subjugates people to the benefit of those who possess and impose it. Consequently, Critical Theorists were critical of the powerful social impact of capitalism—such as inequality, poverty, and tensions between socioeconomic classes—and sought answers from Neo-Marxian *social* theory for understanding and combating problems relating to economic class divisions and conflicts. Note: *Neo*-Marxian social theory *critiques* and *corrects* the economic and political failings of doctrinaire Marxism and is a key theory in the modern sociology of social class dynamics. However, analysis of class conflict by Critical Theorists is accepted and supported by input from various social and intellectual sources, such as Weberian[21] and Phenomenological Sociology,[22] Pragmatism, and Existentialism.

It is only natural, then, that it is critical of the power exerted by schools with the imposition of selected, predigested knowledge that is the basis of traditional schooling and social values, and with the social organization of school-enforced learning, which is too often totalitarian in its imposition of socially "accepted" knowledge that perpetuates the social status quo and its advantages for dominant classes. As a result, Critical Theory focuses on "emancipatory" themes by which students and society can be freed from the oppressive domination of schooling and its traditional meta-narratives.

The influence of *ideology* on people's thinking, particularly capitalism, leads to a "false consciousness" that leaves people satisfied with their relative poverty in life (compared to the very rich) rather than willing (and educationally able) to contend with its oppression of them. For Critical Theory, "ideology" is understood not just as a system of ideas, but as the system by which the interests and values of a *dominant class* are imposed on lower social classes as being in their own best interests, whether or not they agree or have been asked.

> Ideology refers to knowledge and practices which serve the interests of some groups or sections of society but not the interests of all. Ideology gets its power from the fact that this one-sided interest is disguised as either being actually in the interest of all or outside the realm of human control altogether—as a fact of nature. . . . [T]he most powerful form which ideology can take is to be taken-for-granted—to be not only natural but unquestioned, even unarticulated. (Young 1990, 28).

Unquestioned or unarticulated amounts to a "false consciousness" that accepts the ideology ("that's just the way things are"), even though it is oppressive.

Importantly, a dominant class need not be dominant in numbers but is dominant in its power to influence the lives of others in its sphere of influence by using it to promote taken-for-granted "false consciousness" of less powerful classes.[23] Only when the ideological world breaks down can it be reconstructed (e.g., World War II fascism led to the Marshall Plan; the Great Depression led to Progressivism; Postmodernism led to the breakdown of the aesthetic meta-narrative).

We often hear today mention of the "1%" of capitalists ("makers") whose never-ending quest for more and more wealth negatively dominates the lives of the poor and lower precariat classes ("takers"). Yet the "false consciousness" of these lower classes either gives credit to the 1% for what little comforts they do have (e.g., giant TVs) or suffer their condition in silence (rather than joining the "revolution of the proletariat," as Marx had predicted). Meanwhile, their consumerism profits the 1%, and the poor go deeper into credit card debt.

Ideology has also gotten stressed throughout these pages in connection with aesthetic theory as an ideology of a dominant class. This reference has been to the class, small in numbers but big in power, of 'classical' musicians, the cultural elite class of aesthetes, critics, connoisseurs, and professors who, though often knowing little about aesthetics, operate with their own aesthetic "false consciousness," indulged in under its auspices.[24] They dominate the practices of higher education in music just about everywhere in the world and promote only "serious" music for study. Gifted students (often with a background in pop music or gospel singing—with a natural aptitude) who aspire for advanced study, but whose singing has not been 'classical', are often rejected for entrance (Kosa 2012). The sole exception may be jazz studies, though even then, jazz majors are often expected to submit to studio lessons of the "classics."

Not surprisingly, then, is the ideologically dominant power blindly adopted by school music teachers under the advertising slogan "music education as aesthetic education" (MEAE). The problems with the dominance of this ideology have been addressed throughout these pages. First of all, references to aesthetic this-and-that at best attract only the published disputations of aestheticians. However, secondly, other philosophers have shown these theories to be faulty in their isolation of music from life and on multiple other grounds (Elliot & Silverman 2015). And, in any case, contemporary artists not only ignore aesthetic theories but also often studiously oppose them.

First, there is the problem of the theoretical abyss of countless competing aesthetic theories. As for guiding curriculum, supposed aesthetic benefits do not have overt consequences. There is no evidence of 'aesthetic learning' that has (supposedly) improved 'aesthetic responding' (e.g., Director: "Play it again more aesthetically!"). Such instruction lacks overt bases for evaluating benefits and progress—including evidence to students and parents that they are 'aesthetically' improved. Second, this lack of evidence is especially a handicap for students who are attracted to ensembles. They typically number only a small percentage of school enrollment, and they get fewer in number as the ensemble participants move through school. But the vast majority show no empirical evidence of aesthetic enhancement of their musical choices and tastes upon graduation. Third, the public (i.e., taxpayers) sees no results that tax money is well spent; school concert audiences are mainly of family and schoolmates.

This has led to a condition that second-generation Critical Theorist Jürgen Habermas (1975) has called a *"legitimation crisis."* Such crises, he points out, arise when institutions fail to provide their promised benefits (e.g., bank failures during the Great Depression and in 2008). Using "immanent critique," the *publicly claimed benefits* of an institution (its ideological claims) are used as *criteria* for its critique. Does it produce what it promises? Thus, ideology critique judges how well the institution meets its advertised claims for student benefit. Claiming aesthetic benefits is easy; demonstrating the claims is impossible! At least banks were regulated by new laws until the politics of 2016 deregulated them.

In music education, therefore, the wonderful-sounding *advocacy* claims of MEAE fall (literally) on deaf ears of the taxpaying public who can't notice and therefore don't appreciate the benefits of "aesthetic education" (and perhaps do remember their own futile school experiences with school music). Parents caught up by the "basic-studies" mantra may believe that music and art are somehow "basic" to their children's "well rounded" education. But they can't point to the actual benefits such a supposed foundation serves, only that their children have "had" it in school, like chickenpox, and are therefore immune from cultural ignorance.

The "legitimation crisis," of course, is the resulting difficulty school music has in getting support from taxpayers, administrators, and education ministries as a legitimate school subject. Claims that music education is the "icing on the cake" and not really "essential" (as in, e.g., "essentialism") leads to fruitless advocacy from the National Association for Music Education (NAfME) that "music is basic"—a contention that suffers from all the claims of "basic education," such as basic to what? If not to lifelong musicing, then to what?

Another issue is *what* or *whose* musics get included in the curriculum. Only "classics" or easy-listening show tunes, the latest Disney song track, and the like? Or music from a greater breadth of society? Music education, as traditionally offered, only adds one more *dominant ideology class* that is controlling students by including only or mainly "classics" and "classical"-like music and ignoring all the other musics that exist in any community. As we have seen, this brings into play the *hidden curriculum* where students "learn" that *their* musics lack the authorized respect of "the Establishment" needed for inclusion in the curriculum.

In the U.S. and many other countries, music education is dominated at all levels by school performing groups. Music directors are out in front of the pubic (and fellow professionals). Considerable emphasis, therefore, goes to how impressive the ensemble sounds. In states, with ranked levels of music (always, it seems, I through VI), high grades (of soloists and groups) are usually reported to the local papers (extrinsic rewards?). Local reputations of directors get recognized, and directors become ever-more cognizant of their public status, especially in the eyes and ears of other directors.

It wasn't only once that a pitch-deficient but enthusiastic singer (i.e., loud) in the elementary chorus was asked by the teacher *not to sing* in concert but to smile and move his lips. Ensembles at later stages often are entirely dominated by the director's musical needs and reputation. Some students quit when the musical demands made at later levels require serious practicing and rehearsing, or when the director lapses into what I call "musicianism." This is the disposition that puts a priority on *concert* results ahead of *educational* gains beyond concerts (Regelski 2012a). Students (or sections) are singled out for shaming, rehearsals get boringly fragmented with copious stopping and starting to perfect along the way, and the director makes all musical decisions. *Musicianist directors teach to protect music from students!* Such oppressive and insulting behavior is understandably opposed by Critical Theorists, not to mention many other teachers whose dedication to students first stands in sharp contrast.[25]

Music selection that favors the personal tastes of directors and classroom teachers is also an issue. Aside from promoting misbehavior on the part of students who resist such curricular offerings, the situation is unmistakably *unequal*. That's not to say that, for example, all education should include rap, rock, and reggae! "Music" has long been a singular noun (but collective, like "food" or "law"), and as a result the collection of "musics" we increasingly acknowledge today have gotten ignored. Critical Theory argues that "music education" should return in praxis to "music*s* education."

The MayDay Group of music educators is an international group of scholars and professors committed to nine action ideals for promoting Critical Theory in schools. Its two Journals, *Action, Criticism, and Theory (A.C.T.)* and *TOPICS for Music Education Praxis*, and its website offer articles, ideas, and topics for ideology critique and for application to teaching. All are online, free, and easily accessible.

There is a second source of Critical Theory: the *Critical Pedagogy* movement of Brazilian educator Paulo Freire with its emphasis on the economic and social repressions of schooling on society. Its roots are in Latin American socioeconomic contexts and "liberation theology." This blending of Catholic social theology and neo-Marxist critique of social and economic inequality, particularly regarding the poor and subjugated classes of developing countries, is unwelcome by governments and by the South American Roman Catholic Church—although Pope Francis, an Argentinian, seems somewhat more welcoming.

Like Critical Theory, Critical Pedagogy's concern is with the social and economic oppression by power elites, and thus with *empowering* students through schooling to free themselves from it. Again, the troublesome power comes with what is *transmitted* through the knowledge taught in schools (or not) and the methods used to transmit it: a false consciousness upholds the status quo (because it is familiar), no matter its negatives. The proposed action ideal of Critical Pedagogy is a transformation of students through schooling that will transform their roles in society as critically discerning citizens and thereby transform society. At the least, the ideal is to prepare students for oppressive practices in the society into which they will graduate. Here, "prepare" means not just coping but also in some way changing or at least resisting such repression (Kincheloe 2009).

Critical Pedagogues recognize that a teacher's role in *schooling is always a political action*! It always involves a consideration of the population whose children attend government-supported schooling. The danger is that the polity can be partisan—for example, oppose evolution or resent musics from religious cultures or immigrants (your Mariachi group better have some local names in it). U.S. landlords who own property in a district but who don't live in it often resent school taxes; the same may be true of retired people who don't have grandchildren in school. Loud voices in a community may be racist and sexist and resent any attention given to ethnicities and immigrants they dislike.

Critical Pedagogy sees curriculum as being acutely aware of such politics and seeks to overcome them. The focus, instead, is on *social justice* and *equality*. Therefore, curriculum and instruction are keenly sensitive to social inequalities, and where possible opposed.[26] American history, for example, is subjected to a whitewashing or downplaying of negatives by textbooks in American history in favor of those that are uplifting to today's national self-image (Loewen 2018).

Be aware that "John Brown's Body" is an abolitionist and Northern Army marching song of the Civil War, and that "This Land Is Your Land" has lyrics written by communist sympathizer Woodie Guthrie when he got tired of hearing "God Bless America" during the Dust Bowl years of the Great Depression. Don't just sing songs like this; research them for contemporary understanding. For example, the American communist movement was attractive to many in the labor union movement in the Dust Bowl years after the Great Depression and before World War II. But you're not likely to read much about it in school history textbooks, only about the "Red scare" after World War II. Who was "John Brown," and how did he become identified with Northern abolitionism? Marching song? A musical praxis!

Reconstructionism and both Critical Theory and Critical Pedagogy, in sum, are acutely attentive to social conditions outside of school. "Critical" curricular thinking recognizes and addresses that world. It focuses on dealing with pressures on students from any powerful elite (including prominent "culturalists"[27] from within the ethnicity who demand 'purity', not independent thinking).

Summary

Music teachers can easily embrace Reconstructionism and Critical Theory/Pedagogy by simply focusing on musicing, without a taint of aesthetic, class, or ideological impositions. The curricular question is only the important one of including musicing that is noticeably representative of community or national and ethnic affiliations. Efforts in music classes and ensembles to address social injustice and inequality are also of mainstream interest to both Reconstructionism and Critical Theory/Pedagogy. It is clear too that both theories are commensurate with an ethical disposition that seeks transformation, not transmission, of injustice and inequality.

6
Curriculum as and for Praxis

Preliminary Considerations

So far, the practical and ideological liabilities of Idealist, Realist, and Neo-Scholastic assumptions for music curriculum have been stressed. In sum, the aesthetic meanings and values advocated are so intangible, so implausible as to present overwhelming practical problems for the planning, delivery, and especially assessment of instruction for all students. The controlling variables are typically abstractions, and instruction tends to be abstractly "about" not "of" music (musicing). Also, by definition, aesthetic experience is covert and not directly observable, as musical praxis is. As a result, instruction cannot be evaluated for success, nor students held accountable for learning.

The educational styles introduced in the last chapter are also consequential. The first, basic-studies/essentialism, and its roots in the three traditional philosophies of Chapter Two present an ongoing challenge to curriculum reform of any kind. An entire industry of textbooks, teaching aids, and online lesson plans for sale stands in the way. General music textbook series (that include scripted musical activities) and instrumental "methods series" have the same function of de-professionalizing the music educator into a figure who only "delivers" recipe-like lessons with no regard for the effectiveness or lasting effects of learning.

Perennialism seems to take two forms. First, as described earlier, priority is given to the "Great Works" of the standard repertory of Western music. It is difficult to determine whether music educators—especially general music teachers—stress this repertory due to any philosophical reasoning associated with the traditional philosophies (it may well be that they enjoy those old 'war-horses' from their past, or maybe those are the only works familiar to them) or whether their selection is preprogrammed by the recipe-like listening lessons and CDs that accompany "textbook series." Plans purchased from the Internet, and similar 'one-time' lessons.

These selections, all of them from the museum of "Great Works," may also be featured as a result of simple habit, or a habitual belief that all students should be "exposed to" *Carnival of the Animals* or *Pictures at an Exhibition* as though aesthetic appreciation automatically wears off somehow onto students.[1] Meanwhile, among many aesthete elites, such program music fails to equal the aesthetic heights of absolute music.

School ensembles also often focus on a limited repertory, often the works chosen from state music association–ranked lists of difficulty for adjudicating performance by school groups and students. "Difficulty" level is someone's idea of the technical challenges;[2] an exceptional technical performance can be lacking in musicality. But the temptation of directors is to return to the same scores every so often—this abetted by saving the costs of buying new music. The selection, in any case, is often judged according to estimates of student (and audience or competition) relevance more than to pedagogical values chosen to expand students' current tastes and abilities. In any case, some aesthetes complain that, by nature, school groups cannot achieve the 'aesthetic' artistry of mature performers and that, no matter how notable the achievement for a school group, students cannot reach the highest aesthetic experiences that the music supposedly offers.

These aesthetes have suggested that listening to the best performances of the best music is more aesthetically educative than ensembles. Of course, listening can be done in addition to performance, but it is doubtful that listenership is ever given its due emphasis, especially when the literature isn't a part of the CD repertory people listen to and collect (most band/wind ensemble music, I would guess[3]). Directors often rely on "reading clinics" where publishers expose their newest publications for teachers to read and order. But Critical Critics worry that this *commodification of music by capitalism* has undue influence over what music students perform.[4] Teachers out for "something new" may well fail to judge availability for advancing the ensembles to new levels of musical achievement or for guiding them to the interests of compositions that are outside familiar taste preferences.[5]

A solution to these issues is at hand—one that is within reach of most musically well-trained musician-teachers: devise curriculums that teach a pedagogically focused and progressive range of musicing! This solution still leaves the teacher with the responsibility of choosing the musicing to be used and promoted. But the many advantages of the contemporary perspectives examined in Chapter Three find ready fulfillment just from the benefits and processes of musicing. However, such musicing must always be under the conditions of intentionality, consummatory peak experiences, and pragmatic criteria.

Existentialism and phenomenology are addressed when students "identify" musicing as an integral part of their Self, that is, their "musical Self." Their *personhood* depends on music as among the highly regarded B-needs of life. This refers not to those who are plugged in with earbuds to stave off the tedium of their lives. It is personhood defined by "I am a musician," "I love all kinds of musicing," "I choose to spend *good* (i.e., re-creational) *time* with musicing," and personhood guided by the existential experiences of sharing music with like-minded others.

As to competition, observations of adolescents show that (aside from sports) students from pre- through late adolescence are not as much competitive as they are *comparative* with peers. Therefore, unlike competition, progress can be built by fostering cooperative learning and "comparetition."[6] Pragmatism is natural in music with its emphasis on practical, functional results where students increasingly progress to musical independence and become self-directed learners, motivated by intrinsic musical benefits, not gold stars or grades.

Critical Theory and Postmodernity are addressed by not imposing on students the tastes, judgments, and personal preferences of the teacher. And that goes for choices in ensemble rehearsals: "Which tempo would you choose for this section?" Experiment with several to reach a decision—often the one the director had in mind. Then discuss the "why" of differences. And "change" is the motive—a change from the 'endullment' of *a*nesthetic teaching: a "unit" on the 25 greatest composers. Music teachers who don't still live in the moments of musical inspiration and 'calling' that led them into teaching music need to reclaim that sense of "aha" for their students. Too many 'delivery'-minded music educators cover the same territory year after year, with the same enthusiasm, as if driving a subway train along the same route.

A praxical curriculum of musicing, whether in general music classrooms or ensembles, is an improvement over the tediousness of curriculum predicated on traditional philosophical thinking and theory. Praxis *naturally* embraces the benefits of the 20th-century perspectives of Chapter Three. And it concerns Progressive, Critical Theory, and Postmodern criteria that lead to *musical emancipation* from the deadening effects of curricular traditions whose "shelf life" or "use by" date has long ago expired. Let musicing speak for itself and you'll see rewards for yourself (professionally) and your students (musically).

Dimensions of a Praxical Curriculum

Since praxis theory regards music as arising naturally, then *observable* musical results benefit from planning, executing, and evaluating via "authentic assessment."[7] In fact, curricular thinking informed by praxis theory engages all three distinctions concerning curriculum pointed out earlier: an action-articulated formal curriculum, what is actually included in instruction, and the action of "doing" that shows learning.

A formal curriculum guide for praxis should not merely be a document to please administrators. Curriculum for praxis involves, instead, the planning that serves just as a blueprint serves carpenters. In the case of schooling, however, the instructor is architect, builder, and building inspector—and especially needs to meet the satisfaction of those for whom instructional efforts served—students. In practice, a written curriculum for praxical teaching is quite short, direct, and pragmatic.

Three dimensions and their criteria for a curriculum

A curriculum, to be effective, should be clear about the following three particulars.

> The *action* or *praxis dimension* proposes a range of several musical praxes understood in *holistic* musical terms and typically exemplified by 'real life' types of applications and authentic assessment.

1. WHAT PRAXES will be the focus of learning? The curriculum guide first originates in the attention by the instructor (or cooperating faculty) to describe in general, everyday music teacher terms the particular kind(s) of musical praxes toward which the curriculum is directed. This action dimension describes **what praxes** the curriculum proposes to be learned (i.e., is worth learning for the students' present and future musicing). This, of course, also helps avoid wandering off into other realms of praxis.

These kinds of praxes (musicing) are general *action ideals*—as we've seen, not in the sense that "ideal" is fanciful, impractical, illusory, or Utopian. Action (or regulative) ideals in philosophy are ideal in the sense that there can be no single instance nor any ultimate state of perfection that could ever be reached (e.g., good parent, good health). Action ideals for curriculum are directly akin to the guiding or regulative ideals of the helping professions (nursing, therapy, etc.). Therefore, they guide or regulate the students' praxis in question always *toward* intended and generally improved pragmatic ends that can take no single or ultimate form; they can always take improved or other forms (for example, other good strums as per the occasion).

2. The COMPETENCY DIMENSION qualifies *WHAT STUDENTS ARE ABLE TO DO, newly, or better as a result of instruction*.

> TO BE ABLE TO.
> "each praxis" identified in the Action Dimension is then described with criteria guiding particulars of particulars of instruction. These competencies also describe the musicianship at stake; implied is *independent musicianship*.

The COMPETENCY DIMENSION outlines in functional, easily observable terms[8] the musicianship necessary for students **to be able to** (agency) take part, autonomously of the teacher or other assistance, in the praxis in question, that is, progress toward or achieve *independent musicianship* (the realistic competencies of which are governed by the age group's growth-typical abilities and competence).

Such specifics are expressed in holistic terms and rely on the teacher's developed musical sense and informed knowledge of a musical practice (i.e., what is a good strum for the music, where to breathe in shaping a phrase). Thus, these descriptions need not be so detailed as to become atomistic or piecemeal, thereby losing sight of the holistic functionality of the musicianship envisaged. They are, however, stipulated in *action* terms, as observable 'doings'—what the student can DO—not simply as abstract information and certainly not as "aesthetic responding." Teachers who persist in believing in aesthetic fantasies should assume them to be the natural joys of musicing, which are observable (the attitudes below)![9]

3. The ATTITUDE DIMENSION points to the pleasures, affectivity, and musical interests inspired by instruction.

> TO WANT TO. Finally, in recognition of the potential downside of the "hidden curriculum" and the importance of inspiring students for lifelong learning with the benefits and joys of the 'play' of music, the Praxical Dimension ideals are described in terms of the personal *attitudes, values, and personal rewards* and interests instruction will foster in leading to competency in the praxis in question. This Attitude Dimension rules out pedagogies and other practices that "turn off," students, or discourage meeting their musical B needs.

It is concerned to make clear, not leave ignored nor taken for granted, *the affective* and other "good time," motivating conditions *instruction needs to model* if students are **to want to** and ultimately **choose to** continue to be involved in the musical praxis in question. Praxis theory is, therefore, progressive for being focused on B-needs that fuel lifelong learning.

In sum, (a) the curriculum will be clear in action terms *what* musical praxes are at stake,[10] as regards both any individual lesson or rehearsal and as a consistent, overall plan of action (praxis). (b) Then the musicianship skills and knowledge needed to partake in such praxes are made clear to students as a basis for all instruction. Students need to know what *musicianship gains* are at stake in a given lesson/rehearsal, as a prompting of their intentionality for learning. For example, a (short) introductory 'experiment' of having students intentionally perform amusingly flat then gravely sharp is a more interesting lead-in than scales to a rehearsal for performing a passage in tune (and probably more fun—with a purpose and pragmatic result). (c) Not be ignored or overlooked are the *conditions of instruction* that will promote the attitudes (i.e., values) that will most likely lead to intentionality where students *want to* improve, want to savor the musical results of praxis and practicing, and where such peak-experiences (consummations) lead to future motivation. "No pain, no gain" may work for sports or in a conservatory, but it isn't a good motto for school-based music students,

Rather than a curriculum often overloaded with details, these three dimensions are easily planned (or agreed to by a planning group) and can serve as the basis for instruction over the class or ensemble's school year. Such a relatively simple demand for curricular planning also and naturally incorporates virtually all of the best aspects of the curricular perspectives analyzed in Chapters Three and Four, and of Progressivism and Critical Pedagogy discussed in Chapter Five. There is no need to plan all the details covered here. *Just the engaging of musicing will naturally incorporate the most desirable parameters.* However, the pitfalls of mind-sets described in earlier chapters that work against students' progress should be kept in mind, lest you be tempted to fall into the mind-set of traditional philosophies and status quo theories of curriculum. Can you list those you will mindfully avoid?

In schools where multiple music teachers are responsible for different kinds and levels of instruction, agreement is usually quickly reached on a praxical curriculum. Then, educators in different buildings and levels, and with different instructional focuses (band, chorus, strings, and general music), can pursue their teaching assignments according to personal methods, with assurance that they are still all on the "same page" in terms of curriculum.[11] The inability or unwillingness to go with the flow of the staff is a reason for concern, although a dissenter may have his or her version of a praxical curriculum. This is possible, and certainly not negative, *if* that version at least parallels the staff decision while perhaps diverging (e.g., adding more) according to relevant teacher competency, for example, adding jazz symbology in theory class (not just "common practice" theory).

An Example Modeling a Praxis-Based Curriculum

Curriculums depend on action ideals, already multiply explained as guiding ideals that have no final one-time fruition and, thus, that are ongoing—just as being a "good friend" is ongoing. As a very general example, the following model of a curricular action ideal for recreational singing (drawn from an actual curriculum) for a grade 7 through 9 (nonselect) mixed chorus (SA{T}B)[12] may be instructive. Keep in mind that several other action ideals relative to listening, individual vocal progress, literature, and the like might be an integral part of the curriculum for this chorus instruction. The following model is but one among many action ideals (slightly edited) an in-service graduate student deemed practicable for the students, time, resources, and other relevant conditions she faced.[13]

RECREATIONAL SINGING: *Singing for individual and social pleasure*

ACTION DIMENSION (e.g., **what** praxes are intended)
Church and community choirs, "sing-alongs" (e.g., campfire and social clubs), patriotic and community singing (caroling), singing with and for friends and family, karaoke, singing by ear, participating in musical worship services

MUSICIANSHIP DIMENSION (e.g., "to be **able** to")

1. Matches pitch accurately, easily, and consistently
2. Stays in tune with others and accompaniment
3. "Reads" music well enough to use score to learn the part after several times through
4. Stays on own part in the presence of other parts
5. Uses healthy vocal production
6. Accommodates changing voice problems when instructed (boys *and* girls)
7. Tone quality is pleasing, not forced or strained, and blends
8. Sings in style (i.e., is vocally and musically flexible) appropriate to typical literature
9. Contributes suggestions (prompted or not) for interpretation decisions and corrections

10. Adapts to new literature despite initial unfamiliarity with the style (etc.)
11. Picks up songs efficiently "by ear" without a score (e.g., from recordings)
12. Can harmonize by ear for community singing

ATTITUDE DIMENSION (e.g., "to **want** to")

13. Enjoys and looks forward to singing; comes to class on time
14. Unembarrassed (even boys) to sing (even solos) for peers, family, and audiences
15. Auditions for featured parts (e.g., with 'solos' in a piece distributed between several soloists)
16. Is comfortable with and enjoys singing with others
17. Eagerly learns traditional and new literature in a variety of styles
18. Accepts the importance of and works to improve vocal technique, music reading, stylistic, and performance insights and styles
19. Seeks or accepts opportunities to sing, especially outside of school (e.g., church, run-outs outside the school day)

Rubrics

A rubric describes criteria according to various levels of achievement that provides feedback (to teacher and student, even parents), diagnosis, and evaluation. The use of rubrics can help to document progress, especially under administrative demands for some appraisal of student performance. An example from "beginning" to "proficient" is as follows:

- Matches pitch from piano or other voice
- Matches three to four notes within the student's vocal range
- Matches five-plus notes
- Matches an octave or more of an actual tune or choral part

If the aforementioned criteria are arranged in a horizontal grid along with other rubrics that rate curricular accomplishment, a checkmark can register the observed competence per each student (see Regelski 2004, 266–267). Instead of numerical or letter grades, labels such as "Beginning," "Developing," "Proficient," and "Wow" can be used (easily evaluated simply by walking down a section of singers or players, listening and entering the result on the checklist). Obviously, such ratings provide more feedback than a "naked" grade

Figure 6.1 Model of Bar Graph for Evaluating Rubrics

(e.g., "Matching pitch: B–"; "Knows fingering for all keys: C+"). Rubrics can also be of even more value in portfolio forms of reporting progress.

Converting rubrics into bar graphs, with "proficient" shown in a bar below and the student's present progress recorded above (or the reverse), may satisfy administrators for whom such tangible "scores" are imperative (is there a rubric for smiling to please the principal?). Such bar graphs seem to be more congenial to students than checks on a rubrics list (and are more flexible for the teacher to use since in-betweens can be graphically indicated). The bar graph represents "proficiency" of a rubric (derived from the curriculum) *for a given level* (e.g., middle school mixed choir), and the dashed line above would be the teacher's evaluation (the arrowhead portends progress) (Figure 6.1 above). This system works well with portfolio assessment and individual sessions with a student (e.g., evaluating several such competencies). Subsequent evaluations can (hopefully) extend the rating line.

Here judgments are relative to the teacher's experience with previous or similar students. In any case, such formal evaluation should be of minor concern to teachers and students alike; at most such *learning feedback* of development reminds the student of the praxical criterion at stake. Depending on the age level or ensemble, more than three conditions of improvement can be graphed.

Discussion

Different teachers would likely have different musicianship criteria in mind, according to the typical conditions of their particular situations. And other action ideals may be planned: for example, estimating attitude dimensions for "outside listening" (in the school library and at home), which is predicated on promoting long-term habits. For example, students can be assigned to listen to other compositions by the same composer, and similar compositions by other composers ("Dies Irae" from the Verdi Requiem, the Mozart Requiem, and the Berlioz Requiem; compare those to "Amazing Grace," the so-called "Albinoni Adagio in G minor," or "The Saints Go Marching In" as funeral music). Provide praxical ideals for the array of other instruction at various levels. One school I know well teaches music reading to all students via keyboard in grade five and six (ages 9–12) piano classes; others may use handchimes or recorders at that level. All schools should teach music reading for future use, without overlooking singing/playing by ear, improvisation, and "blue notes" when relevant.

In addition to concern with a formal guiding document, praxis theory will point to the organization and delivery of instruction based in effect on the already mentioned *apprenticeship model,* where the action ideals in question denote a *practicum* (Elliott & Silverman 2015). Therefore, and again, impractical, detailed, and overly detailed lists (e.g., U.S. National Standards) and piecemeal approaches to skills and information (U.S.-style "core curriculum") give way instead to the *holistic* immersion of students in the types of musicianship and musicing central to the musical praxes in question.

For sure, such involvement at first will be quite rudimentary, but it will always be at least a holistic approximation of the intended praxical (action ideal) outcome. Instead of a so-called *spiral curriculum* that supposedly revisits 'concepts' at ever-higher levels of abstraction or difficulty, *praxical sequencing* systematically presents ever-more realistic practical challenges of literature that feature the ultimate praxical consequences intended: for example, cross- or alternate fingerings, new chords and keys, and strums, according to the student's present status.

Newcomers to a praxis-based class can have their first experiences simplified, for example, playing only the root for chords provided on an arrangement, or every "G" in a melody—thus following along (for more details, see Regelski 2004, 213–234). With the rest of the class enthused about the praxis, they can often help the newcomer to quickly become a qualified contributor to the class efforts, perhaps more easily than they originally experienced.[14]

In this manner, the knowledge and skills addressed by instruction are ensured to be *actually useful*—a factor contributing not only to the efficiency of instruction but also to evaluating the *authentic effectiveness* of learning. Furthermore, briefly isolated moments of focus—for example, emphasis on this or that detail of technique (e.g., tonguing, alternate fingerings for intonation, pure vowel tone, articulating consonants/tonguing)—never lapse into "for its own sake" preoccupations or *drills,* but rather are always musically and naturally integrated in and through the appropriate musical context and level of praxis.

Rather than drill such isolated technical details as 'warm-ups' (e.g., scales and Latin vowel sounds), warm up on a new Bach chorale per week, or some similar musically interesting piece that also gets the *musical* 'chops' in gear.

In band, play it *ppp* and then full-out *fff*, both with a focus on good tone and intonation; double-tongue it. In chorus, perform it on chosen vowel sounds, without consonants, etc. Save technical improvements for *musically situated problems when the relation of technical drill to musical improvement is cause-and-effect clear to students* (e.g., a point when tonguing is blurred, when a vowel sound is imprecise). And of considerable consequence to this holistic approach is the fact that at each subsequent level, the joys, interests, and benefits of the music in question are fostered and modeled for the future; at the same time, ever-new heights of praxical functioning are often naturally evident and self-rewarding. Student choices of literature help this process.

Expert exemplars may be models—as are, for example, sports heroes for young athletes. But in schools, the next highest level of musical expertise beckons in the form of the models provided by the next class level or age group.[15] Ultimately, perhaps only a few younger students will aspire to and, as a result, achieve the expertise of more expert models whose accomplishments have informed the beginners' formative years (e.g., the select chorus, jazz ensemble) and go on to further study. Nonetheless, with such models, many others will be able to and will want to remain musically active, albeit as amateurs. Furthermore, despite failing to reach expert status, their praxical insights will allow them to be entirely more 'critically' informed and interested as informed listeners to the artistry of professionals. This kind of appreciation, then, is guided by the praxical musicianship that results only from actually engaging in a praxis; it does not develop as dilettantism apart from such engagement.

Listenership is an important praxis of its own. It has its own conditions, criteria, and "goods," and therefore profits from its particular curricular practicum. Students in performance-based instruction (solo or ensemble) benefit greatly from a *listening practicum* as part of their curriculum.[16] It benefits their skill development by contact with models, levels, literature, and the like that are presently outside their reach. It also provides for a future of listening, particularly on the part of graduates whose future circumstances may not allow time in adulthood for ensemble membership (university students). Assigned listening in the library or at home has already been mentioned, but it can be useful to ask for students' feedback about a composition assigned for listening.

Of course, general (classroom) music instruction also needs its particular listening practicum. But this needs to include performing and compositional praxes of various kinds and levels that inform listening in productive ways. Instead of having listening as the *sole* intended consequence of the general music curriculum, a praxical approach to general music class will focus instead on developing an interest in and nurturing the skills for various kinds and levels of performing and creating music for recreational purposes (recorder, harmonica, ukulele, electric piano, melodica, dulcimers, ethnic instruments from home, etc.). Whether using folk instruments or composition software, general music students, in a praxis-oriented curriculum, should not be denied the joys and pleasures of making music—including composition, too often left out of instruction. The bottom line in general music class as elsewhere in the praxical view of curriculum is a pragmatic concern with the kinds of holistic, 'real life' musical praxis students can do at all or better, with more enthusiasm, as a result of instruction (see Regelski 2004).

This attitude dimension leads to the final distinction in connection with curriculum "as and for praxis" (Regelski 1998). In addition to (a) a formal curriculum guide and (b) instruction predicated on an apprentice-like practicum in one or more types of musical praxis, a praxis-based curriculum and the instruction it guides both need to be (c) regularly evaluated in terms of students' actual learning (i.e., "authentic assessment" via rubrics) and, if found wanting, adjusted. Praxis-based approaches to curriculum are inevitably rich in demonstrated competencies of an authentic kind. As a result, the degree and benefits of praxis-based music education are quite evident, even dramatically so, to students, their parents, administrators, and other observers (e.g., taxpayers). Students can and do engage in one or more authentic musical praxes with self-evident acumen and satisfaction—at the very least in response to the psychological "need for achievement" (N-Ach) that is important to students' self-esteem.

An N-Ach is a premise of *personality theory* that describes the human *need to be good at something* meaningful to Self (of any age). It accounts for "achievement motivation"—intrinsic (interest, intentionality) and extrinsic (enjoying the acknowledgment of others)—associated with countless fields of human endeavor. Music is just such an interest, whether it be excelling musically or being a member of a teen taste group that prides itself on the exclusivity of members. N-Ach is held to be especially important in the healthy development of adolescents who need to be good (in the eyes of peers, or their own minds) at something (e.g., skateboarding, music). It accounts for their compelling personal or social interests—from music to computers, sports, scouting achievements, and the like. And it usually entails a like-minded peer group of similarly achievement-minded peers (e.g., a peer group of skateboarders who practice and "show off" for each other; cohorts of technology nerds). Some teachers even believe that N-Ach affects those students who aspire to only being good at being bad—misbehaving and getting peer attention.

Concluding Perspectives

Curriculum as and for praxis requires a hypothetical or experimental mentality.

The *formal curriculum guide* is in effect a *hypothesis*—more precisely, an interrelated complex of several action ideals as hypotheses—concerning what of all that could be learned is most worth including in instruction (for an age group or level). For praxical approaches, the answer is pragmatic: the holistic musical praxes that are most likely to be able to make a positive musical and personal difference in the lives of typical students. These intended 'good results' are hypothesized as the action ideals of the curriculum.

The *instructional phase* of the curriculum is also *hypothetical*: the methods and materials of instruction are first hypothesized as being the most likely of available means for local circumstances (e.g., schedule, materials). Instruction, however, requires *practice*! It is remarkable how often music teachers who have spent so much time practicing musical skills simply expect their methods and materials to just "work" without dedicated practice.

It is not methods and materials that "work." Like any tools, their use for better or worse determines their effectiveness. In music, such instructional tools are effective (or not) according to when and how well "practiced" they are applied. Despite what some texts and "how to" and 'delivery'-oriented teachers contend, methods and materials are only tools and need to be adeptly practiced and employed in a well-conceived curriculum if they are to succeed in producing the intended results. Teaching as a professional praxis, then, is also concerned with ethically qualified results.

Following, first, the thesis of praxical value, then, second, the hypothesis of selecting the most likely instructional methods and materials, the final phase in this process is the *test* or *experimental 'proof'*—*viz.* authentic assessment—of the success and worth of the first two hypothesized variables (*viz.*, the curricular action ideals involved and the instructional means employed). *Reflection* on a less-than-successful lesson (or series of lessons), then, should consider the following:

- It might be that the curricular ideals theorized are valid (well reasoned) but the instructional means chosen were not.
- Or it might be that the methods were not properly put into praxis by the instructor, given the circumstances.
- Or it might be that the ideal can't be achieved given the limitations (e.g., scheduling, budget) of a particular teacher situation.

- Or it might be that the ideals themselves may have been unrealistic, unobtainable, or otherwise unworkable. If so, they need to be re-hypothesized in light of past practice and the predictable challenges of the near future.

The experimental (tentative) nature of this Pragmatic cycle is not to be confused with "experimenting" on students, since it also perfectly describes, for instance, the professional praxis by which a doctor diagnoses and treats patients (diagnosis, treatment, follow-up observation). As mentioned earlier, then, Pragmatism is sometimes referred to as *experimentalism* or *instrumentalism* in recognizing that knowledge and skill are instrumental in bringing about pragmatic ends-in-view, that is, action ideals (Regelski 2017a).

Over time, certainly, the evolution of music and society, new technology, and changes in students' backgrounds, attitudes, schooling circumstances, and the like necessitate periodic and systematic review of curriculum—especially over the career of a music educator. Teachers who teach in the same patterns and paradigms as when they were beginning teachers are either very gifted or deluded—they'd like to think the former but most likely the latter is true. Curriculum, in this view, is not a free-standing premise that remains unaffected by changing circumstances; as frequently stipulated, it is "ideal" exactly in the sense that there is no ultimate, once-and-for-all-times "good" or final curriculum. Consequently, there is a constant need for ongoing connection to ever-fluctuating and evolving socio-musical needs, conditions, and criteria. Children and music are certainly going to change.

Given the intrinsic and evident sociality of music and the important role music provides in both creating and reflecting the structures of society and sociality, a philosophy of curriculum as praxis most fully accounts for the exceptionally profound and ubiquitous role of music in human life. Similarly, then, a praxis-based curriculum, such as is suggested here, provides the kind of pragmatic benefits of music for life that is pointed to by a praxis-based philosophy of music. All kinds and degrees of musical praxis are validated, and music education curriculum planning and use become an educational praxis that is properly and fully committed to inclusiveness of musics, meanings, and values, not to the kinds of exclusiveness pointed to by "pure gaze" aesthetic assumptions, or "what works" 'delivery' methods.

Music education as praxis assumes the value and importance of music as praxis. It is qualified according to the ethics of phronēsis and cognizant of the fact that while there is no legal "malpraxis" in teaching, students who "drop out" of ensembles and "mentally" in class are evidence of not having been positively affected by instruction. They are like patients of doctors who don't agree with the diagnosis or treatment—in our case to the allure of future musicing—and ignore it.

The instructional challenge of praxis *includes* rather than *excludes* students so that music studied in school is understood by students as *music for us,* for our lives, for the musical "good times" of a life well lived. Instruction for only the select or 'talented' few fails any ethical criterion. A praxical curriculum will instead be devoted to helping *all* students find some forms of musicing that contribute to lifelong musicing—including extra efforts to retain potential drop-outs. Approached in this way, music and music education have much more to contribute than has been realized by traditional formats of music curriculum and "music education as aesthetic education." It thus holds forth the promise of having more impact on individuals and society than has been the case following outdated, traditional curricular planning and instruction.

Notes

Preface

1. COMMENTARY. What later will be explained as "methodolatry," the devoted adherence to a certain method where the successful 'delivery' of a lesson as per the prescriptive method is assumed to have resulted in successful, relevant, and long-lasting learning. Too often this is not the case and any 'fun time' for students is not "good time" (literally 'worth-while' time) in terms of long-term learning.

Chapter 1

1. Some exceptions are Elliott & Silverman (2015); Regelski (2016b); Hodges (2017). Regelski (2004) offers a curriculum *model* for middle school general music classes, grades four through eight, that can be extended for upper grades; its chapter on teaching classroom instruments is also applicable to beginning instrument lessons.
2. Throughout, *double* "quotation marks" will be used for unattributed, common expressions (e.g., "best practices," "tricks of the trade"). They are also used when citing a word as a word (e.g., what is called "curriculum"). *Single* 'quotation marks' denote *so-called* or *supposedly* (e.g., 'good music', 'true', 'real', 'good methods'). Commas and periods will follow the single quotation mark. This is an important distinction to be observed by the reader.
3. Eliott and Silverman (2015) spell it "musicing." Christopher Small's usage (1998) puts more emphasis on the social phenomenology of what he spells "musicking," a take-off on the old English "musick."
4. DEFINITION. "Authentic assessment" tests learning through the "authentic" application being taught. The authentic assessment, say, of swimming lessons is being able to swim; the authentic understanding of key signature is tested by consistently correct performance.
5. COMMENTARY. "General music" is known as "classroom music" in some countries, and in some places it is taught by classroom teachers who are not trained musicians—often to their discomfort.
6. COMMENTARY. Known in some countries as "practicum" or "pedagogy" classes. Whatever the term, emphasis seems rarely on the pragmatic results of the instructional practices at stake and how they are to be evaluated in the short and long term. Such "methods" of instruction usually focus on the 'delivery' of student or "what works" and "best practice" plans to university classmates who, of course, do not react as school-aged children would.
7. COMMENTARY. This varies from country to country. In some countries solfeggio is successful (Estonia). In other countries music reading is taught via recorder (Japan), simple wind instruments, or keyboards (see Knappenberger 2016 for details of such a curriculum in action in small-town America). In the United States, however, results of six-plus years of classroom music are at best spotty, especially among male students (thus a perpetual shortage of males for church and community choirs).

8. In a graduate class, students were assigned to take one of their "professional" days to observe a classmate teach. When discussing their observations, disagreements and tensions erupted because what most had observed had been vastly different from how they planned and delivered their own lessons. Few felt they had learned from the observation. University researchers in Europe videotaped hours of what *they* took to be models of good teaching. When shown to other university professors at an international conference, dissention over the 'goodness' of the lessons was considerable.
9. DEFINITION. See Turino (2008) on "presentational" vs. "participatory" musics. Briefly, the former *rehearse* to present music to concert audiences; the latter exist as a mainly musical form of *sociality* among the musicians (and participating listeners' comments and enthusiasm during the music—e.g., caroling, "jam sessions," "garage bands").
10. IDEA. Listening opportunities and assignments in the school library can help compensate for this. Lists of recorded music suggested to buy for home collections also starts the habit early of collecting music other than the current commercial fare.
11. COMMENTARY. Oddly, student and guest recitals in U.S. schools of music often require attendance. Apparently, there's no interest in musics other than for one's own instrument or performances by friends! I asked a returning student who had been studying in London how she enjoyed the choral music there. She said she hadn't heard any: she attended only clarinet recitals, her instrument. A study reported that for students at Julliard, the second most important amount of time after their own practicing was spent listening at the practice room doors of their competitors.
12. COMMENTARY. "Conveyance" here should not be confused with *delivery methods* (methodolatry). Nor should it be understood solely in terms of "transmission" theories of curriculum that are concerned only to transmit knowledge from the past to students (e.g., getting information from the teacher's mind into a student's notebook without touching anything in between). For sociological details about transmission vs. social transformation in schools, see deMarris & LeCompte (1990, 5–43).
13. COMMENTARY. In what follows, "agency"—that is, being an agent—refers to being *one who acts* (praxis), one who creates actions (praxes) that engage the world and people in it. "Change agents" are those whose actions or action roles seek to change given or traditionally accepted conditions. Education is, or should be, a profession concerned with "change agency": changing students' levels of knowledge and ability and thereby changing musicing in society.
14. COMMENTARY. This widespread practice is accused by education sociologists of "deprofessionalizing" teaching, of turning well-meaning professionals into factory-like workers. The widespread practice of selling or sharing lesson plans on the Internet also leads to the same results: not individuals exercising their own professional, praxical knowledge but 'delivering' recipe-like, "pre-fab" instruction that 'covers' U.S. (National Association for Music Education) national standards.
15. Or, in countries where an education ministry creates a vague set of *guidelines* regarded as the national curriculum, where the teacher has to create a personal, functional curriculum that fills in details the national curriculum leaves out, for example, Finland, internationally renowned for the success of its schools in comparison to other countries.
16. TRUE STORY. An exception: a first-year teacher, a graduate of mine, designed a middle school general music curriculum predicated heavily on compositional software and 'recreational' instruments (i.e., nonband or orchestra instruments, guitar, ukulele, recorders, plucked and hammered dulcimer, etc.). The board of education approved it without

question (probably not even reading it). Then the teacher filed a budget request to fund all the instruments, hardware, and software, and the board had little choice but to go along with the request. That clever teacher is now a principal.
17. DEFINITION. In educational psychology, "readiness" is the present competence needed for a student to be able to succeed with a new and usually more advanced lesson.
18. Nonetheless, common discourse identifies "teaching" with "instruction." But herein "teaching" will be used very occasionally when "instruction" is clumsy in a sentence. I use "educator" too, but it actually has the same challenges of actually "educating" in accountable ways.
19. TRUE STORY. I once complained to the music history professor that the students I had in choral conducting classes had no idea of the historical nature and social role of Renaissance madrigals as concerns their performance. He agreed with my understanding but exclaimed, "Well, I taught it to them ['delivered' a lecture?]; if they didn't learn it, it's their fault."
20. DEFINITION. Behaviorism is a psychological theory, once popular in education, that denied cognitive processes of learning in favor of only observable (behavioral) results. The "mind/brain" was conceived to be an input-output mechanism (a black box). The outward demonstration of instructional input, then, was the focus, not the cognitive bases (see, later, Pragmatism's steps three and four) that made such behavior possible. Cognitivism and constructivism have since replaced behaviorism, but the tangible and observable results of learning still are relevant to a curriculum that seeks to promote notable, long-term abilities for musicing. "You know" the fingerings for the clarinet when you can DO them.
21. "Institutional grammar" structures the hidden curriculum the same way grammar structures language. That's apparently always the case with any institution: its grammar—rules of organizing behavior—is sometimes socially overwhelming and often tacitly controls our behavior in that institution (e.g., the grammar of racism, fascism, and white supremacy)—or of teachers in schools!
22. Conversations between adults do not proceed in this way. In a discussion, you time your contribution to the spaces, or to the relevance of what you have to say. Organizing a discussion in a school class should be like conducting a discussion for a business decision. As will be seen, this adjustment of school to the predicates of life is a feature of progressive education.
23. COMMENTARY. Japanese music education has been conflicted over teaching Western music or traditional Japanese musics. The music of Sibelius is more likely to be taught in Finnish schools than the music of his contemporaries from other nations. This is one consequence of Nationalism in music, and evidence against "absolute" music. DEFINITION: "Absolute" music is supposedly socially unconditioned and complete in itself, with no connection to extramusical concepts or meanings: simply a sonorous structure existing only to be contemplated by concert audiences—no nationalism, story, picture, etc. Even the words of art song and opera are denied "pure" aesthetic merit.
24. DEFINITION. "Perfect intervals" are those pitches that occur in the scales built on each of the two pitches: for example, C occurs without an accidental (i.e., "perfectly") in the scale of F, and F occurs "perfectly" in the scale of C. Thus, the interval C to F (C to the fourth degree of the C scale, F) is called a "perfect fourth." The same is the case for perfect fifths (C to G). Surprised? Kind of irrelevant, as is the distinction.
25. IDEA. The maxim of celebrated piano virtuoso Yves Nat, teaching at the Paris Conservatoire in the 1950s, was "*Toute pour musique, rien pour la piano*" (roughly: "It's all about music, not about the piano"). CD liner for *My Personal Favorites*: *The Jacques Loussier Trio Plays*

Bach, Telarc 35319-02, 2014. Loussier, a conservatory piano student of Nat, is internationally noted for having popularized "crossover" jazz based on classical favorites. *IDEA*. Worth a listen, especially for high school listening lessons.

Chapter 2

1. COMMENTARY. In the U.S., students were (and in some places, still are) segregated into "tracks": college preparation, mainly secretarial for women, and in rural areas "agricultural" for boys. It almost took an act of God (and my father as a member of the board of education) for me to be able to take typing class, otherwise offered only for "secretarial" students. I am forever grateful for "the" most important influence on my publishing efforts.
2. For example, J. S. Bach's *Goldberg Variations* as performed by Glenn Gould late in his career can be difficult to reconcile with mainstream interpretations (or even with his youthful performances). COMMENTARY. A recent proposal argues that it is not performance *of* notation that is "the music" but the performance itself *as* (or is) "the music" where each performance creates an original musical experience, not an interpretation. Think about that (see, e.g., Nicholas Cook). This idea is influenced by postmodernity, discussed in Chapter Four.
3. Reimer was a key contributor to the Silver Burdett "Song Series," that featured formal listening lessons and singing over composition or performing on classroom instruments.
4. DEFINITION. The Latin term "aisthesis" for "knowledge derived from the senses" is referred to throughout this text. It originates in the Realist philosophy of Aristotle but was hijacked as the basis of speculative aesthetic theory in the mid-18th century. Aristotle is also the source of the Virtue Ethics discussed later and of the idea of *praxis* that is the basis of praxis-based philosophies of music and music education, today and in the entire history of music. Aisthesis is "sentient knowing." However, sight and hearing were "primary" senses since, unlike the others they didn't compromise the sensory input by having to touch the body.
5. COMMENTARY. Late in his career, following new interest in Pragmatism, philosopher Hilary Putnam relinquished his earlier support of *direct Realism* and took the position that although the world of matter is independent of the human mind, the structure of the world *as we come to know it*—its division into labeled kinds, individuals, colors, conditions, and categories—is a result of the experiences of it picked out and (sometimes) labeled by the human mind; that is, by language. He called this "internal reality," because the world *as we know it* is not outside but internal to us.
6. For more about Pragmatic/Internal Realism, see Putnam (1990, 3–43), Putnam & Putnam (2017, 140–158), M. Johnson (1987, 194–212), and the section on Pragmatism in the next chapter.
7. COMMENTARY. But not "aesthetic realism," which is another somewhat bizarre theory (see Eli Siegel). Also, "realism" in visual art deals with life-like representations of the natural world.
8. "Doctors of the church" were saints and other dead theologians of renown.
9. COMMENTARY. Rhetoric was originally viewed as an art of persuasion, a skill that gives the pleasures of logical argumentation (e.g., formal debate contests) beyond the argument at stake. Today, it often means "empty" arguments undertaken just to argue.
10. COMMENTARY. For example, sociology of music typically studies what musicology intentionally ignores: music's sociality. Ethnomusicology studies the intersection of ethnicity

and musicing, also studiously ignored by musicology and aesthetics. These newer disciplines were established to cover the many gaps in traditional musicology and aesthetics for the sociality of praxis. That they continue to be ignored by schools and conservatories of music is testimony to the threat they represent to the "music" taught in those places that is made to have appeared from Mars, in denial of its social roots.

11. COMMENTARY. Faculty referees need not agree with a thesis (thus admitting new knowledge to the discipline), but their challenges to its defense probe the depths of the candidate's knowledge and reliance on the discipline in defense of the thesis. The question is whether or not the thesis is defensible (not necessarily proven). In the U.S. the defense is usually carried out privately in a conference room or office; in other countries it is public event, but one that celebrates the thesis completion more than probing it, often more theatrically than scholarly.

12. TRUE STORY. Consider the futility of the experienced eighth-grade general music teacher who taught a class lecture "unit" entitled "The 25 Greatest Composers," giving students the rationale that "Someday you'll be at a party where people are talking about composers and you'll be able to join in." I was waiting to see the student teacher in the next lesson. Based on what I saw in that one lesson of the "unit," each of the 25 greats got a lecture on their life, listing of major compositions ("it will be on the test"), and a listening example (no discussion) to an excerpt of one of their most famous works.

13. TRUE STORY. A third-year university student preparing for a recital was asked to present a Beethoven sonata 1st movement for a music appreciation class as an example of "sonata form." The professor, understandably by Neo-Scholastic premises, preceded the performance by asking the pianist to demonstrate the first and second themes and the beginning of the development section for the class. Beyond the opening theme, she had no idea of the key ingredients of the form as usually taught, although she was using an edition that analyzes the form in depth for performers. But she played well.

Chapter 3

1. DEFINITION. *Epistemology* is the subdiscipline of philosophy that studies the nature and extent of knowledge. First, what does it mean to know something? And then, how do we acquire knowledge? Also considered is skepticism, the worry that we cannot know anything for sure at all. See the discussion later of Postmodernism, which essentially claims that all we know are words.

2. COMMENTARY. Then why have studied them? A reasonable question. TRUE STORY in answer: While studying piano, composition, and conducting at the Antwerp (Belgium) Conservatory, I lived with the family of a Dutch Reformed minister. One room in the house was off-limits even to family. I asked why and my "father" unlocked it and showed me. There were books on all four walls—all of them dealing with religions other than Dutch Reformism! When I asked why, he smiled cannily and said, "Know thy enemies!" As to the traditional philosophies, so much of their 'baggage' remains in today's schools that readers who want to challenge this status quo are best prepared to "Know their enemies," the lingering remnants that I hope they will be working against and will avoid repeating.

3. TRUE STORY. A beginning, middle school band teacher was criticized by her (all-male) colleagues in a small city school system for including a selection of chamber music groups along with the band in her first winter concert. They complained that she was "not good

enough to 'pull off' a full band concert" when, in fact, small chamber groups were part of her curriculum for encouraging lifelong interest in chamber combos. She moved on to another school system where she could implement her curricular ideas without harassment from stuck-in-the-mud old-timers.
4. DEFINITION. The *activity theory* of Lev Vygotsky is a related educational psychology and denotes the socio-historical field as a "zone of proximal development" that guides and assists learners in that "zone" (class) who interact. Vygotsky, thus, is known for his *social* construc*tionism* (cooperatively learning by drawing from the resources of a group of peers or instructors). Piaget, in contrast, is distinguished by his *genetic* construc*tivism*: an individual student's knowing unfolds or evolves over time according to the biological maturation of four stages: Sensorimotor, Pre-operational, Concrete operations, Formal operational. The reader's familiarity with Piaget's stages is extremely relevant to curriculum, and they also indirectly condition Vygotsky's influence on activity theory.
5. COMMENTARY. Student "inattention" is usually to a boring lesson; otherwise, they agentively stare out the window, pass notes, talk, doodle, etc.
6. COMMENTARY. When others have characterized such thinkers as "existentialists," most rejected the label. Those who may think themselves to be "existentialists," by that very self-labeling, usually are not! That would subscribe them to a preformed doctrine. Some philosophers and literary figures have expressed existential themes but resisted being identified with it as a formal "ism" (e.g., Camus). Phenomenology has three schools of thought, and existentialism develops as one of them. The other two are transcendental and realist, way off topic for present purposes.
7. COMMENTARY. Obviously, some clergy teach their own certainties and are uncomfortable with "leap of faith" conditions. They oppose theologian Kierkegaard and the ordinary understanding of "faith" in any aspect of life.
8. COMMENTARY. Too often, statistically at least, the conclusion that love (a noun or "thing") is a *static* condition one is "in" (like a closet) is often the beginning of the end—with divorce seven years later (the "seven-year itch"). "Falling in love" in this all-too-typical theory of love can be like a plunge into an open manhole; once falling "in," how or whether to get out is the problem. "Lov*ing*," on the other hand (a verb form, a doing or praxis like music*ing*) is an active and responsive relationship and adjusts to and profits from changes in life's circumstances (e.g., from adjusting to a new baby, to growing old together).
9. Not to be confused with Idealism, where the ideals were abstract cognitions, like "treeness." *Action ideals* are the bases of much of our most noble and notable everyday conduct: we work toward their realization (e.g., good parent) while recognizing that such 'goods' can never be perfectly realized yet are worthy guides for our ongoing intentionality.
10. COMMENTARY. Consider, for example, the herd mentality of Nazism and Fascism, or today's white supremacism, racism, and anti-Hispanic ethnic ideologies.
11. In his masterpiece, *Being and Time*. Being-in-the-world supposes not a factual state (a *what* I am) but a *who*: he calls this Dasein, German for "being there," as a "who" thrown into life not of his choosing. Simpler and much more entertaining is the short, satirical novel *Being There* by Jerzy Kosinki (1983) where the main character, "Chance," a simple-minded gardener who utters profound-sounding comments (actually nonsense about politics as gardening), is thrown into a world of money and power outside his garden that is not of his choosing and attains superstar status by chance.
12. From the very last page of his novel *The Stranger*.

13. As for the theories of Vygotsky and Piaget (mentioned previously and in a later chapter), the constructionism of Vygotsky is more consistent with existential constructivism since it operates in the socio-historical world and is not the simple result of maturational biological processes, as with Piaget.
14. COMMENTARY. Explore the psychological theory of "Dramaturgy" (Irving Goffman), also known as "life as theater," where we are constantly on some public 'stage' playing a "script" to a certain public (e.g., our in-laws) either that we have written or that was written for us (is socially expected) and agreed to; for example, the "script" of student musician calls forth many expected roles.
15. DEFINITION. A model is a simplified representation that explains the working of a real-world process—in the present case, the development of Self.
16. The lack of this last D-need results in bullying, and peer acceptance is extremely influential to a young and developing Self (and neurotic older Selves). In the Covid-19 pandemic of 2020, distance learning experiments resulted in a lack of bullying.
17. DEFINITION. Cohort: an aggregate group or clique sharing mutual interests and status (e.g., band members, cheerleaders, church friends, teachers room, and fellow computer "nerds").
18. WARNING. High-functioning students who feel they have not lived up to their own high standards are often among those attempting suicide. They often give away prize collections to their best friends—a warning sign!
19. COMMENTARY. It is important to consider that such needs are never "finally" met. Musicians who were highly recognized in their schools are in for a surprise in their first year of university studies where everyone enjoyed that local status but some are more advanced. Freshman auditions for ensembles usually reveal this reality.
20. "Why aren't my students interested in what I teach?" Or, "Why don't my students practice?"
21. Thus, classmates from whom they learn in Vygotsky's Zone of Proximal Development are "peer teachers."
22. IDEA. For instrumental music teaching it contributes immeasurably if an accompaniment can be provided. The tune alone is only half "the music." Piano skills of instrumental teachers are often weak. But accompanying software is available that "follows" a student, and of course student pianists can be enrolled to accompany recording an MP3 file of each tune of an instrumentalist's personal progress. Pianists can add to their personal MP3 album of Greatest Hits.
23. COMMENTARY. "Ends in view" have a special role in Pragmatism. Promoting student intentionality is the pedagogical challenge of pragmatic and existentially oriented teachers—not gold stars and the next concert. Ends in view entail the realization of a *present*, musical end in view, not long-term accomplishments—though those may eventually become part of subsequent intentionality. In music, longer-term ends in view often have to be modeled (e.g., the *Haydn Trumpet Concerto* as a listening model for trumpet students). Recorded examples of previous students in the same school playing the same literature are also motivating and provide an aural model.
24. COMMENTARY. There are no extrinsic awards for the musicing of most adult amateurs. If a student's motivation has been largely extrinsic, interest is short-circuited with graduation. Adult groups may engage in festive cooperation (e.g., barbershop competitions, university-age football marching bands), but the motives that propel their efforts are the intrinsic and social rewards of rehearsing together and enjoying mutual musicing. A group of university professors got together regularly to drink beer and sing amusing Old England catches and glees, the scholarly specialty of the leader. When one proposed giving a concert, the

others objected because then they'd have to rehearse. The leader, Prof. Mac Nelson, died in February 2019, and a memorial performance of catches and glees was held that spring. I don't know if it was rehearsed or if the group continues without him.

25. COMMENTARY. This common motivational strategy "rewards" *quantity* of practice instead of *quality* of practice and, among other problems, leads to "practicing" (i.e., mindless repetition) that is just filling time, not devoted intentionally to solving musical problems—as identified by student or teacher—and progressing. Practicing skills need to be taught, not just assigned.

26. COMMENTARY. Some directors approve of losing such students whom they believe are dragging down 'the program'—called, by one director, "the cream of the crap." Such existentially inauthentic decisions not to offer them further help are also professionally unethical. Ensemble directors alone in schools are allowed this weeding out of weak or disinclined students.

27. COMMENTARY. Perfectly dictated over the years by the wealthy cultural patrons who, with the rise of public concerts, trained audiences to sit quiet as though in intellectual reverie; not conducting along with the music, not tapping their feet to the syncopations or savoring refreshments during the concert. Opera audiences took a bit longer to tame. This contrast of audience behavior with "pop" and jazz performances is undoubtedly a major turn-off for the audience behavior of restless youth.

28. Not to be confused with the educational theory of "reconstructionism" explained in Chapter Five; see Dewey (1971).

29. This audiation also allows all of us to recognize a tune for singing, or playing "by ear." But, in musical performance, that aural image is the intentionality that guides action. Singing and some wind instruments are especially dependent on audiation. Woe to brass instruments faced with an exposed entrance.

30. This is the process of pragmatic learning and also applies to the Zone of Proximal Development (ZPD) of Vygotsky as regards experience and shared observations of a group, and thus learning in or as a group.

31. IDEA. Frequently the problem is the *transition* of getting from one note's fingering to the next fingering. Then it doesn't help to correct only the mistaken note and begin playing again from that corrected note. Going back a few notes or measures to *practice the troublesome transition* is needed, not just correcting the wrong pitch or rhythm and starting again from that point. Thus, practice skills need to be taught in the lesson: for example, ask students to demonstrate their practicing of a few measures (that need it!), and then correct any practicing strategies that are faulty, such as the aforementioned example, which is very typical, even for adult learners. Advanced learners (and good sight readers) take into consideration ever-larger segments of the notation; problems can occur at the 'seams' between such segments.

32. COMMENTARY. In mid-career called "internal" Realism by Hilary Putnam, and later called "transactionalism"—transactions between the mind with the scientifically known physical world (not direct reality).

33. COMMENTARY. We don't always announce our intentions. However, in guiding practicing of students it is helpful to have the student state what she thinks needs fixing and how she intends to reach those intentions. Discussion then confirms the degree to which the ends were achieved (by her present means) or need more or different strategies. The vacuity of aesthetic education is seen in the apocryphal student assignment, "Play it more

aesthetically." "Put more feeling into it" is roughly like telling a beginning skier to "keep your balance." It is obvious that the expectation is ridiculous.

34. For an account of Dewey's theory of emotion, see Alexander (1987, 136–141); for the theory itself, see Dewey (1860/1894).

35. COMMENTARY. An aesthetic theory claiming that art/music exists "for its own sake" (not to serve any use, sociality, purpose, etc.), only to be *contemplated* in leisure time, according to "aesthetic distance"—a state of *personal disinterestedness* that removes the experience from a direct relationship to one's life. "Such "absolute music," as it is called, is "music alone" (Kivy 1991)—music about music—and even words (of vocal/choral music) and titles (of program music) compromise the "purely musical" nature of the experience. It is characteristic of Idealist conceptions of art. More follows on this extreme claim.

36. As mentioned earlier, Elliott (1995) conveys the same understanding of music as a verb form, except for spelling it "musicing." Sociologist Small's spelling is a play on the Old English "musick." Herein, Elliot's spelling is adopted for its relation to musical praxis in his publications. Small's concept reflects phenomenological sociology, addressed briefly later, and includes more than just the sounds of a performance.

37. Again, the term was derived from Aristotle's "aisthesis," or knowledge gained from the senses (*interoception*: knowledge of inner states of the body), a rather advanced notion in Aristotle's Greece where "knowledge" had more typically meant Plato's Ideal Forms. Baumgarten wanted to argue that what he called "aesthetics" was knowledge of the beautiful through poetry (see Summers 1987).

38. Explained across two publications: *The Critique of Pure Reason* and *The Critique of Judgment* (translations abound). The latter denies aesthetic claims of the time and credits the arts simply with promoting the *free play of imagination* and an experience of "pleasure."

39. COMMENTARY. Semiotics explores the importance of signs and symbols (beyond just language) in communication. *Spatial* semiotics studies the *symbolic meanings* conveyed by arrangements of space. For example, in the past, classrooms organized space with the teacher's desk and chalkboard in the front and students' desks fixed unmovably in rows—like soldiers in marching formation, a symbol of regimentation and of a focus on teacher-directed learning and teacher-talk. Today's desks are moveable and designed to fit together for group work. The semiotics of music in schools are vastly different than that same music in other spaces. Likewise, the spaces of concert halls are designed with the meanings of concert listening primary. Their changes over architectural history demonstrate different historical conceptions of listening (for details, see Johnson 1995). Many churches are displays of spatial semiotics: compare the virtual exuberance of a Baroque church with the austerity of a Lutheran church during the Catholic Counter Reformation.

40. For a postmodern analysis of the "aesthetic project," the politics, and other social ingredients of art, see Postmodernist Rancière (2009a, 2009b).

41. DEFINITION/IDEA. The idea relies on an image of a physical scaffold where, like with a ladder, successfully reaching each more advanced level enables attaining the next step. At first, teachers will help with the scaffolding of problem solving, but ultimately it will be a natural sequence enacted by the student's growing skills. Practicing is the time devoted especially to student progress, and as such, effective practicing strategies and scaffolding need to be taught. Have the student identify a passage that is causing difficulty and watch him practice it; then correct unproductive strategies and promote better use of practice time. In a group setting have one student "practice" a few measures, and have the other

students comment on the strategies—or better, demonstrate better ideas. Rotate the student demonstrator during the group's lesson time.

42. COMMENTARY. Don't let conventions of language mislead. Going for a forest walk (in order) "to experience" its tranquil beauty is, in fact, already guided by intentionality (the anticipated goal of *an* experience of tranquility) and thus will be the basis for "an experience" of its natural quiet. And falling on the ice may demonstrate the future need for more care, but that wasn't the intentionality. We do learn from some nonintentional experiences.

43. COMMENTARY. What you take from your first experience with a tree accumulates with all subsequent experiences with "trees." That is the process of *induction* at work in formulating concepts (or Piagetian *schema* or groups of concepts). Induction of music starts with the very young (even hearing in the womb), and they typically have many musical concepts already in their minds—for example, just calling activities "music" or being 'naturally' attuned to local pitch praxis (tonal or microtonal) and other details.

44. Notice again the absurdity of telling students from the podium to "sing more aesthetically." Even "play more musically" is without criteria that can benefit students for the future. Independent musicianship includes the skill and knowledge needed for competent musicing in the absence of a teacher or other leader. (That's one of the benefits of chamber groups.) The goal of ensembles is to acquire independent musicianship, not to function as part of a machine-like performance. Questions and choices are needed to facilitate this independence.

45. IDEA. But ensemble players down in the sections may have no ends-in-view except following the director's insistence on certain details of the ensemble's performance. What if there were a brass quartet (+ euphonium?) playing, say, transcriptions of Bach chorales or even more adventuresome music, for example, Copland, *Fanfare for the Common Man* (but you'll have to arrange it for them from the brass ensemble version!)? Then each player is musically responsible for her exposed part.

46. Again, Small spells this socially extended "musicking" after the Old English "musick."

47. COMMENTARY. In science, the failure of a well-done experiment is a positive result; it removes the need to test that hypothesis again. Similarly, in learning as "experimental" (Pragmatism), reflection on mistaken actions and awareness and understanding of what was wrong contribute to learning not to do that again.

48. IDEA. Some small schools, probably very few in number, invite participation of retired adults to regularly join nonselect high school ensembles, thus branching into community music education. Only administrative negativity may work against this. For schools too small to have, say, an orchestra, chamber groupings of various kinds are an excellent alternative. Chamber musicers will often make more personal progress than if they had been in a large ensemble.

49. IDEA. Even during full rehearsals, it is instructive to spontaneously select, say, a double SATB group from the whole choir to perform a selected passage for constructive comments by the rest of the ensemble. Similar selected groupings can be heard in instrumental ensembles, not just the auditing of a part that has been struggling.

Chapter 4

1. "Practice theory" offers social and philosophical accounts of human action and agency and analyzes contemporary culture and its institutional practices (e.g., Bourdieu 1990; Schatzki

et al. 2001; Wenger 1999). While "practice theory" accounts for an affective component (Reckwitz 2017, 114–125), unlike praxis it lacks an inherent ethical dimension. When practice theory principles are applied to schooling, ethics have to be considered in addition. The terms "practice" and "praxis" are distinguished by the former's lack of an ethical criterion (e.g., the practice of carrying an umbrella when rain is predicted). Otherwise, practice theory is a welcome contemporary addition supporting praxis theory.

2. Philip Alperson was a former editor of the *Journal of Aesthetics and Art Criticism*, so his scholarly qualifications are not in question.
3. Elliot (1995; and its sequel, 2015). The second edition, with coauthor M. Silverman, goes into far more detail about the praxical bases of curriculum (e.g., musical personhood, different types of knowing supporting praxis, and much more). My initial publication along praxical lines was on "Action Learning" (Regelski 1982a, 1982b). Specifically emphasizing praxis was my 1996 "Prolegomenon to a Praxial Theory of Music Education" that stated a research agenda concerning praxicalism that concludes with this book. Following that Prolegomenon, I have continued to feature the various advantages of praxical theory—using an alternative adjective "prax*ical*" for its resonance with "prac*tical*." Meanwhile Elliot has focused since 2015 on various other interests. My reaction to Elliott's 1995 book is seen in my 2001 review, "Accounting for All Praxis." See Goble (2003) for a comparison of Elliott and Regelski. Most of my observations in the 2001 review have been addressed in the 2015 second edition—really a substantially new book.
4. COMMENTARY. An in*sight*, for example, which is assumed when "I see" means "I understand." Aristotle's era considered vision to be the primary source of knowledge. Hearing was regarded as a second primary sense. The other three senses were considered secondary because they were dependent on physical contact with the source of knowledge and thus defiled by subjective (bodily) impurities.
5. For more on this idea see Arendt (1988, 273, 302), where the "speechless wonder" associated with *thaumazein* is used as all but a synonym for theoria.
6. For a discussion of the *vita contemplativa* of theoria in comparison to the *vita activa* of praxis, see Arendt (1998, 12–17 and Arendt Chapter 6).
7. COMMENTARY. The situation of many classically trained musicians might be characterized in such terms. For example, section string players in professional orchestras acquired considerable technical training for virtuoso careers. Instead, as orchestra members, their contribution is usually not individuating or personal; that is, they may not feel like much more than organ pipes are to the organist save for the pleasures of being a part of the whole. Some may resent the "services" they have to perform to earn a living (union thinking for such "workers") and look forward, instead, to what often amounts to recreational performance of chamber music—which they may do for free. For a discussion of this problem, see Kingsbury (1988, e.g., 123–126, 141–142). Similar situations obtain for just about all vocational roles for performing, and by definition in the Aristotelian sense, they all fall short of the individual and individuating satisfactions of praxis to be described later. Except for solo parts, large school ensembles suffer from the same lack of individuating results, unlike chamber literature.
8. For example, producing the proper pitch, a good tone, in tune, the proper meter and tempo, with complete control over the dynamic requirements, etc.—all according to the style or praxis.
9. QUOTATION. Howard (1997, 42–54) makes a distinction "between high technical proficiency and technical *competency*. One can be technically competent without being highly

proficient and it is quite possible to have technical competency, even high technical proficiency, without musicianship or artistry—derisively labeled 'mechanical' performances" (46–47, italics original)? TRUE STORY. A high school student I knew belatedly fell in love with the saxophone. He practiced, intensively, without a teacher with the intention of being accepted in a university music program. He wasn't, due to the highly mechanical technique he had developed. A kinder judgment might have accepted his developed skills and worked to develop his musicality.

10. COMMENTARY. The reference here is strictly to dimensions of "technique," or technē per se: for example, the surgeon who stitches incisions badly, or the conductor who cannot hear errors in students' performances. These 'standards' of technical accountability are matters of technē. Standards of accountability for music praxis will include technē but add other criteria and requirements for artistry.

11. 'Right results' can't be detailed in advance; degrees of excellence regarding people are usually subjective, and as action ideals take no singular form at any particular time. 'Right results' serve the needs of those affected by a praxis.

12. Interestingly, Aristotle categorized physicians as dealing with technē—no doubt because the heuristics of diagnosis according to scientific premises did not yet exist, and "doctoring" was seen as more of a craft or technology than as what we today recognize as professional praxis.

13. IDEA. Not just the next new tune in the methods book; or maybe the same tune, but with an emphasis on improving tone, or the use of alternative fingers; or a tune from the 'real world' outside of school to spur on momentary lapses of motivation. For small group lessons, two to three students can study the same piece and perform it for the others, which then acts as a commentating audience. Then the others in the group play their piece. This can be done, of course, even when all students are studying the same piece, and it develops critical listening skills.

14. The format and use of the national 'standards' (2014) proposed by the National Association for Music Education (NAfME), then, do not facilitate praxis. In fact, slavishly pursued by teachers as a quality control checklist, they amount only to matters of technē, that is, "delivery" ("I did those, now on to the next"—to paraphrase an actual comment). However, the 'standards' might serve as very general pointers for local curriculum development that properly takes the form of action ideals of a holistic and pragmatic musical nature rather than a fragmented succession of lessons. Remember: *The standards of praxis* are *standards of care*!

15. Amateuring is to amateur as musicing is to music. See Regelski (2007).

16. TRUE STORY. A student teacher returned from her first day teaching elementary general music and exclaimed, "It was such fun; I can't believe they actually pay people to do this." I've often wondered whether she kept that enthusiasm. Another remarked, "I was in seventh heaven—but why did I spend years in the practice room instead of being with children more?" I doubt her piano skills were wasted on students.

17. Study by music medicine shows that beginning students' holding of the instrument puts pressure on arms and jaw muscles to hold the embouchure in proper alignment. The result can be embouchure disfigurations that affect at least tone if not articulation, as the instrument droops more and more. And physical harm can result for young and developing bodies. This is all the more reason to take a short rest break, a good time to listen to a recording of the next tune (to promote audiation) or of advanced performers on the instrument.

18. Quoting an in-service teacher in a graduate class. He went on to be president of the state music teachers association. Another gem, from the same source (a band teacher): "I'd rather eat live rats than teach general music."
19. "It's my practice to use the Oxford (serial) comma in writing." Your practice may be to rake leaves left- or right-handed. The "practice of medicine" sounds as problematic as "practice teaching" (practicing on children?) once did. How much more profound does "teaching internship" sound?
20. TRUE STORY. A second-year music education student in my adolescent psychology class jumped up and as she rushed from the room angrily shouted, "Just teach us to teach! All this shit about kids is nonsense!! I don't even like kids!!!" She was never seen again; perhaps she transferred and is teaching somewhere, or became a professional oboist.
21. COMMENTARY. "Secondary" because they detail the conditions of phronēsis, which *is* primary; in fact, as regards criteria of professional competence, they are actually primary.
22. For example, students who never learn to "match pitch" are musically 'handicapped' when singing carols, church hymns, etc. Instrumentalists whose musicianship is insufficient to learn new music on their own are also 'handicapped' in this regard.
23. This duty is difficult to meet in a large ensemble. It is met more readily by an infusion of solos, duets, trios, etc., involving a range of musics for student choice-making. Chamber ensembles formed from the larger ensemble can perform their practicing for the ensemble, thus engaging critical audience listening.
24. COMMENTARY. For example, where a student is obliged to switch instruments when doing so is not in the best educational and musical interest of the student and serves only to improve ensemble instrumentation. Or (TRUE STORY) where students are recruited on instruments strictly with a view to the needs of the ensemble, for example, the fourth-grade student who came home with a brief slip from the band teacher, "_____ (name) has been selected, on the basis of musical achievement tests [?], to study the _____ (euphonium)." The father, a nonmusic professor, asked me what it was all about. A duty is also failed when students who play certain instruments are denied school opportunities due to a lack of ensembles for those instruments, or must learn an 'accepted' instrument to be in an ensemble (and sell that accordion!). Similarly, pianists who end up as a choir's full-time accompanist are not having their needs as singers met, although the opportunity to accompany does impart musicianship skills that are likely to serve them outside of school and as graduates.
25. "Applied ethics" take into account the ethical implications of *real-world* praxes, for example, medical ethics, business ethics and police ethics.
26. Most notably, Aristotle's *Nichomachean Ethics* (see, e.g., Reeve's translation, 2013). For a survey of other virtue ethics, see Vardy & Prosch (1999, 94–122); for contemporary relevance, see MacIntyre (1981).
27. TRUE STORY. A jazz group (a string quartet!) hired for dancing played tempi and changing meters unsuitable for dancing (but no Finnish tangos, a major enthusiasm in Finland—no relation to either the music or steps of other Tango traditions), thus drawing complaints from the dancers. It was "good jazz," but not "good dance music." Different praxes! I enjoyed listening, but the dancers objected (oddly so in that very patient country). Contrarily, an old-time, three-chord, Chicago blues group was in concert under a tent and losing audience interest. Recognizing this, the leader said, "Is there a law against dancing?" which got the audience up and enthusiastically dancing on the grass. I was still bored. This was music "good for dancing" but not "good for concert listening."

28. Bourdieu also traces the sociological/historical "Genesis of a Pure Aesthetic" (1993, 254–266), thus demonstrating that *aesthetic theory itself was a social construction* of the 18th to 19th centuries and not at all a matter of purely philosophical reasoning or discovery. Socially it was a perfect fit for the rising merchant middle-class aspirations to be 'classy' and thus to deny such status to nonconnoisseurs.
29. COMMENTARY. Sociologists of music know that to understand a particular culture, you need to understand its music: why it exists, where and when it is created, by whom, and what the criteria are of "good" music for that culture. On the other hand, understanding a culture's social practices and institutions is key to understanding its music. Thus, music and culture are inextricably intertwined! What will judgments be of today's musical life and culture 100 years from now?
30. As does even the idea of "pain" (and emotion and feelings in a particular language culture), which in many respects is conditioned by sociocultural variables (e.g., Kövecses 2000).
31. For example, technological improvements in instruments (piston valves); performing Bach on the modern grand piano or marimba; the lush Samuel Barber *Adagio for Strings* used in the war movie *Platoon*; two piano synthesizers and drum set replacing a pit orchestra for musicals; etc. Familiarity bred by recordings can be a major downside when a listener is influenced in hearing a new performance of a work that is otherwise very familiar from repeated hearings of a recorded version.
32. Some religions disapprove of "music" per se but condone in their religious praxis what other cultures describe as sung "prayer."
33. For detailed analyses of music and sociality see, for example, Martin (1996), Shepherd (1991), Shepherd & Wicke (1997), Regelski (2016a, 2016b), and the scholarship from sociology of music and ethnomusicology. COMMENTARY. These disciplines are not usually taught in (most U.S.) university schools of music, probably because they contradict the "pure gaze" premises of aesthetic theory usually taken for granted in such programs. In some places "music education" as a scholarly discipline is taught in departments of social and cultural theory, not in "schools of music" for performers only (e.g., Örebrö university in Sweden).
34. See Regelski (2016a, 2016b, 2017b), Bourdieu (1993, 1984—the latter on "[social class] Distinction" and "The Aristocracy of Culture," 11–96).
35. COMMENTARY. When performed publically for Western audiences, such musics become "concert music" for listening (a different praxis) and no longer serve (for concert audiences, at least) their original situated, praxical values. Performers still can give evidence of the originating praxical functions—for example, performances of "Kodō," the Japanese *taiko* drumming ensemble—the physicality of whose mesmerizing concert performing is, for them, a spiritual discipline, even in concert. Their audio recordings suffer from the lack of seeing the sheer physical exertion of the praxis, but a DVD captures some of it.
36. See DeNora (2000, 91–108; p. 92) on "exosemantic correspondences" between music and the body: for example, sound tracks for aerobics are carefully preplanned to alternate stress and release, and all kinds of dancing exhibit this correspondence, especially today's improvisatory dance moves.
37. For more on "good time" see Regelski (1997) and Lakoff & Johnson (1999). The "good time" described in both should not be confused with mere "fun time." It equals a judgment of "worth-while."
38. *IDEA*. "Modeled," because music in school does not have the same governing social conditions that exist outside of school (e.g., jazz in a club). Thus, with praxicalism, choral

music in schools having sacred texts is *not* a part of the doctrinal situatedness or spatial semiotics of religious praxis in a worship service: it is music, not religion. Standing for Handel's *Hallelujah Chorus* confuses music as praxis with religion (worship) as praxis. See if you can defend that concept in words of your own convincing to a school board or complaining parent dealing with the question of religious texts in school-based choral music. The easy answer compares choral music with a sacred text to the script and actions of a villain on TV, in the theater, or in film: obviously the actor is not personally a villain, and the chorus is similarly not a church choir. Choir robes confuse the situatedness of a school music praxis.

39. In Piaget's theory an experience that is "understood" by an existing schema (idea, conceptual entity) is *assimilated* and thus that concept is strengthened. An experience that is new can be *accommodated*, thus adjusting the original concept and allowing more such experiences to be assimilated to the concept, thus modifying it to more broadly understand new experiences. School students will already have a concept of "tree" until they have an experience of a bonsai tree, the size of which then must be accommodated. Then "trees" can be big or tiny.

40. "Rhythm bands" are teacher-directed instrumental class performances performed usually on classroom rhythm instruments that are either not real instruments or scaled down to student size (hand drums). These "activities" are supposed to teach "the concepts" of rhythm and meter (e.g., "steady beat"). But the fact that they are incredibly easy to organize demonstrates that most students typically already have the metric knowledge supposedly being taught. Students who lack the skill are very difficult to assist to improve in the group context.

41. Depending on when "modernity" is judged to have ended, the era following it is today commonly referred to as "postmodernity." The expression "postmodernism" started off referring to a style of art that rejected the values of the 19th century but today often also includes postmodernity. I'll try to keep "postmodernity" and "postmodernism" clear: the first as an era following Modernity, the second as a movement in the arts, architecture, literature, and even music. Complications abound, but that is the nature of postmodern discourse.

42. Krisztof Pendercki makes this claim for the new musical "language" of his *Threnody to the Victims of Hiroshima* (1960). Now (2020) it is comparatively tame considering musics today that depart entirely from standard notation and relish dissonance, aleatory, stochastic, and minimalist departures from tonality—even eschewing atonality.

43. Meta-narratives are all-embracing historical systems, taken-for-granted ideas, accounts, assumptions, and uncritical indulgences that *legitimate the status quo* by which dominant social and ideological groups control other groups. This is discussed in greater detail in what follows.

44. COMMENTARY. The chances of entering the "standard repertory" (or making a career in composing) seem slight, and one-time listening is perhaps the rule for all but commissioned compositions. Some conductors perform new works twice, in expectation that familiarity will be gained. This depends, however, on the length of the work, many of which are short compared to the standard repertory, perhaps in recognition of the difficulties posed for audiences. Composition professors are often dependent on colleagues and former students for performance of their works and earn their living as teachers of composition. Thus, universities and college campuses are primary sites for much new music.

45. Reminder: "Absolute music": the habit of music for music's sake conveying no story, representation, or conceptual connections to life, just formal arrangements of sound

for contemplation. COMMENTARY. However, even absolute music is "for" the listening pleasures of audiences entertained by such listening and thus serves that "good for" use in attracting their allegiance and its social role in culture.
46. DEFINITION. *Scientism* claims that only science reveals authoritative and 'certain' knowledge and truth. *Positivism* regards as 'certain' knowledge only what can be verified by the senses. Both resist or doubt humanism, art, religion, and the liberal arts as sources of reliable knowledge.
47. COMMENTARY. Some languages seem to have no past tense and no future tense. Speakers apparently live in an ever-now present tense without cause and effect. However, the language itself may not have, say, a future tense, but the culture nonetheless plants seeds. Thus, individuals in such a language culture have intuitions on which they act that are nonverbal or traditional.
48. DEFINITIONS. The "uncertainty principle" in physics holds that you cannot observe the location of a subatomic particle and its momentum at the same time. Also, "the observer effect" states that just observing an event changes it. "Hawthorne Effect": When factory lighting was gradually improved, worker productivity went up. But when the lighting was slowly turned down again, worker productivity continued to rise—presumably because the workers knew they were being observed. This "observer effect" is somewhat related to the uncertainty principle since any observation influences the status of what is being observed, thus disturbing usual ideas of "truth" or "fact." It also seems likely that the observer effect of "stage fright" is learned at some stage of a performer's study; young children, for example, show no such problems, and plenty of professionals thrive on their presence before an audience—and any "tensions" are not about memory lapses or technical stumbles but those commanded by musical artistry.
49. DEFINITION. In philosophy, "facticity" is one's body, place, past, social position, and fundamental relationship to *the Other*. "The Other" (though not plural) refers to other human beings and the (social) reality they share of *differences* from one's own self-actualized image. In sociological theory, "facticity" is the result of treating an idea (concept, etc.) as though a physical thing (e.g., "institutions").
50. COMMENTARY. Hawking proposes an alternative to both "realism" and "anti-realism." He concludes that scientific or cognitive "models" the mind constructs, even though not of 'reality', guide understanding and the generating of knowledge about 'reality' and how it functions *when the models yield effective predictions*; for example, a mental model of the world as round rather than flat generated exploration and explained much about our knowledge and experience of the physical world (Ferguson 2017, 422–423). As the Buddhists say, "The finger pointing to the moon is not the moon," and the scientific model is not the 'reality', only a pointer.
51. "Mental models" have something in common with what is known as concepts, except that in science, models predict results that are confirmed by extensive experimentation. Concepts, in distinction, predict, but only what is already premised by the concept (e.g., the conservative's concept of poverty as resulting from laziness). Concepts like that in life, however, deserve to be treated as scientific theories put to a pragmatic test: does music education really improve school learning or are music students already good students? Concepts often devolve into "beliefs" that have little evidence to support them (e.g., about welfare mothers driving Cadillacs).
52. DEFINITION. "Neo-Pragmatism" is a postmodern version of Pragmatism, especially sharing the idea of pragmatic reality, the questioning of absolutes, and a focus on the social mind,

consciousness, and beliefs. It focuses on words *as used and understood*, not on experience per se. A Neo-Pragmatic Self is a localized cloud of beliefs, feelings, and ideas that are untethered to any central structure holding them in orbit. However, the cloud is relatively stable and dislodged only through the winds of opposition and change. See, for example, Richard Rorty (1998).

53. COMMENTARY. For example, Arctic dwellers develop concepts (and sometimes words for them) for qualities of "snow" that are central to their survival, that are not in the vocabulary or experience of those living in a world without snow. FACT. The developmental timing of the concepts of space and time varies in 18-month-old infants according to their language (Weist et al. 1997, a study of Polish, Finnish, and American babies).

54. DEFINITION. Not to be confused with *multiculturalism,* which stresses the assimilation ("melting pot") of groups into *one* sociocultural ensemble: think of an orchestra as a model. *Cultural pluralism* respects and supports cultural identities that are retained (and maybe restrained) while fitting with wider social values and laws but that can enhance the rest of a society or nation: think of an "Italian Fest" celebration of Italian cooking that even non-Italians enjoy. Also note the seductive appeal of Irish/Scottish dance tunes when you can't help tapping your foot with the rhythms.

55. IDEA. Was the U.S. Civil War about freeing slaves in the South (the standard historical account) or, as claimed by Southern revisionist historians, was the South defending states' rights and limited national government? What to teach? While the 'fact' will never be agreed to, both claims can be considered in arriving at an understanding of the complexities involved (as usual, with human affairs) and their continuing social relevance. Schooling should be directed to thinking through such vital complexities, not clear-cut, true/false answers (e.g., sources of poverty, forms of government, global warming). Is some music, without words, immoral? You'd better be prepared to deal with that challenge.

56. For example, those who stress their own LGBTQ+ status as a so-called lens through which to propose both critiques and corrections for music education from their "perspectivism"—the conclusions of which are also urged on non-LGBTQ+ thinkers (see, e.g., Gould 2004; Allsup 2016).

57. DEFINITION. "Precariat": Portmanteau for a socioeconomic class faced with a '*precari*ous' existence of job insecurity, intermittent or underemployment, and living in debt at and sometimes below the fringes of poverty or barely above it. What is schooling like for children living in such homes? Or their access to music?

58. TRUE STORY. A fifth-grade child appeared at her first group clarinet lesson with a set of two new, professional-quality A and B-flat Selmer clarinets in a case given to her by her grandparents.

59. TRUE STORY. District elementary school teachers decided to forego grading in favor of a portfolio combined with parental conferences. Unexpectedly, several district parents, who were teachers but taught in another school system, mounted an aggressive challenge arguing that their children (whom they assumed to be top students) would be penalized by grade-less school records when they applied to colleges or for jobs. They argued, then, for the continued use of grading. The teachers won the support of their union and board of education members. COMMENTARY. A serious ethical *faux pas* is committed when students who own their own instruments and take private lessons are put into competition (or allowed to make challenges) for ensemble seating with students lacking those advantages.

60. TRUE STORY. The memoir of Steve Jobs's daughter (Brennan-Jobs 2018) recounts a teacher who, after giving back tests and homework, had students publicly announce their grades,

which he then entered into his computer in front of the entire class. Negative looks and comments were directed at those reporting low grades. Intended embarrassment, or too lazy to enter the grades in his records on his own? Either way, seriously unethical.

61. COMMENTARY. The advantages that students who own their own instruments have in "challenge systems" for ensemble seating over those without such lessons have already been noted! But further discrimination arises when the school instrumental teacher teaches all instruments, while some students are fortunate (i.e., parentally funded) to study privately with specialists. And what of those children whose parents drop them off for concerts but don't stay to hear them?

62. COMMENTARY. School tax is the only tax in the U.S. that people can vote on. And the services schools provide are determined in part by the school budget. For example, should taxpayers provide free lunch (and sometimes breakfast) for students from poor families? Should the school own instruments for poorer students to use in ensembles? Is it fair that recruitment efforts ignore instruments that are not typical in band or orchestra? And why are history textbooks whitewashed of negatives of U.S. history, for example, genocide of Native Americans (see Loewen 1987)?

63. COMMENTARY. It is important to recall, again, that knowledge we have "retained" from successful past experiences for future use (Pragmatism's stage 3) becomes *assimilated* into ever-more inclusive concepts (or schema). Thus, when assimilated knowledge fails to deal with a problem, a new successful solution gets *accommodated* and thus reconstructs that concept (i.e., alters it usually in subtle ways but sometimes in dramatic ways). This is the case at least according to Jean Piaget's genetic construct*ivism,* which unfolds as the student grows older and more experienced concepts are "updated by accommodations from new experiences." With Lev Vygotsky's social construct*ionism,* new knowledge is gained over time by interaction in a social milieu and, as structured by the teacher, is cooperatively acquired. Piaget dominates North American educational psychology; Vygotsky dominates European educational psychology. And the differences of class pedagogy are immediately noticeable—especially with the U.S. low standing in international comparisons (e.g., Program for International Student Assessment—PISA scores).

64. COMMENTARY. Money: A society agrees that those pieces of paper and metal called "money" are valuable and this facilitates a wide range of worldwide social dealings predicated on that social agreement. However, libertarians argue that gold should stand in government treasuries (commodity money) to support government-issued (fiat) money.

65. Preparing for a concert does motivate students, and to family members, it is evidence of that effort. But concerts offered on such grounds are dead ends, unless students' skills and musicianship last beyond the events that end with graduation. Even so, the dropout rate between elementary groups and senior high school groups is typically considerable. Of what value has ensemble participation been to them? As to the survivors in high school groups, their musicing typically ends with graduation. A praxical curriculum focuses, instead, on musicianship that lasts into adulthood and facilitates continuing musicing.

66. IDEA. A beginning is a webpage that covers musical life in the school and other musical opportunities in the community. Such information might include instrumentalists interested in finding another with whom to play duets, the availability of an accompanist for home musicing, local events, information about music in the local library (e.g., CDs and DVDs), etc. Students can easily mount and maintain such a site as a separate section of a school's website through high school music classes.

Chapter 5

1. *COMMENTARY*. Is a chord spelled (upward in C major) D, F, A, C a ii_7 chord or a IV^{+6}? The first is a minor seventh chord; the second a major chord with an added sixth. What is the reality? Are the harmonic implications of each considered in context or is only one taught as "fact"? Theorists of music disagree in their collegiate textbooks. In context for jazz players it describes F^6. Why is 18th-century "common practice" taught at all and not the symbology and uses common to today's musics? Or both? Why aren't the findings and premises of the sociology of music or ethnomusicology included in teacher preparation? Why is music history not concerned with *doing* history (e.g., students researching the technical development of their instruments and its impact for what they can do musically)?
2. *TRUE STORY*. Music teachers in a large, rural district were criticized by colleagues for giving up their "free period" (granted by union contract) to work individually with students on solos, pitch matching, college auditions, etc. They then decided to take a more active role in union politics, which led to the contractual redefinition of a "free period" as "free to choose" how teachers use that time. Other teachers can still read newspapers and talk about sports events or gossip if they like.
3. *DEFINITION*. A vernacular dialect also called "Black English" by linguists in North America. There is, of course, a long history of its use in speech and literature that is often ignored—except maybe by white teens who borrow some expressions as part of being what they think is "cool."
4. Some countries wisely start second and even third languages in elementary school, the age at which there is a natural 'window' in the brain for language learning and after which a new language is progressively more difficult to learn.
5. *COMMENTARY*. Postmodernism challenges even the 'objectivity' of science, regarding findings more as agreed-upon ideas than as 'facts'—doubting both the validity of science and claims to objective knowledge (see Rosenau 1992). Cultural conservatives share postmodern dismissal of "facts" when, as a group, they reject out of hand the scientific evidence for global warming, as do those who argue the dangers to children of vaccination.
6. Consider a thought experiment. What if a student judged by the status quo/establishment to be worthy only of vocational education, condemning him to a life of blue-collar labor, were to be, say, given to a tutor—or qualified home schooling—to educate. Is it not entirely feasible that the student, despite ups and downs of motivation and achievement, would become eligible for university study? Such individual attention is not possible in comprehensive general education, but it would demonstrate that many students are capable of more than a vocational track—given their individual profiles of learning. What if this were a situation to be judged for your own child? By the way, I was 11th in a class of 21 at graduation. Music and sports cleared the way for me, a decidedly late bloomer who thrived on the collegiate experience.
7. The authors listed for school textbooks are not always those who wrote the text. Many ghost-writers are employed, especially for texts originally written by deceased authors whose writing needs to be updated to meet, not scholarly standards, but the often political criteria of local, state, and city boards of education. See Loewen (2018) for the scandalous commodification of history textbooks. And imagine the publisher's dilemma these days providing textbooks for biology, given the public debate over evolution and creationism.

8. Not to mention, why 'cover' Shakespeare at all? This commitment is a given—an imposition on students of Neo-Scholastic and Perennialist deification. Why not any number of more recent plays by great playwrights?
9. *Idea*. In a rehearsal, record a passage of the ensemble's performance. Play it back directing students to listen "critically." *With no discussion* repeat the passage according to "What can you or your section accomplish with musically improved results"? *Then discuss* briefly what (if anything) was improved, how, etc. (Repeated over time, criteria of "musicianship" will become ever-more clear to students.)
10. Robert Bilder is a clinical neuropsychologist and a director of the Tennenbaum Center for the Biology of Creativity in Los Angeles who studies creativity and the brain.
11. *Idea*. The question of how to finger a new note should lead immediately to how to use a fingering chart for the instrument, thus promoting independence.
12. *True Story*. I saw a father outside a motel rearranging his SUV already filled with camping equipment while his son and wife watched. And the last thing he put in was a guitar in its case. I said to him: "It's great your son brings his guitar along on a vacation." He said, smiling: "Son? No way! That's *my* guitar!"
13. In various formats, in academic contests an academic question is asked of teams from two different schools. The first team answering correctly is awarded a point. The total determines the winner.
14. Two competing class teams in a spelling bee may be an exception. Still, the student who fails to spell the decisive word can experience a sense of failure. "You're so dumb, we lost."
15. *Definition*. "Social learning theory" involves learning through social interaction with others where learning is an attempt to adjust to complex social situations. In teaching (and therapy) emphasis is on modeling by the teacher (or therapist). It is not mindless, however, but cognitively organized according to expectations formed in prior experiences as per constructivism. For more on social learning theory, see Albert Bandura in educational psychology texts (e.g., 2017).
16. Imagine three concentric circles: the innermost represents what little the student can *already* do unassisted; the next circle out is the ZPD where doing more is accomplished with the *help* of peers in groups or the teacher; the outside circle represents what the learner *can't do* with or without help.
17. Again, envision a scaffold where work at a lower level is a step to the next more complex level, and so on with subsequent levels until musical independence is gained.
18. *Definition*. Advance organizers: Guidance provided as a lead-in to a lesson; information that is said to be necessary for students to contend with a lesson focused on new knowledge or skill. Advance organizers usually involve connections to past lessons or make comparisons.
19. See Loewen (2018) for a shocking exposé of textbook publishing in American history.
20. During World War II leading members moved to the U.S. to avoid Nazism and joined the "New School of Social Research" in New York City (today called "the New School"). Some stayed in the U.S., while others returned to Germany after World War II.
21. *Definition*. According to sociologist Max Weber, *an action is "social"* when the agent takes into consideration the reactions of others to it and accounts for those reactions (positive and negative) in completing the course of an action's resolution.
22. *Definition*. Phenomenological Sociology is the study of the acts of intentionality as revealed in the lifeworld. This discipline goes beyond merely informal reports and language

and instead deals formally with how intentionality *becomes conscious of itself* and the results of this self-reflection for the lifeworld.
23. COMMENTARY. Consider the degree to which music educators have been subjected to the dominance of a small but powerful class of professors, most of whom are not experienced with, nor often concerned with the realities of school music teaching. How much time of the teacher education program went into performance excellence of the 'classics' (studio instruction and ensembles) versus into studies of teaching? What was the point of it all? Jobs for musicians unable to achieve a career as performers? Most don't even try and aspire in their postgraduate studies, instead, to employment as professors. Then they label their instruction as "professional" studies!
24. TRUE STORIES. Take note of the music professor whose students were expected to come to lessons in formal attire (suit, formal dress, etc.)—apparently to honor the seriousness of the music being taught in lessons, or the "discipline" expected of "serious" students. Another student was accepted at a major U.S. conservatory. In her first "get to know you" lesson, when asked by the woman teacher about her life plans, she mentioned that the following summer she planned to be married. She was abruptly "shown the door" with the critically overbearing observation that music must be her life: no place for family!
25. IDEA. See the DVD *Whiplash* (2013, SONY Pictures Classics Release/Bold Films) for an Academy Award portrayal of a brutal jazz ensemble director who is exactly what is meant here by a "musicianist." If the finale suggests to you that all the psychological mistreatment of the student musician might have been worth it for him, you're on the way to musicianism or are already there!
26. Recent U.S. news (January 2019) tells of a teacher who tried to remove LGBTQ+ language and bias from the curriculum. She was fired. You have to know the depth of institutional prejudice in a community to carefully address it. Otherwise, your professional integrity may be compromised.
27. COMMENTARY. "Culturalism" in general holds that ethnic groups all have certain traits that, overall, *exclusively define them* (e.g., all Polish-Americans are alike). There may be some everyday sense to this (e.g., food preferences; but Polish-Americans eat spaghetti). However, in sociology and anthropology, such *essentialist accounts* of cultural identity are challenged (see Regelski 2002). Some outspoken leaders within a cultural group, however, may politicize a group for *cultural purity and ideology* (e.g., Ku Klux Klan, White Nationalism, Black Panther Party), and against either multiculturalism (a concept that suffers from its misunderstood reliance on "culturalism") or cultural pluralism. However, be attentive: a Native American chief informed a group of professors that the music of his (Seneca) culture should be taught in the "longhouses" of the tribe. He stressed that only tribal members could understand their song lamenting the extinction of the carrier pigeon—a catastrophe for their tribe's pantheism. He admitted, however, that he was appreciative that his son was learning jazz in the public school and that he and his son were traveling to a jazz concert.

Chapter 6

1. If inclined to "program music," try instead Debussy, *Children's Corner Suite,* the movements of which offer a lot more musical detail worth educational focus. Compare Debussy's elephant segment ("Jimbo's Lullaby") with the elephant in *Carnival of the Animals*.

2. *Commentary*. Not to mention the disputability of such rankings, which are arbitrary and manage to change by committee over time from one level to another. The first movement of Beethoven's "Moonlight Sonata" is not really easy!!
3. It is ironic, given the popularity of school and university bands and wind ensembles, that so little literature exists on CD that is as widely available as choral and orchestral recordings. That, in itself, is a question worth considering, for if graduating students don't continue to play, without teacher provided listening lists they also can't collect wind literature CDs for their personal listening pleasure. But the truth may be that such literature, though promoted by schools and university ensembles, has no (economically viable) audiences for either recordings or collecting. If so, why the single-minded emphasis in schools?
4. *Commentary*. Critical Theorist, music critic, sociologist, and composer Theodor W. Adorno critiqued what he called the "commodification" of even the standard repertory of 'classical' music available on recordings and as printed music, where music is purchased and supports the commercial "star system" of virtuoso soloists and conductors. Along with his composition teacher, Schoenberg, he believed music was best "heard" inwardly by simply studying (audiating) the score. He also dissented from the value of jazz and thought J. S. Bach's admirers went overboard with their enthusiasm. His musical values were not shared by other Critical Theorists. Critical Theorist Walter Benjamin carried on a substantial correspondence contesting such issues.
5. For example, the high school choir that performed one of R. Murray Schafer's "soundscapes" at a university concert with the composer in the audience!
6. *True story/Idea* for comparative learning. At a concert of select chamber choirs from different schools singing for an audience mainly of each other, one school 'esteemed' for its madrigal choir performed a selection of madrigals. Another choir from a smaller school but with singers of equal ability performed a variety of lively works (spirituals, jazz arrangements, etc.). The next year, when the event was repeated, the madrigal choir performed a balanced program of styles, with no madrigals. You should believe students rehearse more intently for an audience of peers. In comparative terms, they had been impressed with the other choir's equally accomplished flexibility, showmanship, and general musicianship as exhibited across the several styles. (The final number of the concert has the massed choirs perform a masterwork together.)
7. *Definition*. To reiterate, "authentic assessment" uses doing the praxis at stake as the criterion for evaluating learning. Phrasing has been learned when students observe phrasing as notated. "Observable" here means that, say, a child's "good manners" are seen in action (or not) at the dinner table, in the same sense that "loving" is observed in action (or not) beyond "I love you" pronouncements. Thus, the "love of music" ("music appreciation") can only be seen in action—in observable actions of loving music. Praxical assessment always involves "authentic assessment" of the learned skills and knowledge "in action." The Nike slogan "Just do it" is apt for assessing praxis.
8. *Commentary*. This is NOT the collapsing of concepts into behavioral functions (behaviorism) but the typical expectations we have that actions are expected to produce results when promises or predictions are made; a curriculum is a form of promise/prediction to produce certain tangible benefits for students' musicing. The difference between action theory and behaviorism is the intentionality of the individual student that *mindfully* promotes a desired result. The student's knowledge of fingering, then, is seen in correct fingering in appropriate situations; it is not a "concept" of correct fingering. This expands to music (parts) where alternate fingerings are used for style, intonation, or ease.

9. *True story*. A principal who had to evaluate all teachers three times a year admitted to this author that he had NO IDEA what to comment on when viewing music rehearsals and concerts. His only criterion was that students were smiling (Even with instruments in their mouths? I didn't ask). Another principal brought the regimentation of his previous manner of band directing to bear on all teachers, regardless of subject. They soon learned that their scheduled observations had to have a structured format different from their usual praxis. (What is the equivalent of "first, warm up on scales" for a history teacher?)
10. Not as a handout or syllabus, but "in action" by the teacher's lessons and expectations.
11. *Commentary*. Deciding whether music reading should rely on solfeggio (fixed or moveable "Do," hand signs or not), numbers, or pitch names (among other choices) could be a stumbling block. But the curricular ideal is that the students learn to read music, by whichever method. Over time it will be clear whose methodology is most successful, as will the need (or not) for a staff discussion.
12. If need be, the director might have to devise a {T} part from, at least, some higher passages of the Baritones ("Bari-tenors} and lower passages of the Altos (or when either may need support or share the tune from time to time).
13. I respect the thinking of in-service teachers I have had. They reflect the challenges they face every day and in terms reflective of their individual values and concerns. Regelski (2004) features an entire K through 6 general music curriculum of this nature. Time erases names, but I am indebted to students for many ideas and examples herein.
14. See Regelski (2004, 257–267) for details in general music classes. There is no reason that the same pedagogy can't be used with newcomers to beginning instrumental lessons (213–234).
15. *Idea*. It is important then, for example, that elementary students regularly hear the performance of middle school students and that the latter hear performances of high school groups. If possible, some public concert performances should also be school-time assembly events where the ensemble can perform for an audience of age-group peers, and in an evening repeat the performance for an adult audience. *Guided listening program notes* can help students (and parents) to listen more attentively. Have them written as an assignment by students in high school music theory classes. For example: "This composition begins quietly and simply, then builds in complexity and dynamics, and finally returns to its original ideas of appealing, quiet interest: then the calm is broken by a finale that completes the musical moment. This ABA + finale (coda) is an effective way of developing musical ideas."
16. *Idea*. For example, at least critical/analytic listening to recorded passages of their own playing (during a rehearsal) for reflective praxis (e.g., perform a passage, listen to the recording, perform again to improve without director input), but also listening to at least models of the ensemble medium by accomplished groups (especially high school and collegiate—the next levels they can relate to), with attention to details of performance as their own action ideals and with appreciation for future listening. Chamber groups formed from within an ensemble can rehearse their literature interests (e.g., a woodwind quintet) on their own time, then perform in rehearsal for the full ensemble, and even as part of concert programs. Middle school students listening to recorded performances of high school ensembles greatly benefit by having the score for their part to follow.

References and Further Reading

In-service teachers have to "come to grips" with whatever topic most challenges their 'comfort levels' of both curriculum and teaching. Both challenges should, in any case, be traits of a professional approach to teaching music as praxis—improving conditions of phronēsis. And remember, teaching as praxis for music as praxis requires practice and remaining updated. The following identifies useful readings for in-service and doctoral candidates. Entries marked with * are suitable for interested pre-service readers and ** indicates readings especially relevant to this monograph.

Adler, Mortimer J. 1994. *Art, the Arts, and the Great Ideas*. New York: Macmillan.
**Alperson, Philip. 1991. "What should one expect from a philosophy of music education?" *Journal of Aesthetic Education*, 25 (3): 215–229.
———. 1994. "Music as philosophy." In *What Is Music? An Introduction to the Philosophy of Music*, edited by Philip Alperson. University Park: The Pennsylvania State University Press.
Alexander, Thomas M. 1987. *John Dewey's Theory of Art, Experience and Nature: The Horizons of Feeling*. Albany: State University of New York Press.
*Allsup, Randall. 2016. *Remixing the Classroom: Toward an Open Philosophy of Music Education*. New York: Teachers College Press.
Arendt, Hannah. 1998. *The Human Condition*. 2nd rev. ed. Chicago: University of Chicago Press.
Aristotle. 1998. *The Nichomachean Ethics*. Oxford: Oxford University Press.
Bilder, Robert. 2019. "States Consider Longer School Recess, and the Adults Aren't Complaining." https://www.nytimes.com/2019/02/28/nyregion/longer-school-recess-connecticut.html
Brennan-Jobs, Lisa. 2018. *Small Fry*. London: Grove Press.
**Bourdieu, Pierre. 1984. *Distinction: A Social Critique of the Judgement of Taste*. Translated by R. Nice. Cambridge, MA: Harvard University Press.
———. 1990. *The Logic of Practice*. Translated by R. Nice. Stanford, CA: Stanford University Press.
*———. 1993. *The Field of Cultural Production*. New York: Columbia University Press.
*Bowman, Wayne. 1996. "Music without universals: Relativism reconsidered." In *Critical Reflections on Music Education*, edited by L. R. Bartel and D. J. Elliott. Toronto: University of Toronto/Canadian Music Education Research Center.
*Broudy, Harry S. 1991. "A Realistic philosophy of music education." In *Basic Concepts in Music Education II*, edited by R. Colwell. Niwot: University Press of Colorado.
Csikszentmihalyi, Mihaly. 1990. *Flow: The Psychology of Optimal Experience*. New York: Harper & Row.
*DeNora, Tia. 2000. *Music in Everyday Life*. Cambridge: Cambridge University Press.
**Dewey, John. 1860/1894. "The theory of emotion." In *John Dewey: Philosophy, Psychology and Social Practice,* edited by Joseph Ratner, 214–251. New York: G. P. Putnam's Sons.
*———. 1925/1989. *Experience and Nature*. LaSalle, IL: Chicago: Open Court.
*———. 1934/1980. *Art as Experience*. New York: Perigree/Putnam.
———. 1971. *Reconstruction in Philosophy*. Enlarged ed. Boston: Beacon Press.
*deMarris, Kathleen B., and Margaret D. LeCompte. 1990. *The Ways Schools Work*. 3rd ed. New York: Longman.
*Dissanayake, Ellen. 1990. *What Is Art for?* Seattle: University of Washington Press.

*———. 1992. *Homo Aestheticus: Where Art Comes from and Why.* New York: Free Press/Macmillan.
*Dixon, Robert. 1995. *The Baumgarten Corruption: From Sense to Nonsense in Art and Philosophy.* East Haven, CN: Pluto Press.
**Dunne, Joseph. 1993. *Back to the Rough Ground: Phronēsis and Technē in Modern Philosophy and Aristotle.* Notre Dame, IN: Notre Dame University Press.
Elliott, David J. 1995. *Music Matters: A New Philosophy of Music Education.* New York: Oxford University Press.
**Elliott, David, and Marissa Silverman. 2015. *Music Matters: A Philosophy of Music Education.* 2nd ed. New York: Oxford University Press.
Erskine, John. 1944. *What Is Music?* New York: J. B. Lippincott, Co.
Farley, Christopher John. 1999. Quoting Ani DiFranco, *River of Song* (PBS 1999), in "Sounding the waters." *Time*, 153 (1) (January 11): 95.
Ferguson, Kitty. 2017. *Stephen Hawking: His Life and His Work.* Rev. ed. London: Penguin. Direct quotation from Tim Folger, "The return of the Invisible Man," *Discover Magazine*, July/August 2009, 44.
*Gatto, John T. 2017. *Dumbing Us Down: The Hidden Curriculum of Compulsory Schooling.* LaVergne, TN: Ingram Publisher Services.
Glynn, Ian. 2013. *Elegance in Science: Beauty and Simplicity.* Oxford: Oxford University Press.
*Goble, J. Scott. 2003. "Perspectives on practice: A pragmatic comparison of the praxial philosophies of David Elliott and Thomas Regelski." *Philosophy of Music Education Review*, 11 (Spring): 23–44.
Gould, Elizabeth. 2009. "Dis-orientations of desire: music education queer." In *Music Education for Changing Times*, edited by Thomas Regelski and J. T. Gates. New York: Springer.
Habermas, Jürgen. 1975. *Legitimation Crisis.* Boston: Beacon Press.
*Harari, Yuval Noah. 2018. *21 Lessons for the 21st Century.* London: Jonathan Cape.
**Hill, D., P. McLaren, M. Cole, and Glenn Rikowski, eds. 1999. *Postmodernism in Educational Theory: Education and the Politics of Human Resistance.* London: Tufnell Press.
*Hodges, Donald A. 2017. *A Concise Survey of Music Philosophy.* New York: Routledge.
*Howard, Vernon. 1997. "Virtuosity as a performance concept: A philosophical analysis." *Philosophy of Music Education Review*, 5 (1): 42–54.
*James, Aaron. 2013. *Assholes: A Theory.* Boston: Nicholas Brealey.
*Johnson, James H. 1995. *Listening in Paris: A Cultural History.* Berkeley: University of California Press.
*Johnson, Mark. 1987. *The Body in the Mind: The Bodily Basis of Meaning, Imagination, and Reason.* Chicago: University of Chicago Press.
*Kincheloe, Joe L. 2009. *Critical Pedagogy.* 2nd ed. New York: Peter Lang.
*Kingsbury, Henry. 1988. *Music, Talent, and Performance: A Conservatory Cultural System.* Philadelphia: Temple University Press.
**Kivy, Peter. 1980. *The Corded Shell: Reflections on Musical Expression.* Princeton, NJ: Princeton University Press.
———. 1991. *Music Alone.* Ithaca, NY: Cornell University Press.
*Knappenberger, Kent. 2016. "Music for life." *TOPICS for Music Education Praxis.* http://topics.maydaygroup.org/2016/Knappenberger16.pdf.
*Kosa, Julia E. 2012. "Listening for whiteness: hearing racial politics in undergraduate school music." In *Music Education for Changing Times*, edited by Thomas Regelski and J. T. Gates. New York: Springer.
*Kosinski, Jerzy. 1983. *Being There.* London: Black Swan/Penguin.
Kövecses, Zoltán. 2000. *Metaphor and Emotion: Language, Culture, and Body in Human Feeling.* Cambridge: Cambridge University Press.
Langer, Susanne K. 1977. *Feeling and Form.* Macmillan.

*Light, Andrew W., and Jonathan M. Smith. 2005. *The Aesthetics of Everyday Life*. New York: Columbia University Press.
*Loewen, James W. 2018. *Lies My Teacher Told Me: Everything Your American History Textbook Got Wrong*. 2018 ed. New York: New Press.
Määttänen, Pentti. 2015. *Mind in Action*. New York: Springer.
**———. 2017. "Emotions, values, and aesthetic perception." *New Ideas in Psychology*. http://dx.doi.org/10.1016/j.newideapsych.2017.03.009 (Accessed July 2020).
MacIntyre, Alasdair. 1984. *After Virtue*. 2nd ed. Notre Dame, IN: Notre Dame University Press.
**Mandoki, Katya. 2007. *Everyday Aesthetics: Prosaics, the Play of Culture, and Social Identities*. Burlington, VT: Ashgate.
*Martin, Peter J. 1996. *Sounds and Society*. Manchester: Manchester University Press.
*Maslow, Abraham. 1962/2011. *Towards a Psychology of Being*. New York: Martino Press.
**Mead, George Herbert. 2015. *Mind, Self, and Society—The Definitive Edition*. Edited by Charles W. Morris, annotated edition by Daniel R. Huebner. Chicago: University of Chicago Press.
**Norris, Christopher. 1990. *What's Wrong with Postmodernism: Critical Theory and the Ends of Philosophy*. Baltimore: Johns Hopkins Press.
Peirce, C. S. 1931/1958. *The Collected Papers of Charles Sanders Peirce*. Edited by C. Hartshorne, P. Weiss, and A. W. Burks. Cambridge, MA: Harvard University Press: 1931, Volume 5, paragraph 2.
**Polanyi, Michael. 1962. *Personal Knowledge: Towards a Post-Critical Philosophy*. Chicago: Chicago University Press.
**Popp, Jerome A. 1999. *Cognitive Science and Philosophy of Education*. San Francisco: Caddo Gap Press.
*Proudfoot, Michael. 1988. "Aesthetics." In *The Handbook of Western Philosophy*. General editor, G. H. R. Parkinson. New York: Macmillan.
Putnam, Hilary. 1990. *Realism with a Human Face*. Cambridge, MA: Harvard University Press.
Putnam, Hilary, and Ruth Anna Putnam. 2017. *Pragmatism as a Way of Life*. Cambridge, MA: Harvard/Belknap.
**Rancière, Jacques. 2009a. *The Politics of Aesthetics*. Translated by G. Rockhill. London: Continuum.
**———. 2009b. *Aesthetics and Its Discontents*. Translated by S. Corcoran. Cambridge: Polity Press.
Reckwitz, Andreas. 2017. "*Practices and Their Affects*." In *The Nexus of Practices: Connections, Constellations, Practitioners*, edited by Allison Hui, Theodore Schatski, and Elizabeth Shove. London: Routledge.
Reeve, C. D. C. 2013. *Aristotle on Practical Wisdom, Nicomachean Ethics VI*. Translated, with Introduction, Analysis, and Commentary. Cambridge, MA: Harvard University Press.
*Regelski, Thomas A. 1973. "Self-actualization in creating and responding to art." *Journal of Humanistic Psychology*, 13 (4): 57–68.
*———. 1981. *Teaching General Music: Action Learning for Middle and Secondary Schools*. New York: Schirmer/Macmillan.
*———. 1983a. "Action learning." *Music Educators Journal*, 69 (6) (February): 46–50.
*———. 1983b. "Action learning versus the Pied Piper approach." *Music Educators Journal*, 69 (8) (April): 55–57.
*———. 1996. "A prolegomenon to a praxial theory of music and music education." *Finnish Journal of Music Education*, 1 (1) (Fall): 23–38. Reprinted in *Canadian Music Educator*, 38 (3) (Spring 1997): 43–51.
*———. 1998. "Action Learning: curriculum and instruction as and for praxis." In *Proceedings of the Charles Fowler Conference on Arts Education*. College Park: University of Maryland Press.

**———. 2001. "Accounting for all praxis: an essay critique of Elliott's music matters." *Council of Research in Music Education, Bulletin*, 144 (Spring): 61–88.

*———. 2002. "'Critical Education,' culturalism and multiculturalism." *Action, Criticism, and Theory for Music Education*, 1 (1): 1–40. http://act.maydaygroup.org/articles/Regelski1_1.pdf

*———. 2004. *Teaching General Music in Grades 4–8: A Musicianship Approach*. New York: Oxford University Press.

*———. 2007. "Amateuring in music and its rivals." *Action, Criticism, and Theory for Music Education*, 6 (3): 22–50. http://act.maydaygroup.org/articles/Regelski6_3.pdf

**———. 2009. *Music Education for a Changing World: Guiding Visions for Practice*. Edited with J. T. Gates, with an Introduction and Conclusion chapters of my own. New York: Springer.

*———. 2012a. "Musicianism and the ethics of school music." *Action, Criticism, and Theory for Music Education*, 11 (1): 7–42. http://act.maydaygroup.org/articles/Regelski11_1.pdf

*———. 2012b. "The good life of teaching or the life of good teaching." *Action, Criticism, and Theory for Music Education*, 11 (2): 42–78. http://act.maydaygroup.org/articles/Regelski11_2.pdf

*———. 2016a. "Music, music education, and institutional ideology: A praxial philosophy of music sociality." *Action, Criticism, and Theory for Music Education*, 15 (2): 10–45. http://act.maydaygroup.org/articles/Regelski15_2.pdf

*———. 2016b. *A Brief Introduction to a Philosophy of Music Education as Social Praxis*. New York: Routledge.

**———. 2017a. "Pragmatism, praxis, and naturalism: the importance for music education of intentionality and consummatory experience in musical praxes." *Action, Criticism, and Theory for Music Education*, 6 (2): 102–143. http://act.maydaygroup.org/articles/Regelski6_2.pdf

*———. 2017b. "Autonomania: music and music education from Mars." *Contemporary Aesthetics*. http://www.contempaesthetics.org/Volume 15

*Reimer, Bennett. 2003. *Philosophy of Music Education*. 3rd ed. Upper Saddle River, NJ: Pearson Education Inc.

Remhof, Justin. 2018. *Nietzsche's Constructivism: A Metaphysics of Physical Objects*. New York: Routledge.

*Rice, Timothy. 2014. *Ethnomusicology: A Very Short Introduction*. New York: Oxford University Press.

Rorty, Richard. 1998. *Truth and Progress: Philosophical Papers*. Vol. 3, p. 9. Cambridge: Cambridge University Press.

Rosenau, Pauline M. 1992. *Post-Modernism and the Social Sciences: Insights, Inroads, and Intrusions*. Princeton, NJ: Princeton University Press.

*Saito, Yuriko. 2007. *Everyday Aesthetics*. New York: Oxford University Press.

*Schatzki, Theodore R., Karin Knorr Cetina, and Eike Von Savigny, eds. 2001. *The Practice Turn in Contemporary Theory*. New York: Routledge.

Schwadron, Abraham. 1967. *Aesthetics: Dimensions for Music Education*. Washington, DC: Music Educators National Conference (today NAfME).

**Searle, John. 1998. *Mind, Language, and Society*. New York: Basic Books.

**Shepherd, John. 1991. *Music as Social Text*. Cambridge: Polity Press.

Shepherd, John, and Peter Wicke. 1997. *Music and Cultural Theory*. Cambridge: Polity Press.

**Small, Christopher. 1998. *Musicking: The Meanings of Performing and Listening*. Hanover, NH: Wesleyan University Press.

Smith, Gareth Dyland, and Marissa Silverman. 2020. *Eudaimonia: Perspectives for Music Learning*. New York: Oxford University Press.

**Summers, David. 1987. *The Judgement of Sense: Renaissance Naturalism and the Rise of Aesthetics*. Cambridge: Cambridge University Press.

**Turino, Thomas. 2008. *Music as Social Life: The Politics of Participation.* Chicago: University of Chicago Press.

*Väkevä, Lauri. 2000. "Naturalizing philosophy of music education." *Action, Criticism, and Theory for Music Education,* 1 (1) (April 2002). http://act.maydaygroup.org/articles/Vakeva1_1.pdf

*Vardy, Peter, and Paul Grosch. 1991. *The Puzzle of Ethics.* Rev. ed. London: HarperCollins/Fount Paperbacks.

Von Drehle, David. 2019. https://www.washingtonpost.com/opinions/its-time-to-rethink-what-teachers-are-for/2019/02/12/771ccbaa-2f04-11e9-86ab-5d02109aeb01_story.html?utm_term=.651e822762ac&wpisrc=nl_opinions&wpmm=1

Weist, Richard, Paul Lyytinen, Jolanta Wysocka, and Marja Antanassova. 1997. "The interaction of language and thought in children's language acquisition: a cross-lingual study." *Journal of Child Language,* 24 (1): 81–121.

Wenger, Etienne. 1999. *Communities of Practice: Learning, Meaning, and Identity.* Cambridge: Cambridge University Press.

Westerlund, Heidi. 2003. "Reconsidering aesthetic experience in praxial music education." *Philosophy of Music Education Review,* 11 (1): 45–62.

Wittgenstein, Ludwig. 1953/2017. *Philosophical Investigations.* London: Macat Library.

———. 1966. *Lectures and Conversations on Aesthetics, Psychology and Religious Belief.* Edited by C. Barrett. Los Angeles: University of California Press.

Young, Robert. 1990. *A Critical Theory of Education: Habermas and Our Children's Future.* New York: Teachers College Press.

*Zillmann, Dolf, and Su-lin Gan. 1997. "Musical taste in adolescence." In *The Social Psychology of Music,* edited by D. J. Hargreaves and A. C. North. New York: Oxford University Press.

Index

For the benefit of digital users, indexed terms that span two pages (e.g., 52-53) may, on occasion, appear on only one of those pages.
Figures are indicated by *f* following the page number

action, vi
Action Learning, 3, 74, 96–98
   apprenticeship, 79
   general musicianship, 97–98
   independent musicianship, 97
   intentionality, 42, 69–70, 97
   transfer of learning, 97–98
activities vs. actions, 70
activity, human, 2
advocacy, 8–9
aesthetic(s), 21
   absolute music, 22, 68
   aesthetic/musical idea, 24
   aesthetic theory of art, 68–69
   body excluded, prioritizing mind, 24
   emotions (aestheticized), 27–28
   extramusical, 45–46
   formalism, 51
   ideology, 50, 125
   performance *of* or *as* music, 24–25
   social origins of, 67, 68
aesthetic hierarchy, 22–23, 23*f*
   orthodoxy, 17–18, 19, 27
aesthetic meaning is intangible, 137
agency, vi
aisthesis, 20, 78
"art for arts sake" 68–69

Baumgarten Alexander, vi
"best practices" 2, 4

Four C's (Haari), 73
chamber music, 25–26, 74–75
Christian existentialism. *See* existentialism
commodification of music, 78
Common Core, 1
comparetition, 139
concepts, teaching activities, 25–27, 70–71

contemporary perspectives, 77–78
   Ethics of School Music as Praxis, 85–86
   Aristotle's Four Secondary (intellectual)
      Values, 85–86, 86*f*
   consequentialism, 87
   duty (deontological) ethics, 86–87
   phronēsis, 81–82, 86
   virtue ethics, 89
      musicianism, 90
      precision for amateurism, 90
      virtue of praxis, 91–92
music as praxis, 77–78
practice theory, 77–78
praxis, 77–78
praxis ("virtuous doing"), 81–86
   action ideals, 83
   ethical criterion, 81–82
   phronēsis, 81–82
   praxial/praxical knowledge, 83–86
      four intellectual criteria, 82*f*
      reflective knowledge, 83
   readiness, 83
   "right results" (Aristotle), 81–83
   unrepeatable/individualized, 84–85
   serves people's needs, 81–82
   "standards" of (ethical) care, 82, 83
technē, 79–81
   action feedback, 80–81
   applied theoria, 80
   apprenticeship/practicum, 80, 146
   instrumental/operational knowledge, 81
   learning feedback, 80–81
   makes 'things' 79–80
   musicianship training, 81
   observational learning, 80
   poiēsis (excellent making), 79–80

contemporary perspectives (*cont.*)
    supervisory oversight, 80–81
    technical accountability, 81
  theoria, 78–79
    contemplation, 79
    practical theory, 79
critical philosophy, ix
Critical Theory, ix, 139
  critical pedagogy, 89
  false consciousness, ix
  ideology critique, ix
cultural naturalism, 63–64
curriculum, ix
  alignment: horizontal, vertical, 10
  curricular basics, 1–7
  curriculum philosophy, ix
  ensembles, ix–x, 7, 138
    "averaging effect of large numbers" 8
    concerts as curriculum, 4
  music education, for, ix
  as philosophy, 15
    axiology, 15
  theory, ix, 1
Curriculum Models from Educational Theory, 117–18
  basic studies/essentialism, 118–21
    'Basics' of Idealism, Realism, Neo-Scholasticism, 120, 121
    Basic to what? 119
  conditions of instruction, 142
  educational theories influencing curriculum, 118
  Perennialism, 121–23
    curriculum of sages of past the same for all, 122
    disciplined mind (as per Neo-Scholasticism), 122–23
    recall of abstract, inert 'facts' 123
    timelesss "great ideas," "great works" 121–22
    transmission of ready-made knowledge, 122
  praxical curriculum, 137, 139–40
    action or praxis dimensions (3), 140–43
      action, praxis, 140
      attitude, 141–42, 148
      authentic assessment 118, 148
      competency, 141
      rubrics, 144–45
    model, 144

Progressivism, 123–28
  Action Learning, 127–28
  active learning, 124
  against traditional educational practices, 124
  authoritative not authoritarian, 124
  child-centered, whole child, 126
  cooperation not competition, 126, 127
  democratic teaching, 126
  existentialism, 127–28
  learning by doing. project method, 126
  music as social praxis, 127–28
  problem solving, 124–25
  ZPD Zone of Proximal Development, 127
Reconstructionism and Critical Theory, 128–35, 139
  against oppression and unequal social power, 129
  critical of knowledge as power to subjugate people, 129–30
  democratic solving of social problems, 128
  emancipatory themes, 130
  empowering students choose their own histories, 128
  Frankfurt School of social theory and philosophy, 129
  ideology critique, false consciousness, 130
  "legitimation crisis" (Habermas) of MEAE, 132
  MayDay Group of Critical Theorists in music education, 133
  metanarrative of aesthetics is social elitism, 131
  overcoming ill effects of capitalism, 130–31
  transformation s. transmission, 128
  unequal power of social classes, 128
  whose music (socioeconomic class) to teach? 132–33
curriculum vs. syllabus, 9–10

delivery lessons, 1, 2–3, 4, 5, 9, 86
  methodolatry, 3–4, 88, 91
drills, 146

epistemology, 41
essentialism, 23
ethics, ethical, 2–3
  criteria, 2–3

existentialism, 41, 138–39
   absurdity (angst. anxiety), 44–46, 47–48
   Christian existentialism, 43–46
      Kierkegaard, Søren, 43–46
   existential authenticity, 46
   existential *in*authenticity, 44–45
   false-consciousness, 46
   humanistic existentialism, 46–51
   humanistic psychology &
      existentialism, 51–59
     Being needs. 'B-needs' 54, 138–39
       intrinsic/inner-directed, 52*f*, 54
   Deficiency Needs. 'D-Needs' 51–54, 52*f*
      extrinsic/other-directed, 51–54, 52*f*
   Maslow's Hierarchy of needs, 51–53, 52*f*
   Marcel, Gabriel, 46
   meaning-making, 45–46
   Myth of Sisyphus Camus, 45–44
   perspectivism (Nietzsche), 49
     music curriculum, 55
       attitude dimension, 56
       authoritarian. 56
       authoritative, 56–57
       intentionality, 42, 56–57, 69–70
       music as social praxis, 54
       personhood, 55–56, 138–39
       recreation as *re*-creation, 57–58
       technique drills, 58
   self-actualizing choices, 48–49, 50
   social constructivism, 41–42
expressionism, 27–28

formalism, 27

"helping professions. 4
"hidden" 12
holistic musicianship (wholism), 141

Idealism, 18–28
   Christian soul, 18
   concept teaching, 26–27
   Idealism and the music curriculum, 19
     beauty as aesthetic forms, 21
     intellectual study, 20
     not for usefulness, 18–19
     rational judgment, 20
     transmission of status quo, 21
     ideas more real than sentient experience
       (aisthesis), 20
   Luther Martin, 19
   social activities, 84

independent musicianship, 71
intentionality, 42, 69–70
"it works" 2, 84

Kant, Emmanuel, vi
knowledge
   conceptual (Piaget), 42
   culturally created, 42
   personally reflective, 42
   practical, 42
   propositional, 42

lead teacher, 73
lifelong learning, 3–4
listenership praxis/practicum, 8, 25, 147

malpraxis, 2–3
MayDay Group, 109
music as social praxis, 26–27, 92–96
   "classical music" is "good time" 95
   different musics "good for" different "right
      results" 94
   humans are intensely social, 92
   musical "good time" is "worth-while"
      94, 138–39
   no "pure gaze" (absolute music), 94
   sociality, 92, 95
   social sounds become "music" 93
music appreciation, 14
musical meaning, 15–16
musicing, 67

Neo-Scholasticism, 33–38
   analytic truth, 35
   Aristotle, 34
   Dominicans, 34
   deductive logic, 34
   disciplined thinking, 34
   discipline of history and theory, 33
   Franciscans, 34
   good life in harmony with
      reason, 35
   humans are rational, 35
   inductive logic, 34–35
   lecture (*lectio*), 33
   music curriculum, 35–38
   Neo-Platonism, 34
   rational knowledge, 34
   school, scholar, scholastic, 33
   synthetic truth, 35
   thesis, professing, 33

Neo-Scholasticism and music
    curriculum, 35–38
  excellent making (technē), 35–36
  good taste from rational study, 27, 36
  mix of Idealist/Realist aesthetics, 37–39
"No Child Left Behind" 1
19–20th Century Philosophies of
    curriculum, 41–75

Perennialism, 137
phenomenology, 41, 42
postmodernity, 98–115, 139
  metanarratives "deconstructed" and
      transformation of schools, 109–15
    "deconstructs", challenges narratives of
        discrimination, 109–11
    favors emancipatory interests over
        metanarratives of power, 112–13
    rejects vestiges of Idealism, Realism,
        Neo-Scholasticism, 112
    social construction of knowledge. 109
    supports plural perspectives, 111
    transformation for future, not
        transmission pf past, 112
  modernity, 98–100
    belief in progress, 99
    knowledge as power, 99
    scientific, 'objective' knowledge, 100
  music appreciation reconsidered, 115–16
    appreciation as musicing
        regularly. 115–16
    music praxis outside of and after
        graduation. 116
  (Post)-modernism, 100, 139
    rejection of bourgeois modernity, 100
  postmodernism and the music
      curriculum, 108–9
    contests social injustice,
        inequality, racial/LGBTQ+
        discrimination, 109
    critiques Eurocentric culture and
        history, 109
  postmodernity and modernist art and
      music, 100–3
    anti-art art, 101–2
    "art" judged "art" by "Artworld" 100, 102
    challenged modernity, 100–1
    composers ignore or reject aesthetic
        metanarratives, 103
    music allied with 'pop' culture, 102
    new musics "deconstruct" traditional
        expectations, 102–3
    no high art/low distinction
        (elitism), 102
    rejects tonality, formalism,
        serialism, 102
  postmodern tendencies, 103–8
Pragmatism, 59, 60, 62, 63–64
  abduction, 61
  actions, choices are meaning-
      making, 59–60
  aesthetic education, 68
  agency, change agents, 60
  all experience potentially "esthetic" 66–67
  anesthetic perils to a 'good' musicing, 66
  an experience, 60, 61*f*
  artful living, 65
  authentic praxis, 60
  Baumgarten Alexander, 67
  connoisseur, 32, 65
  consummatory experience, 71–72
  different kinds of music should not
      compared for goodness. 64
  direct emotion of sound, 67
  "ends-in-view" (Dewey), 71
    choices, 72
  "esthetic" (sic) experience, Dewey "*affect
      quale*" 66
  falsificationism/verificationism, 62–63
  "good music" is "good for" a preferred
      use, 64–65
  mindful problem solving, 61*f*
  naturalizing of meaning/value, 63
  ordinary listeners, 68
  pragmatic/inner realism, 62
  "pragmatic maxim" of C.S.Peirce, 63
  Pragmatism and "artful living" through
      music, 65–69
  to experience, 70, 71
  use confers meaning, 59–60
  values are affordances already in the
      world, 63–64
Pragmatism and the music
    curriculum, 69–75
  banking metaphor, 73–74, 124
  child-centered, 73–74
  lead teacher, 73
  praxis, vi, 2–3
  program(s), 7
  push teacher, 73

praxial sequencing, 146
praxical curriculum, dimensions, 137
"pre-fab(ricated)" 10

Realism, 28–32
  aisthesis, 28
  direct, 28
  ethics follow natural order of universe, 28–29
  music isn't acoustics, 29
  pragmatic/internal realism, 28
  school knowledge is pre-fab, 29
Realism and the music curriculum, 28–32
  connoisseurship, 32
  disembodied meaning, 32
  expressionism, 30–31, 30f
  formalism, 30–31
  intellectual/aesthetic emotion, 31
  intellectual(ized) emotion, 31
  Langer, Susanne K. 31
  meaning in the score, 32
  presentational symbols of feeling. 31

social mind, 24, 30, 31–32
too mature meaning for school ages, 32

scaffolding, 69–70
Searle John, vi
spatial semiotics in music meaning, 69
spiral curriculum, 9–10

taste (musical, group tastes) vi, 27
teaching, 26
three types of curriculum, 9–11
  action for doing (praxical), 11
  formal–written action potential, 9–10
  Idealism, Realism, Neo-Scholasticism compared, 38–39
  instructed, 11
    teaching vs. instruction, 11
traditional philosophical foundations, 5–6, 27–28
  Idealism, 18–28
  Idealism and the music curriculum, 19–28

Wittgenstein, 39

Made in the USA
Monee, IL
28 April 2026

49136501R00118